# MURDER AND MADNESS

# MILITARY MATTERS
## AND
# MANAGED MEDICINE

Memorable Milestones
and Moments

*Allen D. Spiegel*

HERITAGE BOOKS
2007

# HERITAGE BOOKS
*AN IMPRINT OF HERITAGE BOOKS, INC.*

**Books, CDs, and more—Worldwide**

For our listing of thousands of titles see our website
at
www.HeritageBooks.com

Published 2007 by
HERITAGE BOOKS, INC.
Publishing Division
65 East Main Street
Westminster, Maryland 21157-5026

Copyright © 2007 Allen D. Spiegel

*Due to the death of Dr. Spiegel prior to the publication of this work, some items, such as photo credits, are missing.*

All rights reserved. No part of this book may be reproduced or transmitted in any form or by any means, electronic or mechanical, including photocopying, recording or by any information storage and retrieval system without written permission from the author, except for the inclusion of brief quotations in a review.

International Standard Book Number: 978-0-7884-4079-3

# CONTENTS

Preface   v

## SECTION ONE — MURDER AND MADNESS

Introduction   1

- Murder Defense Plea: Brutal Prison Beatings Caused Insanity   5
- A. Lincoln, Esquire and a Chloroform Induced Insanity Plea   21
- Uncontrollable Frenzy and a Unique Temporary Insanity Plea   41
- Politics and the Medical Expert On Insanity   57
- Murderess Insane Due to Being
    "Crossed-in-Love and Painful Dysmenorrhea"   75
- John Wilkes Booth Diagnosed As a Monomaniac   99

## SECTION TWO — MILITARY MATTERS

Introduction   115

- James McHenry: A Fort Named In His Honor   117
- A Red Devil and the National Anthem   135
- A Fighting Doctor Wins the Medal of Honor   143
- Clara Barton: Founder of the American Red Cross   161
- First, and Only, Female Ever Awarded
    the Congressional Medal of Honor   179

## SECTION THREE — MANAGED MEDICINE

Introduction   199

- Managed Medical Care in Babylonia in 1700 BCE   201
- America's First Medical Malpractice Crisis, 1835-1865   219
- A Veritable Oasis in the Desert: New York Medical College   239

Bibliography   257
Index   261

# MURDER AND MADNESS

*Center Section, Listed in Order of Appearance*

William H. Seward

Chart on the faculties of the mind used by Dr. Thomas Spencer

Dr. Amariah Brigham

New York State Lunatic Asylum at Utica

Abraham Lincoln

Leonard Swett

McLean County Courthouse, Bloomington, Illinois

Dr. Andrew McFarland

Teresa (Bagioli) Sickles

Philip Barton Key

Daniel E. Sickles

Sickles shooting Key with Samuel T. Butterworth watching

President Abraham Lincoln

Dr. David Minton Wright

Dr. John P. Gray

Government Hospital for the Insane, Washington, D.C.

Mary Harris

1859 Sharps .32-caliber four barreled Derringer

Joseph H. Bradley, Sr.

Dr. Charles H. Nichols

Dr. John Frederick May

John Wilkes Booth

Booth brothers in *Julius Caesar* in 1864

Post-mortem on *USS Montauk* to identify Booth's body

Dr. James McHenry

Revolutionary War Surgeon's field case

Dr. Benjamin Rush

Plans for a Revolutionary War flying hospital
Francis Scott Key
British fleet attacking Fort McHenry with rockets and bombs
Rear Admiral George Cockburn, the Red Devil
Francis Scott Key, Dr. William Beanes and John S. Skinner
Dr. Bernard J. D. Irwin, U.S. Army Captain
Cochise, Chief of the Apaches
Plan of the tent field hospital, Shiloh, Tennessee
Brigadier General Bernard J. D. Irwin
Clara Barton
U.S. Patent Office, Washington, D.C.
Poster advertising a Clara Barton lecture
U.S. postage stamp honoring Clara Barton
Dr. Mary Edwards Walker in "bloomer" outfit
Front and back view of the "dress reform undersuit"
Dr. Mary E. Walker's two Congressional Medals of Honor
Dr. Mary E. Walker in full formal dress (male attire)
Cuneiform writing from Codex Hammurabi
King Hammurabi receiving ring and scepter from Shamash
Seal of a Babylonian physician
Clay model of a sheep's liver used for divination
John J. Elwell, physician and lawyer
Medical advertisements in the newspaper
Dr. Frank H. Hamilton
Fractured leg with splints and packing
Front view of New York Medical College Catalogue
Dr. B. Fordyce Barker
Dr. Edmund Randolph Peaslee
Dr. Robert Ogden Doremus

# PREFACE

"In ancient times there existed in the country of Serendip, in the far east, a great and powerful king by the name of Giaffer. He had three sons who were very dear to him. And being a good father and very concerned about their education, he decided that he had to leave them endowed not only with great power, but also with all kinds of virtues of which princes are particularly in need."

So begins the enchanting Persian fairy tale of *The Three Princes of Serendip*. King Giaffer sent the three princes on a prolonged journey to acquire empirical experience. They entered into the kingdom of the great and powerful Emperor Beramo. With a combination of wisdom and accidental events, the princes resolve the mystery of the one-eyed camel, retrieve the Mirror of Justice and prescribe a remedy for Emperor Beramo's suffering over the loss of his paramour. After their journeys, the three princes return to Serendip. Upon King Giaffer's death, the eldest son succeeds his father. The middle son returns to the Queen who held the Mirror of Justice, marries her and becomes king. Emperor Beramo sends for the youngest son and offers him his daughter in marriage. After the Emperor's death, the youngest price becomes king of the empire.

British author Horace Walpole read this fairy tale when he was a young boy. In a January 28, 1754 letter to Horace Mann, an envoy of King George II stationed in Florence, Italy, Walpole coined the word *serendipity*. Walpole gave the derivation of the word from *The Three Princes of Serendip*: "... as their highnesses traveled, they were always making discoveries, by accident and sagacity, of things which they were not in quest of ..."

This book recalling historic milestones and memorable moments owes much to the process of serendipity. Many of the events link individuals who appear on other occasions. Initially, the murder by Mary Harris attracted my attention with a few sentences in a note in a late 1800s issue of the *American Journal of Insanity*. Later, upon investigation, Charles Mason, one of her lawyers, led to Clara Barton's story. A specific mention of a court spectator at the Harris trial led to Medal of Honor winner Dr. Mary E. Walker. In turn, this led to the first Medal of Honor winner, Dr. Bernard J. D. Irwin. Irwin directed us to his medical school, the reforming New York Medical College. An official report of the Harris murder trial noted that Mrs. Mary Todd Lincoln sent flowers to the cell of the murderess. At the time General Daniel E. Sickles was often in the White House visiting with the Lincolns. As a practicing lawyer, Lincoln commented about Sickles' trial for the murder of Philip Barton Key. This prompted a purview of Lincoln's law cases and revealed the chloroform induced insanity plea and the expert medical opinion on the sanity of Dr. David M. Wright. Diagnosis of assassin John Wilkes Booth as a monomaniac was a logical follow-up. Lincoln's law career led to the research into the first malpractice crisis in the U.S.

Because of the interaction among the individuals, some material is briefly noted more than once. This merely rounds out the story in each case. Tangential information adds relevance to provide understanding and comprehensiveness of the situation.

Information was adapted, with permission, from the *American Journal of Forensic Psychiatry*, *Caduceus*, the *Journal of Community Health* [Kluwer Academic Publishers; Springer Science and Business Media], and the *New York State Journal of Medicine*.

Lois A. Hahn and Maria Dejesus Callender provided the vital task of speaking to the computers in their own language.

Allen D. Spiegel, PhD, MPH

## SECTION ONE — MURDER AND MADNESS

Throughout the nineteenth century there were accepted medical and legal concepts of insanity in the United States. Jurisprudence of insanity reacted and interacted with societal attitudes and behaviors.

A compilation on madness and morals in the nineteenth century included selections from contemporary experts that covered criminal lunatics, feminine vulnerability, heredity and character, idiocy, insanity, moral insanity and pauper lunacy. With far ranging insight, the causes of insanity considered the effects of age, domestic troubles, education, a female's critical period, occupation, puerperal state, religion, seasons and sex. Medical jurisprudence in nineteenth century America focused on physicians and the law covering medical testimony, malpractice, societal reactions, and the expert witness. Special attention was devoted to medically determined causes of insanity, including emotional insanity. In the 1800s, physicians equated insanity with mental illness. Legally, insane or incompetent individuals were labeled lunatics. Institutions were called lunatic asylums. Today, insanity is a legal concept; mental illness is a medical condition.

Attorneys and physicians seldom met professionally, except in court, to argue about testimony on matters raised in trials. Between 1867 and 1890, the medico-legal society came into existence in five American locations: New York City; Massachusetts; Rhode Island; Chicago; and Denver. Correlations between insanity and crime were a major discussion topic for these groups. Today, discussions of social and legal responsibilities continue with many of the same words and arguments that were used more than a century ago. Behavioral and attitudinal stances of the legal profession, mental health professionals, practicing physicians, the mass media, and the public endured over time.

During the 1800s, American physicians believed insanity resulted from two causes: the predisposing and the exciting. Predisposing causes were paramount and heredity was the most influential. Doctors thought that insanity was almost always preceded by an illness, lack of sleep or poor nutrition. Attending physicians believed that those weakened in body and mind became highly vulnerable to mental illness. Exciting causes included a wide variety of stressful emotional and/or physical incidents.

A preeminent American physician, Dr. Benjamin Rush, believed that madness mirrored inward emotions and turned anger into illness that damaged the brain. Colorfully, Rush illustrated the observable symptoms: "A wild and ferocious countenance; enlarged and rolling eyes; constant singing; whistling and hallowing; imitations of the voices of different animals; walking with a quick step; or standing still with hands and eyes elevated towards the heavens ... the madman, or maniac, is in a rage."

Theories and ideas of Dr. James Cowles Prichard of England and Drs. Philippe Pinel and Jean Étienne D. Esquirol of France, greatly influenced Dr. Isaac Ray in the United States. Although he was a physician, Ray was not legally trained. He was the Superintendent of the Butler Hospital for the Insane in Providence, Rhode Island. However, Ray's publications influenced every major development in the common law of insanity including the M'Naghten rule, the irresistible impulse test, the New Hampshire doctrine, and the Durham ruling. Ray created a diagnostic nosology largely derived from Esquirol. In his 1838 book on the medical jurisprudence of insanity, Ray alternated discussing the medical condition in one chapter and followed with the legal consequences in the next chapter. His topics included partial and general moral mania [disease of affect and volition], lucid intervals, simulated insanity, and the civil questions of confinement and interdiction [incompetency]. Ray defined partial moral mania: "In this form of insanity, the derangement is confined to one or a few of the affective faculties, the rest of the moral and intellectual constitution preserving its ordinary integrity." Specifically, Ray discussed the homicidal monomanic as follows: "Amid the rapid and tumultuous succession of feeling that rush into the mind, the reflective powers are paralyzed, and his movements are solely the result of a blind, automatic impulse with which the reason has as little to do, as with the movements of a newborn infant."

In a two-volume widely acclaimed 1842 medical school textbook, Dr. Robley Dunglison, Dean of Philadelphia's Jefferson Medical College, discussed and defined the three commonly accepted classifications of mental alienation:

*Mania* results when the intellect is completely perverted on all subjects.
*Monomania*, or partial insanity, means that the perversion is restricted to one
    subject.

***Moral insanity*** consists of a morbid perversion of the natural feelings, affections, inclinations, temper, habits, moral disposition, and natural impulses without any remarkable disorder or defect of the intellect or knowing and reasoning faculties and particularly without any insane delusion or hallucination.

Subsequently, the experts began to dicker about moral insanity and the necessity of organic causation for a mental illness diagnosis. Ray continued to be a leading proponent of the doctrine of moral insanity in the United States and abroad. However, during a discussion at the 1863 meeting of the Association of Medical Superintendents of American Institutions for the Insane [AMSAII] only thirteen superintendents ventured an opinion on moral insanity. Five supported the theory and eight rejected the concept. Rejections were primarily based on moralistic grounds including religious, social and legal rationales. A fear was expressed that the profession's reputation would be harmed if the superintendents supported moral insanity as a defense in criminal trials. With this divided opinion among the medical mental illness experts, defense lawyers were fortunate to secure a reputable expert to testify.

Lawyers frequently bolstered their trial oratory about madness with legal, scientific and professional references. Occasionally, attorneys mentioned a failed attempt by a foreign lunatic named Richard Lawrence to kill President Andrew Jackson on January 30, 1835. In addition, they cited the late 1870s successful assassination of President James Garfield by a mentally ill disappointed office seeker, Charles J. Guiteau. With oratorical bombast, learned counsel quoted, from memory, from Shakespeare's *King Lear* and *Richard III* to illustrate acts of madness. Medical mental illness experts contended that chronic insanity of the brain may reveal no physical evidence of the disease. A monomaniac could be insane on one or two subjects and sane on all others.

In this section all the murders are alleged to be caused by insanity. Various rationales explain the madness. In 1846, prominent lawyer William H. Seward defended a multiple murderer. He proposed, for the first time, the argument that his client was insane due to brutal bearings he received while a prisoner in the penitentiary. In 1857, Abraham Lincoln prosecuted a murderer as the defense claimed that an overdose of chloroform caused his insanity. In 1859, defense lawyers argued that a cuckolded husband underwent an uncontrollable frenzy that resulted in a brainstorm causing insanity. This was the first time that a temporary insanity plea was used in a U.S. court. In 1865, a defense plea advocated that paroxysmal insanity was due to being crossed-in-love combined with painful dysmenorrhea. For the first time, a temporary insanity plea was supported by expert medical testimony in a U.S. courtroom. A physician who medically treated John Wilkes Booth in 1863 contended that he was insane when he shot and killed President Abraham Lincoln. During all these legal proceedings, familiar concepts and attitudes emerge repeatedly.

Today, attitudes and concepts remain similar. There appears to be an undercurrent of disbelief when the insanity plea is used in criminal proceedings. Critics throughly reviewed the insanity defense examining the misconceptions about overuse in the courts, the battle of medical experts in testimony, the characteristics of the defendants, the necessity of punishment, the disposition of the acquitted defendants and even the moral basis of the special defense of insanity. A variety of suggested reforms and research have been suggested. Insanity concepts continue to evoke intense pro and con responses today as professionals and the public continue to discuss insanity and murder.

## MURDER DEFENSE PLEA:
## BRUTAL PRISON BEATINGS CAUSED INSANITY

Two sensational murder trials in New York occurred within a few months of each other and the same lawyer defended both men. He used the same insanity defense for both trials. These murder trials attracted a great deal of attention to the medical concepts of insanity and their relation to the law. Essentially, the question was straightforward, but complex: "How can you tell if a man is crazy?"

A plea of insanity as a defense against a charge of murder was viewed with disdain and disbelief ever since the first time the argument was used in a court of law. Public and professional attitudes toward the successful insanity defense persist despite research indicating that "impressive evidence of insanity probably had more to do with acquittals ... than has been commonly assumed."

Early in 1846, Henry G. Wyatt, a prisoner in the Auburn Penitentiary, wrote to William H. Seward pleading for his legal defense on a charge of murder. Wyatt murdered James Gordon while they both were prisoners. Seward agreed to defend Wyatt and maintained that Wyatt was brutally whipped across the spinal column so often that he became insane and irresponsible. Furthermore, Seward claimed that Wyatt was an example of the new concept of moral insanity; insanity caused by other than organic brain disease. During the February 1846 trial, Seward relied upon the warden's official records of the whippings and combined that with expert medical testimony. Although this insanity defense was regarded with suspicion and disfavor, a hung jury resulted and a second trial was scheduled for June.

William H. Seward was a lawyer by profession, a native New Yorker, and a resident of Auburn for most of his life. His fame as a jury lawyer rested on four criminal case defenses, although Seward lost all of them: John Van Zandt in a fugitive slave law case in 1842; Henry G. Wyatt for murder in 1846; William Freeman for murder in 1846; and Abel F. Fitch for conspiracy to destroy railroad property in 1851.

Both, Wyatt and Freeman were Negroes and Seward's defense for both was insanity caused by brutal treatment while in prison. As he defended the two men charged with murder, Seward evolved into a legal expert on the jurisprudence of insanity. Despite his respected legal reputation, Seward declared his misgivings about the law: "I fear, I abhor, detest, despise, and loathe litigation." Nevertheless, he was well known in legal and political circles in Albany, New York City and Washington, D.C. During his political career, Seward was consecutively elected a New York State Senator, the Governor of New York and a U.S. Senator. After declining the nomination for Governor in 1842, Seward practiced law in Auburn with the firm of Seward, [Christopher] Morgan and [Samuel] Blatchford.

In 1843, mental health crusader, Dorothea Lynde Dix, visited Seward seeking his advice on steps to improve the lot of demented people. As New York's Governor, Seward devoted considerable time to mental disease as a state problem and sponsored successful legislation to forbid a trial for the insane.

With this background and while awaiting Wyatt's second trial, a murderous rampage occurred and Seward was plunged into the developing maelstrom.

About 9:30 PM on Thursday, March 12, 1846, William Freeman stealthily approached a farm house in Fleming, about three miles south of Auburn. It was a cold night and the moon reflected on the new fallen snow and the two knives in Freeman's hands. As Mrs. Sarah Van Nest stepped out of the back kitchen door, an unprovoked Freeman attacked her inflicting a single deep wound in her abdomen. She screamed, ran to the front of the house and died in a few minutes. Freeman entered the house through the back door and immediately confronted her husband, 41 year old John G. Van Nest. He stabbed him in the chest and the heart causing his instant death. Continuing his rampage, Freeman stabbed their sleeping two year old son, George Washington Van Nest with such ferocity that the knife passed completely through the infant's body. After this, Freeman attacked Cornelius Van Arsdale, the hired man, and severely wounded him in the breast. Despite his wounds, Van Arsdale managed to drive Freeman from the house into the yard. Once outside, Freeman encountered Sarah's mother, Mrs. Phebe Wyckoff, who had armed herself with a butcher knife. Viciously, Freeman slashed the 70 year old woman inflicting a deep wound. However, Mrs. Wyckoff managed to severely cut Freeman's wrist. Later, he would say: "My hand was so hurt I couldn't kill any more." Although badly wounded, Mrs. Wyckoff ran a quarter-mile across a field to a neighbor to spread the alarm. Finding Mrs. Wyckoff's old horse tethered outside, Freeman mounted it and escaped. He stole another horse when the first one faltered, and reached Schroeppel at 2:00 AM the next morning where he was arrested. On Saturday, March 14, Freeman was driven to the Van Nest home where he was met by a tumultuous, vengeful mob. Shouting for Freeman's blood, they displayed a rope and a lasso demanding that he be lynched. Authorities acted swiftly to spirit Freeman away in a covered wagon. Despite their secretive action, a terrible commotion followed Freeman into the village of Auburn. Frances Seward, the ex-governor's wife, wrote to her sister: "I trust in the mercy of God that I shall never again be a witness to such an outburst of the spirit of vengeance as I saw while they were carrying the murderer past our door." About this time, Mrs. Wyckoff died from her wounds. Freeman had murdered a husband, his wife, their two year old son, and his mother-in-law and badly wounded the hired man.

Within this impassioned environment, nobody could be found to provide legal representation for the man who committed such a monstrous crime. When nobody volunteered their legal services, Seward stepped forward to declare that he would defend the murderer. A Grand Jury indicted Freeman on May 18, 1846 accused of "feloniously, willfully, and of malice aforethought, and from a premeditated design to effect the death of the said John G. Van Nest, did kill and murder, against the peace and dignity of the people of the State of New York."

With Wyatt and Freeman both in jail for capital offenses, Governor Silas Wright ordered a special session of the court under Judge Bowen Whiting for the trial of both prisoners. On Monday June 1, 1846 Freeman was arraigned in the Auburn courthouse and Seward entered a plea of insanity. Seward contended that Freeman became insane due to cruel and abusive beatings administered in jail. During the trial, Captain James E. Tyler testified that during Freeman's first year in jail in 1841 he ordered Freeman flogged for not doing his full quota of work. Tyler described what happened: "I called him up and told him that I was done talking to him. I was going to punish him. I told him to take his clothes off. I turned to get the cat and received a blow on the back part of the head from him ... As I looked around, Bill struck me on the back. I kicked at him and knocked him partly over ... He jumped up, went across the shop, took up a knife and came at me. I took up a piece of wood lying on the desk, went down and met him. It was a basswood board two feet long, fourteen inches wide and half an inch thick ... When I came in reach of him, I struck him on the head flatwise, split the board, and left a piece in my hands four inches wide ... I hit him eight or ten times with the remaining board ... after I flogged him ten or twelve blows ... A black man's hide is thicker than a white man's, and I meant to make him feel the punishment."

After this beating, Freeman always appeared downcast and "went about with his head down." There was a decided difference between the prosecution and the defense as to Freeman's sanity. Seward said that Freeman acted under a blind impulse to avenge the alleged injustice of his imprisonment. Freeman explained the injustice: "I've been whipped, and knocked and abused, and made deaf. There wouldn't any body pay me for it." After deliberation, Judge Whiting ruled that a trial by jury should determine the sanity or insanity of the accused.

Freeman's murderous outburst occurred almost immediately after the Wyatt jury failed to render a verdict. On March 12, 1846, Freeman murdered four people and was charged with murder. Seward worked on both cases at the same time and expeditiously sought out expert medical advice. He persuaded Dr. Amariah Brigham, superintendent of the Utica [NY] Lunatic Asylum to become his prime witness and his personal consultant on insanity. With the Asylum located about 150 miles east of Auburn, this was a major effort on Brigham's part since the trip took thirteen hours by railroad in 1846.

Dr. Brigham studied medicine during several apprenticeships and attended one term of medical lectures at the College of Physicians and Surgeons of New York. Some time later, in 1837, he accepted a special lectureship in anatomy and surgery there. After practicing for about seven years, Brigham continued his education by touring European medical facilities for two years, including hospitals for the mentally ill. In France, he learned the language and his psychiatric thinking was markedly influenced by liberal interpretations of mental illness. In July 1840, he became the superintendent of the Retreat for the Insane in Hartford, Connecticut. When the New York State Lunatic Asylum in Utica was newly opened in October 1842, Brigham became the first superintendent. His psychiatric thought and practice became the forefront of concepts of moral insanity and moral treatment. In caring for patients, Brigham limited the use of harsh medicines and restraints. He applied hydrotherapy, tonics, advocated work and occupational therapy, required educational classes to produce an ordered mind, offered entertainments and amusements, and promoted public education about mental health. Brigham believed that the brain was the organ of the mind and could be affected by psychological and physical causes which could lead to mental illness as well as bodily dysfunction. In 1844, he was one of the thirteen founding members of the Association of Medical Superintendents of American Institutions for the Insane which later became the American Psychiatric Association. In July 1844, he founded the first psychiatric journal in the world published in English, the *American Journal of Insanity*. Brigham remained the editor until his death in 1849.

Brigham sent Seward several books to read in preparation for the trial: James C. Prichard's *A Treatise on Insanity and Other Disorders Affecting the Mind*; Jean Etienne D. Esquirol's Mental Maladies. A Treatise on Insanity; Samuel Tuke's *Description of the [York] Retreat*; and Isaac Ray's *A Treatise on the Medical Jurisprudence of Insanity*. While traveling on the Mississippi river, Seward wrote to his wife on May 9, 1846 commenting that Brigham's material will help with the Wyatt case: "Have been reading ... the works of the fascinating Esquirol, also Isaac Ray ..." Incidentally, Seward's wife assisted with the trial, read the books, marked pertinent passages and also acquired expertise about insanity.

Already defending Wyatt, Seward represented Freeman stimulated by his sense of duty and confident in his fearlessness of intensive heated passions. He took the bold action despite the almost unanimous degradation by his townspeople. On one occasion, boys even threw stones at one of Seward's children. Even Seward's father-in-law and former law partner, Judge Elijah Miller, tormented him with advice to "abandon the nigger." In a letter to Thurlow Weed, his political mentor, Seward remarked: "There is a busy war around me, to drive me from defending and securing a fair trial for the negro Freeman ... He is deaf, deserted, ignorant, and his conduct is unexplainable on any principle of sanity . . Freeman is a demented idiot made so by blows [in prison] which extinguished everything in his breast but a blind passion of revenge."

During the three months that Seward worked on the Wyatt and Freeman cases, he greatly enhanced his proficiency on the subject of insanity. Seward's definition of insanity reflected Brigham's teachings: "Although my definition would not perhaps be strictly accurate, I should pronounce insanity to be a derangement of the mind, character and conduct, resulting from bodily disease."

On June 25, 1846, the trial began to determine whether Freeman was sane or insane. State Attorney General John Van Buren, the 36 year old son of past President Martin Van Buren [1837-1841], and Luman Sherwood, Cayuaga County District Attorney, appeared for the prosecution. Seward and his law partners and David Wright represented Freeman without a fee.

This preliminary trial turned out to be a preview for the murder trial. A host of lay witnesses testified: Freeman's mother, sister, in-laws, and other family members; Van Nest's mother and father; neighbors of Van Nest and Freeman; shopkeepers who knew about Freeman's knives; local townspeople who knew Freeman as a boy; clergymen; investigating police officers and justice officials; fellow prisoners; and jail personnel. Prosecution witnesses testified about the events before, during and after the murders to present the obvious uncontested evidence that Freeman committed the murders. Testimony focused upon a variety of characteristics: Freeman's normal and happy boyhood; his feeble intellect and stupidity; his vacant stare; his idiotic smile; his appearance; his insane aunt and uncle; his change of character; and his behavior before and after being in prison for five years after being convicted, probably falsely, of stealing a horse in 1840.

Reverend John M. Austin, Universalist Church of Auburn, raised the racial prejudice issue in his testimony as he asked: "Is not society in some degree accountable for this sad catastrophe?" He characterized Auburn's Negroes as "victims of unworthy prejudices which compel them to exist under circumstances where they are exposed to imbibe all the vices, without being able to become imbued with the virtues of those around them; who can wonder that they fall into crime?"

John Dupuy, Freeman's brother-in-law, made a similar point: "White men made this murderer [Freeman] what he was, a brute beast; they don't make anything else of our people but brute beasts; but when we violate their laws, they want to punish us as if we were men."

Witnesses testified about exactly the same characteristics but posed contrasting interpretations as to Freeman's insanity. Freeman's smile was labeled idiotic on one hand and the smile he always had on the other. Some noticed tremendous change in Freeman while others said he remained the same as always.

A parade of medical experts from Auburn, Albany and Utica testified. Six physicians found Freeman to be sane while seven medical experts declared that he was insane. After ten days, the jury returned about 8:00 AM on Sunday July 5, 1846 to report that they were deadlocked. One juror could not agree to a verdict of sanity. Judge Whiting then advised the jury that "the main question ... is whether the prisoner knows right from wrong. If he does, then he is to be considered sane." While Seward took exception to the judge's remarks, the jurors were ordered to retire to reconsider. At 8:00 PM on the same day, after about an hour of deliberation, the jurors rendered their verdict: "We find the prisoner sufficiently sane in mind and memory to distinguish between right and wrong." Upon hearing the jury verdict, Seward asked the court to reject that verdict and to instruct the jury to find a verdict on whether the prisoner is sane or insane. Judge Whiting refused and the murder trial began on July 10.

Almost exactly the same lay and medical witnesses returned to testify at Freeman's trial for the murder of John G. Van Nest. Jurors heard from a staggering total of 108 witnesses including seventeen physicians.

Sixty-four lay witnesses testified for the prosecution while twenty-seven did so for the defense. Generally, the witnesses were questioned about exactly the same areas discussed in the preliminary trial on the sanity of the prisoner.

Dr. Leander B. Bigelow practiced medicine for twenty years, was a prison surgeon for seven years and visited Freeman in jail several times. Bigelow knew Freeman's family history and did not consider his laugh as idiotic. His specialty was detecting fakers, or dissemblers, of insanity. He examined Freeman's pulse and asked him a variety of questions. His conclusion: "I am satisfied that he is an ignorant, dull, stupid, morose and degraded Negro, but not insane. I found nothing to satisfy me that the prisoner was insane ... I have no doubt, whatever, but the prisoner is sane."

After examining Freeman in jail, Dr. Jedediah Darrow 'talked with him considerably," and found his memory was good. Under Seward's cross-examination, Darrow confessed: "I have not read anything upon the subject of insanity for a great many years." Further, his opportunities for observing insanity had been very limited. Nevertheless, Darrow stated: "I discovered nothing that indicated that there was insanity about him. My opinion was that he was sane at the time I saw him ... I do not give a professional, but only a common sense opinion of this prisoner."

Although he had seen many cases of insanity, Dr. Charles A. Hyde said "my opportunities for treating it professionally have not been very extensive." Hyde had practiced for twelve years and examined Freeman twice in jail. He found no insanity although Freeman appeared dull and stupid and not talkative. "From seeing him twice, it would be difficult to say that he is insane. I was rather of the opinion that he was not."

Dr. Samuel Gilmore examined Freeman in jail and heard the testimony. He pointed out Freeman's preparation and planning of the homicide with skill and care and his carrying it out as well as any sane man could. Gilmore said this murder indicates great depravity, but not insanity. Although not intelligent, Freeman knew it was wrong to commit murder. "It is my opinion from my examination of him that he was not insane."

Despite being in practice for thirty-five years, Dr. Joseph Clary declared: "I have seen so little of insanity that I don't know as I ought to express an opinion." He visited Freeman in jail three times and noted that his pulse ranged from 120 to 123. Even though Clary was not confident of his opinion, he did declare: "From what I have seen of him it is my opinion that he is sane."

Dr. David Dimon of Auburn visited Freeman six or eight times and examined him at considerable length about his life and the murder. While Dimon found Freeman to be ignorant and depraved, he didn't discover any disturbance of his faculties. Under cross-examination, Dimon did not recollect any prior case where he was called upon to determine doubtful insanity. While he was aware of the questionable smile, the symptoms of dementia and the insane delusion, Dimon saw no evidence of insanity. "I conclude that his mind is now in the same condition that it has been since he was a boy. I discovered nothing about him indicating insanity .. I think he is as sane as ever he was."

In practice for twenty-three years, Dr. Sylvester Willard, examined Freeman six or eight times in jail. He stated that he did not have a great deal of experience in insanity and added: "I don't profess to be an adept, yet I have seen a few insane persons." Nonetheless, Willard did conclude: "I did not find evidence sufficient to make me think him insane."

Dr. Thomas Spencer, Professor of the Theory and Practice of Medicine at the Medical College at Geneva [NY], studied and taught about insanity, visited asylums in London and Paris, and had ten to twelve interviews with Freeman. Spencer noted that "I have bestowed much mental labor upon this case." In the most scholarly testimony of all the prosecution's medical witnesses, he defined insanity as "the deranged, impulsive, incoherent, deluding exercise of some or all of the faculties of mind; suspending the control of conscience, reason, and judgment, over the thoughts, words and acts of the patient." Continuing, he discussed monomania, the prisoner's smile and Freeman's change in character.

In a professorial manner, Spencer used a chart to identify the thirty-six faculties of the mind, divided into three classes: involuntary; voluntary; and intermediate. Involuntary faculties are listed with odd numbers designating the "unbalancing, tempting, affective, and instinctive" ranging from *Sensation* [#1] to *Self-preservation* [#29]. *Conscience* [#36] is the "essential balancing faculty" between the voluntary and involuntary faculties designated by even numbers ranging from *Attention* [#2] to *Will* [#30]. Three intermediate faculties of *Conception* [#31], *Imagination* [#32], and *Association* [#33] are "the essential seat of insanity" while *Sympathy in human weal* [#34} and *Sorrow for human woe* [#35] are aids of conscience in regulating the voluntary faculties. Since all the faculties are united, Spencer connected them all with "imaginary telegraphic wires" on his chart. Spencer compared the acts of the prisoner with the thirty-six faculties of the mind and found all signs and symptoms "to be in a healthy state."

Seward's comprehensive cross-examination raised questions about the impaired mind, moral depravity, pain sensation, mania, walking somnambulism, memory, and distinguishing right from wrong. In particular, Seward questioned Spencer about his visits to asylums and Spencer could recall few facts indicating that he gained any expertise. However, he was quite assured in his conclusion: "I can no longer doubt that the prisoner is sane. I have no reasonable doubt of it."

Next came medical testimony for the defense. Dr. Blanchard Fosgate of Auburn was in practice for eleven years. He was called to the jail to attend to Freeman's severe hand wound on March 16th. Fosgate commented that Freeman did not manifest any sense of pain despite the bad wound. On one visit, Fosgate found Freeman to have an idiotic smile on his face for no reason. Freeman seemed to have no conversational powers; he responded only in monosyllables. "I think he does not comprehend the idea of right and wrong ... he has no moral sense of accountability."

Although he saw patients for twelve years as a Thomsonian botanic medical practitioner, Dr. Levi Hermance was then the assistant keeper of the Auburn prison. He observed Freeman in December 1845 when he sawed fire wood for him. Hermance found Freeman to be in a gloomy, despondent state of mind with singular and strange manners. "My opinion of him last December was that he was a deranged man. Since then I have had no cause to change it - it is my opinion now."

Dr. Lansingh Briggs lived in Auburn, knew Freeman for about eight years before he went to prison and was now a prison physician. Briggs observed that Freeman has less mind than before, that he exhibited little sensibility to pain, and concluded that his mind was impaired and diseased. Under cross-examination, Briggs defined dementia as a gradual diminution or decaying of the powers of the mind. Idiocy was defined as a want of mind from birth. Mania means that mental powers are excited into unnatural activity. Symptoms of dementia and delusion include a downcast look, an aversion to exertion, indolence, loss of intelligence in the expression of the eye, and in the extreme, drooling at the mouth. Freeman believed that society wronged him and owed him reparation. "This delusion, in my judgment, is an insane delusion - the delusion of an insane mind."

After receiving his medical degree from New York University in 1825, Dr. Charles Van Epps continuously practiced in Auburn. He knew Freeman since he was a nursing babe and commented on the change in character. "His smile and general deportment is like persons demented ... I think he was insane at and before that time [July 6, 1846] ... There is not the least doubt that at the time the prisoner committed the act, he was insane."

As the superintendent of the Utica Lunatic Asylum, Dr. Amariah Brigham was the most experienced medical witness regarding insanity; the only real expert medical witness. He visited Freeman several times, heard all the testimony at the preliminary trial, and heard or read all the testimony at the murder trial. In a dramatic demonstration during his testimony, Brigham pointed at a man sitting in court and was proven to be correct as he said: "I see a deranged man there ... I saw him across the court room the other day, and knew from his looks that he was insane." After examination, Brigham found that Freeman was not feigning insanity. He commented that the peculiar pallor, which oftentimes attends insanity, cannot be easily detected from the countenance of colored people. Regarding a predisposition to insanity, Brigham remarked that Freeman had an insane aunt and uncle and heredity was a probable cause. Freeman's character changed from a "lively, active, sociable lad" before entering prison and emerged "taciturn, dull and stupid." Brigham reviewed a number of prior cases to illustrate the actions of insane people. Continuing, Brigham referred to the testimony of earlier witnesses who spoke about insensibility to pain, a rapid pulse, indifference about his fate, and appearances. On cross-examination, Brigham identified symptoms of dementia and partial dementia, labeled Freeman as exhibiting homicidal monomania, spoke about the sudden irresistible impulse, explained the change of character rationale, commented on the smile as evidence of insanity, and defined the role of sleeplessness in insanity. An illuminating dialogue passed between prosecutor Van Buren and Brigham:

    VB:    Do you think stealing hens any evidence of insanity?
    B:    If you should rob a hen roost to-night, I should think you were crazy.
    VB:    And the same of the other counsel, I suppose?
    B:    Yes; for it would be equally strong.

"I believe the prisoner to be insane ... although I have heard sane people talk of revenge, I still think the prisoner was crazy." In a letter to his wife, Frances, Seward said that "Brigham was wonderful" on the witness stand.

    Dr. John McCall, President of the Medical Society of New York State, visited Freeman in jail and examined him. McCall stated that Freeman was not feigning insanity, that his brain was diseased, that there was a familial predisposition to insanity, and that beatings may have injured the brain. He believed that Freeman committed the murder under an insane delusion or irresistible influence and ought not to be held responsible. "From personal observation and also from the testimony, I am of the opinion that the prisoner at the bar, is insane. I have no reasonable doubt of it .. A verdict of a jury in this case, that the prisoner was sufficiently sane to know right from wrong. I do not consider a verdict of sanity. It falls far short of it."

Dr. Charles B. Coventry, a Professor of Medical Jurisprudence in Geneva Medical College, prescribed for the insane and came from Utica [NY] to examine Freeman and to testify. He diagnosed Freeman as a case of partial mania with dementia citing his indifference, the beatings, the predisposition and the supposed feigning. Coventry declared that Freeman "has almost a total abolition of moral faculties ... The prisoner is insane, and has been for a considerable period of time ... I cannot say I have doubt of his insanity then or at this time ... I became fully satisfied that he was insane on the twelfth of March."

Dr. Thomas Hun, Professor in the Albany Medical College, practiced medicine for sixteen years and did not examine Freeman before the jury verdict in the preliminary trial. Consequently, the prosecution objected to Hun's testifying about Freeman's insanity and the judge sustained the objection. From observations in the courtroom, Hun cited the idiotic smile, the chronic disease of the brain, his listless manner, and his inattention to what was happening. Seward proceeded to question Hun using a number of suppositions and Hun repeatedly responded about the hypothetical person: "I should think him insane."

In practice since 1817, Dr. James McNaughton, Professor of the Theory and Practice of Medicine at Albany Medical College and Surgeon General of the State of New York, received his medical education in Edinburgh. McNaughton commented that he could not give a "very positive opinion" of the prisoner's mental condition from only seeing him in court. He said: "...appears to be stupid and foolish ... very feeble intellect ... smile is idiotic ... from his appearance alone, an imbecile ... He is either idiotic or partially demented."

After thirteen trial days, the jury was hard pressed to keep up with the contrasting views of the 72 witnesses for the people and 36 for the defense including eight and nine physicians respectively.

Seward began his summation with elan: "Thou shalt not kill ...whoso sheddeth man's blood by man shall his blood be shed." He then proceeded to answer rhetorical questions and explain issues: "Is the prisoner feigning or counterfeiting insanity?; It is proved that the prisoner is changed; and the prisoner at the bar is insane." During his summation, Seward carefully utilized the testimony of the witness to support his proposition that Freeman was insane. During his impassioned presentation Seward averred that he was shocked "at the spectacle of trying a maniac as a malefactor."

Following, prosecutor Van Buren reminded the jury that "criminal irresponsibility is a question of law, not of medicine ... If the punishment of crime is to be determined by medical rules, the Professors should sit upon the bench and fill the jury box." This reiterated an earlier remark by county district attorney Sherwood that "he did not regard insanity as a subject that was purely or exclusively medical." Van Buren said that all his evidence concluded that Freeman was "in perfect physical health" for the past two years.

Judge Whiting charged the jury and covered both sides. He said: "Sanity consists of having a knowledge of right and wrong ... and in processing memory, intelligence, reason and will ... If sane, he is guilty. If insane, he is not guilty. There is no middle ground." Pointedly, the judge remarked that ignorance is not insanity. In contrast, "evidence of the prisoner's insanity is derived from comparison, from facts and from opinions of medical witnesses."

After retiring, the jury deliberated and rendered a verdict on July 23, 1846. They found Freeman "guilty of the crime wherewith he stands charged in the indictment." Quickly following on July 24, 1846 at 6½ o'clock AM, the judge pronounced sentence: "The judgment of the law is, that the prisoner at the bar, William Freeman, be taken from this place from whence he came, there to remain until Friday, the eighteenth day of September next, and on that day, between the hours of one and four in the afternoon, he be taken from thence to the place of execution appointed by law, and there be hung by the neck until he shall be dead."

Despite the hard fought authoritative defense, both defendants were found guilty. After an initial hung jury, Wyatt was executed after a second trial. Seward believed that the jury punished Wyatt for Freeman's brutal and bloody murders. While Freeman was also found guilty, his execution was stayed as Seward appealed to the Supreme Court on a *Writ of Error*. In the interim, in October, Seward and his wife visited Freeman in jail. She wrote to her sister: "Pray God that he may be insensible to the inhumanity of his relentless keepers. He stood upon the cold stone floor with bare feet, a cot bedstead with nothing but the sacking underneath and a small filthy blanket to cover him."

On February 11, 1847, the Supreme Court reversed the lower court's judgment and ordered a new trial. Four days later, Seward called on Brigham to submit the names of "one hundred of the most intelligent physicians throughout the State of New York and abroad" who might give evidence. At this point Freeman was visited and examined by the Circuit Judge relative to his mental condition. He found the prisoner in a gradual decline of health and strength and declined to try Freeman again. William Freeman remained in chains and died in his cell in the early morning on Saturday, August 21, 1847.

A post-mortem examination of Freeman began about nine o'clock in the morning of August 21. Drs. Briggs and Fosgate, assisted by Drs. Willard and Robinson, removed Freeman's brain from his skull and preserved it in ice to prevent any deterioration. This was deemed expedient since Drs. Brigham and McCall would not arrive until twelve hours later. With Drs. Briggs, Dimon, Fosgate, Hyde, Luce, Van Epps and a large number of lawyers and others watching, Brigham carefully dissected the brain. Brigham prepared a statement which was signed by the other physicians: "Undersigned coincide in the opinion that this organ presented the appearance of chronic disease ... arachnoid membrane somewhat thickened and congested ... medullary portion unnatural dusky color, harder in places, as if par-boiled ...posterior portion appeared diseased and dura-mater unnaturally adherent ... left temporal bone in vicinity of auditory nerve carious and much diseased."

In response to a follow-up request, Brigham made a strong, unequivocal statement about the Freeman case on September 6, 1847: "The whole history of this man, his parentage, his imprisonment, punishment, deafness, crimes, trial, sickness, death and the post-mortem appearance of his brain, establish, most clearly to my mind, and I doubt not to others who are much acquainted with mental maladies, that this was a case of insanity - that Freeman had disease of the brain, and was deranged in mind, from a period some time previous to his leaving prison, until the time of his death."

After Freeman's trial, Seward commented on the intense hostility and verbal abuse from his own townspeople that his family endured during the trials: "I rise from these fruitless labors exhausted in mind and body, covered with public reproach, stunned with duns and protests." Subsequently, Seward's voluntary defenses reaped political advantages and enhanced his legal reputation. New clients flocked to his law firm and their business grew by leaps and bounds. Seward's *Argument in Defense of William Freeman* was published from his notes and went through four printings.

Freeman's trial attracted considerable attention to the insanity plea in a murder trial, and to the subject of insanity in general. Complimentary letters came to Seward. Salmon P. Chase, who became Lincoln's Secretary of the Treasury and Chief Justice of the Supreme Court, regarded Seward "as one of the very first public men of our country ... his action in the Freeman case, considering his own personal position and circumstances ... magnanimous in the highest degree." A zealous abolitionist, Samuel J. May, was equally praising: "Your magnanimous espousal of the case of poor Freeman, and unsparing efforts in his behalf, commanded my admiration." Seward commented on the fickleness of the harsh public reactions to his defense of Freeman: "Less than a year has passed since no execrations were too severe for the people who now judge favorably my conduct, without any regard to the question whether my client deserved death or not."

Despite his notoriety from the Freeman trial, Seward is best remembered for buying Russian icebergs when he was Secretary of State. Continuing to serve under President Andrew Johnson after Abraham Lincoln's assassination, Seward achieved dubious fame for the $7.2 million purchase of 586,000 square miles of land in North America from Russia on March 30, 1867. His acquisition of this domain called, Walrussia, was derisively labeled "Seward's Folly" or "Seward's Icebox." In the *New York Herald*, James Gordon Bennett summed up the conventional wisdom of the day by suggesting that any impoverished European monarch who wanted to sell worthless territory should apply to "W. H. Seward, State Department, Washington, D.C." Seward responded to the ridicule on August 12, 1868 in a speech at Sitka: "[I do not doubt] that the political society to be constituted here, first as a Territory, and ultimately as a State or many States, will prove a worthy constituency of the Republic." In 1897-1898, the Klondike Gold Rush was the first discovery to turn "Seward's Folly" into a fortuitous bargain which was augmented by the later discovery of oil. On January 3, 1959, President Eisenhower signed the act declaring Alaska the 49th state.

## A. LINCOLN, ESQUIRE:
## A CHLOROFORM INDUCED INSANITY PLEA

Before Abraham Lincoln became President of the United States, he earned a comfortable living working as a lawyer for almost twenty-five years. He handled all types of cases and seldom turned away a paying client. Although he was most often pictured with a beard, Lincoln was clean-shaven during his years as an attorney. He did not grow a beard until he became President.

In an unusual 1857 trial, Lincoln and Leonard Swett were the opposing lawyers. Defense lawyers claimed that their client was absolved of willful murder because an overdose of chloroform administered during an earlier surgical procedure caused the accused's insanity. Jurors in this murder trial had to contend with the perplexities and definitions of insanity, the conflicting testimony of expert medical witnesses and the art and science of anesthesia.

For this murder trial, Lincoln assisted the State's Attorney for the Eighth Judicial Circuit in Illinois with the prosecution. A fellow Illinois lawyer on the circuit, Swett was the chief defense attorney. He was an able lawyer with significant personal charm. Coincidentally, there was a strong physical resemblance between Lincoln and Swett. Both men were bony, long and lanky with Swett having a long thoughtful face with a white chin beard. They had similar legal styles in the courtroom including an inoffensive presence and a magnetic effect upon juries.

Before the murder, Isaac Wyant and Anson Rusk feuded belligerently for some months over a contested land boundary. There was "bad blood" between them and their families. After an exchange of excitable words in June 1855, several family members on both sides participated in a brutal confrontation. Rusk shot Wyant in the arm when he thought that Wyant threatened him with a bowie knife. Wyant's left arm was so badly damaged that amputation at the shoulder was necessary sixteen hours later. Attending physicians, Drs. Lemon, John Warner and Christopher Goodbrake, administered chloroform as an anesthetic during the operation. After the amputation, Wyant was "ever after morbidly fearful that Rusk would kill him ... and complained greatly about his head and exhibited many signs of being unsettled in his intellect."

Suffering continuous physical pain and emotional turmoil, Wyant stalked Rusk to the DeWitt County clerk's office in Clinton, Illinois on October 12, 1855. At point blank range, in broad daylight, Wyant brutally fired four shots at Rusk, killing him with a final shot to the head. As Wyant fled the building, he was captured by the sheriff. DeWitt County Court Clerk John J. McGraw secured a warrant to arrest Wyant:

> TO ALL SHERIFFS, CORONERS AND CONSTABLES OF SAID STATE
> Whereas John J. McGraw hath this day made complaint on oath before Daniel Robbins ... that one Isaac Wyant did at the county of DeWitt in the State of Illinois on the 12th day of October 1855 commit a criminal offence by shooting and wounding one Anson Rusk thereby causing his death by reason of said shooting and wounding ... that just and reasonable grounds to suspect that the said Isaac Wyant has been guilty ... prays that a warrant may issue against the said Isaac Wyant.
> We therefore command you, forthwith, to take the said Isaac Wyant and bring him before ... any Justice of the Peace ... to be dealt with according to law. Hereof fail not at your own peril.

Squire McGraw had Constable William W. Williams arrest Wyant while he went to inform the coroner, Dr. Christopher Goodbrake, about the fatal shooting. After hearing the testimony at an examination in Justices' Court by Justices of the Peace Daniel Robbins and Samuel Phares, "it was ordered that the prisoner be kept in close confinement in the county jail to await his trial in the circuit court, the case not being considered bailable." On October 26, 1855, Tazewell County sheriff Thomas C. Reeves "received of William Fuller, sheriff of DeWitt County the body of Isaac Wyant for safe keeping and to be delivered to the sheriff of DeWitt County when called for." A grand jury indicted Wyant for murder on October 19, 1855. In preparing for an obviously sensational murder trial, Wyant's lawyers petitioned for a change of venue in the May 1856 term of the court. In granting the request, the court ordered the trial moved from Clinton in DeWitt County to Bloomington in McLean County. On September 10, 1856, Swett secured a continuance of Wyant's trial to the next court term. Without bail, Wyant remained in prison for about seventeen months until the trial started.

Lincoln's law associate, Ward Hill Lamon, was the State's Attorney for McLean County. Their co-partnership was advertised, probably by Lamon without Lincoln's knowledge, in local newspapers such as the *Iroquois Journal* in Middleport, Illinois:

> ABRAM LINCOLN, *Springfield*            W. H. LAMON, *Danville*
> **LINCOLN & LAMON,** ATTORNEYS AT LAW,
> Having formed a co-partnership, will practice in the Courts of the Eighth Judicial Circuit, and the Superior Court, and all business entrusted to them will be attended to with promptness and fidelity.
> ☞ Office on the second floor of the "Barnum Building"
> over Whitcomb's Store.           Denville, Nov. 10, 1852

    To conduct the People's case against the murderer, Lamon secured the assistance of Lincoln, Clifton H. Moore and Harvey Hogg. To defend him, Wyant retained Leonard Swett and his partner, William Ward Orme. Newspaper accounts of the trial in the Bloomington *Weekly Pantagraph* reveal that Lincoln handled the prosecution almost singlehandedly. Swett directed the thrust of the defense. On the afternoon of March 30, 1857, the trial began and lasted about six days. Jury members included James Adams, Wolford Wyatt, Samuel White, E.V. Augustus, Denton Young, J.L. Brittaman, David Shough, John T. Hill, James Huff, W.C. Warlow, J.S. Barber, and Joseph Shough. During the trial, the jury stayed at the Pike House in charge of police officers. An article in the Bloomington *Weekly Pantagraph* announced "great interest in the progress and result of the trial was manifested by the people, and the Court House was constantly thronged." That local newspaper reported on the trial in comprehensive detail.

    Attracted by the spectacle of a sensational murder trial, winter weather dreary and work weary prairie residents converged upon the Bloomington public square. Each day, all the hitching posts were occupied and people noisily milled about on the town square. With their legal reputations well known to all, spectators jostled for seats to behold the expected robust fray between Lincoln and Swett. Bloomington residents anticipated a "battle royal" between Lincoln and Swett.

    Opening for the State, Lincoln presented a straightforward *prima facie* case of murder. There was an abundance of evidence and witnesses. He used a diagram of the clerk's office to show the murder site to the witnesses and the jury. All six of Lincoln's witnesses were nearby at the time of the shooting. All heard the four shots. All saw Wyant coming or going. Harry Kidder actually was an eyewitness to the whole affair: "I was in the [clerk's] office when Rusk came in .. first thing I saw of the difficulty was the smoke of the pistol ... was in but a short time when Wyant came and opened the door and fired on Rusk ...

appeared about one or two o'clock ... Rusk bellowed two or three times ... Rusk fell on his knees ...defendant shot again ... I caught the defendant and told him he should shoot no more there ...[he] shot three times ... said nothing after I took hold of him ... nothing passed between the defendant and Rusk before the shooting ... Rusk had two pistols; one in his side pocket and the other in his hind coat pocket."

Three witnesses heard Wyant say that he killed Rusk. Constable Williams exchanged words with Wyatt: "Was in Taylor & Bell's store about fifty steps away ... I heard the shooting and knew something was wrong and came immediately ... Wyant was a few rods [about forty feet] from the court house gate when I first saw him with his pistol in his hand ... He had two pistols [revolvers]; one with six loads in it and the other with two loads ... I had a struggle with him to get the first pistol and he gave up the other one ... I took him back to the court house ... I arrested him [Wyant] and told him he had killed Rusk. He said 'Well, if I have killed him, damn his soul, that is just what I came here to do.' ... He begged of me not to take him where he could see the dead man, for he said that his friends would shoot his poor body all to pieces."

DeWitt County Court Clerk Esquire McGraw knew Rusk for several years and noticed Wyant the day before the shooting. He saw Wyant enter the office, heard a pistol and a scream followed by two more shots and another scream. As Wyant came out of the clerk's office he told McGraw that "he had shot the damn rascal that had shot his arm off." McGraw had Constable Williams arrest Wyant and went to inform the coroner, Dr. Goodbrake, about the fatal shooting.

Robert Lewis was a resident of Clinton for six years. He heard the four shots and saw Wyatt after he was taken upstairs. He did not see Wyatt vomit up there. Wyatt told him that he "shot the man who murdered his arm."

Dr. Goodbrake heard the sound of four distinct shots and met McGraw outside the court house. He encountered Wyatt coming out of the court house door. "I was walking tolerably lively and [Wyatt] said something about the shooting, but I don't recollect what it was." As the coroner, Goodbrake testified: "When I got into the office, Rusk was lying on the floor with his head doubled under and his brains coming out. I examined the body and found four wounds occasioned by balls; in the head, shoulder blade, side and arm ... the head wound caused the death, though the shot in the side would have terminated fatally, but not so soon ... head wound ball entered above the left eye and plowed its way through the brain and lodged against the skull on the other side ... I probed the wound with a flexible Gum Catheter."

Dr. Thomas K. Edmundson first saw Rusk's body at the coroner's inquest. He agreed with Goodbrake in his description of the wounds and the cause of death. In passing, Edmundson commented that Wyatt's pistols were old fashioned with barrels that were three to four inches long.

Lincoln presented his evidence and closed for the prosecution in the evening of the first day of the trial as entered in the court record:

Thursday April 2$^{nd}$ 1857

People       }
vs           }    Indictment for Murder
Isaac Wyant  }

This day again came the Prosecuting Attorney and also the defendant in custody of the Sheriff and also came Swett & Orme his attorneys and the jurymen, empaneled and sworn to try this cause being called, each answered to his name. Thereupon the Court proceeded to hear further evidence on behalf of the People, which evidence being closed, the Court then proceeded to hear evidence on behalf of said defendant. And now the said jury again retire being, in charge of a proper officer and the Court adjourned to Friday morning.

Presiding Judge David Davis allowed the defense to propose an insanity plea for Wyant's actions. Swett asserted: "Resting on the ground of insanity, the killing was not controverted." Innovatively, Swett stated that medical experts would testify that an overdose of chloroform resulted in damage to the brain and caused Wyant's ensuing insanity. Preparing the jury, Swett told them that evidence of commonly and professionally accepted irrational behaviors would be presented along with proof of an inherited tendency to insanity. Swett considered historical data to create the chloroform induced insanity plea.

During the time that Lincoln practiced law, the insanity defense was well established and Lincoln certainly saw the defense used in Illinois courtrooms. Furthermore, despite heated objections, "the Supreme Court of Illinois of Lincoln's day upheld the insanity defense and met some of the same arguments that are used against it today."

Believing that Wyant was feigning "the loss of his mentality," Lincoln strenuously objected to the defense's insanity argument.

However, Judge Davis did not change his decision. At the time of the trial, the insanity plea was used, but was still a novel defense. A chloroform induced insanity plea was rarer still. Supporting medical testimony for the insanity defense was said to be unique in Illinois courts.

    Swett augmented his insanity defense with intensive research into the medical arguments consulting Dr. Luther V. Bell, Superintendent, McLean Asylum, Boston, Massachusetts. It is likely that Bell referred Swett to Dr. Isaac Ray's landmark book, *A Treatise on the Medical Jurisprudence of Insanity*, first published in 1838 and then in its third edition in 1853. Ray's book was repeatedly cited by British barristers in the 1843 trial of Daniel M'Naghten for murdering the prime minister's private secretary. Adjudicating an insanity plea, the British Court's verdict resulted in establishing the "knowing right from wrong" principle, a cherished tenet of medical jurisprudence. Ray was an international authority on medical jurisprudence, a colleague in the Association of Medical Superintendents of American Institutions for the Insane, and Bell's New England neighbor as superintendent of the Butler Hospital for the Insane in Providence, Rhode Island. Defining mental illness, Ray declared: "Insanity is a disease, and as is the case with all other diseases, the fact of existence is never established by a single diagnostic symptom, but by the whole body of symptoms, no particular one of which is present in every case."

    Scientific testimony of medical witnesses for the defense exposed Lincoln to professional concepts of insanity as caused by chloroform anesthesia. Swett displayed an extraordinary mastery of the intricacies of anesthesia, medical science and mental disease without ever hearing the word, psychiatry; the term was yet to be coined. In advocating Wyant's insanity plea, Swett introduced nineteen witnesses: five relatives; five friends; six physicians; the sheriff; the county clerk; and even Swett himself. Those who were present when Wyant was shot in the arm described the raucous brawl and the mortal threats. Wyant's friends and family testified about his multiple irrational behaviors. His symptoms included: a constant fearfulness that the Rusks were going to kill him; picking his head until the scalp was bloody with festering sores; frequent and unexpected tantrums; being flighty, rambling and unconnected; continuously talked to himself and others; and underwent a total change in disposition. His sister surprised the jury with a grotesque fact. In an emotional outburst, Wyant demanded that his buried arm be dug up from the graveyard and brought in to him. Wyant's physical complaints included: a roaring in the head; ringing in the ears; facial twitching; constipation; feverish excitement; sleeplessness; loss of appetite; and general continuous and phantom pains. Six physicians repeated and magnified the medical symptoms while incorporating the bizarre behaviors observed by the friends and family members.

Wyant's sister, half-brother and an uncle told of a hereditary predisposition; two uncles were unbalanced; one went "queer in the head after not getting a girl he had sparked."

Five physicians testified about the harmful effects of too much chloroform during anesthesia. Dr. Lemon told about the amputation as well as about chloroform: "[Wyant's] arm was fractured with wound below the elbow ... arm amputated sixteen hours after the wound ... Drs. Warner, Goodbrake and myself present ... chloroform administered ... took long time in administering it; thought it not good for anything ... sent son to get bottle of ether while prisoner continued breathing the chloroform til it worked ... Books say that injury produced from chloroform causes uneasiness about the head including picking ... when it [chloroform] injures the brain, it destroys the mind ... there are some recorded cases of permanent insanity from the use of chloroform ... insanity one of the probable effects of injury from use of it."

In Lincoln's cross-examination, Dr. Lemon testified further: "Did not examine bottle [of chloroform] until four or five weeks after death of Rusk ... not much experience of the effects of chloroform ... most of information drawn from books ... inference is that anything producing insensibility affects the brain ... one case of insanity mentioned in books ... don't know what kind of insanity chloroform produces."

Physicians who attended Wyant's amputation and post-operative recovery visited him four or five times a day during his convalescence. Wyant's constant brooding over the loss of his left arm further unhinged his mind.

Dr. Parks recounted his experiences using a combination of ether and chloroform to make the compound less dangerous. He commented that it is probable that chloroform injures the mind. However, Parks couldn't mention a single case where a male was rendered permanently insane by the use of chloroform. In keeping with medical beliefs, Parks declared that females and nervous males are more susceptible to insanity.

Dr. Roe declared that the "tendency of chloroform is to effect the brain and nervous system ... instead of deadening his [Wyant's] animal passions, it [chloroform] had the effect to revive and excite them ... I think that chloroform given in any quantities leads to insanity ... picking of the head is often an accompaniment of insanity ... all morbid feelings are evidences of insanity." Under Lincoln's cross-examination, Roe agreed that "It is a very difficult matter to judge insanity; the books lay down this. I know of no case of a male being made insane by chloroform, though it has occurred." He concurred that females are more susceptible, particularly during childbirth, "when there is a greater tendency to insanity."

Dr. Spencer's experience included dealing with the insane when he was in charge of the Insane Hospital in Albany, New York for two years. He testified that "Among the symptoms of the abuse of chloroform are pain or ringing in the head, listening to fancied noises, etc. I have seen a case where this was the prominent trait of the insanity."

On seeing Wyant for the first time, Dr. Hoover "was called to him by his peculiar appearance and manner. His muscles were twitching in his face and he was picking at his head ... he talked but was rambling and disconnected."

Five physicians, including two experienced asylum superintendents, did not hesitate in agreement that Wyant was insane. Hoover said: "I have no doubt in my mind that Wyant was insane when I saw him ... satisfied from his manner that he was insane ... his appearance denoted it." Agreeing, Roe declared: "I have heard the testimony in this case and from that testimony I am satisfied that Wyant was insane at the time of the commission of the offence. I think he is insane ... I have no doubt of his being insane since the shooting of the arm." Spencer concurred: "From the evidence, I think Wyant was insane." Parks concluded that the "symptoms of insanity mentioned by the physicians are evidences of insanity." Dr. Andrew McFarland, Superintendent, Illinois State Hospital for the Insane, Jacksonville, said: "There are reasonable grounds to believe from the evidence that he was insane when he killed Rusk."

During Lincoln's cross-examination of the medical experts for the defense, he questioned whether Wyant was feigning insanity. Hoover announced his position: "I don't think he was feigning insanity."

McFarland's expert opinion was conclusive: "Insanity is sometimes successfully feigned, but not where there is an opportunity for experienced persons to witness the attempts at feigning. I have no fears in this case that insanity had been feigned."

McFarland was Swett's star witness. He had a medical degree from Jefferson Medical College in Philadelphia, was a former superintendent of the New Hampshire Asylum for the Insane from 1845 to 1852, Illinois state asylum superintendent since 1854, and a specialist in the study of the mind for twelve years. After all nineteen defense witnesses testified, McFarland was asked "to summarize all the points, great and small, that went to show the defendant to be insane." Speaking with self-assured authority, McFarland identified several conclusive medical rationales for Wyant's insanity: Wyant's change in character from courageous to cowardice; his wakefulness and watchfulness; the propensity of a heredity predisposition; ringing noises in the head; his picking his head constantly is of more importance than would appear to ordinary man; his vomiting after shooting Rusk evidences insanity; and his charging his sister with shooting off his arm. "I conceive it to be the natural tendency of chloroform to paralyze the brain. The secondary effect is to carry that paralyzation beyond recovery or to fatality. The first effect of it is to blunt the sensation of feeling. I consider that it effected Wyant from the amount inhaled and the length of time inhaling." McFarland told the jury that Wyant's condition used to be called a "sanguineo-nervous temperament" but physicians now ceased to talk of temperament. In addition, McFarland revealed that he had experimented with the effects of chloroform upon the mind including its use with "extremely excited maniacs."

Independent of each other, Lemon, Parks, Roe and Spencer all expertly concurred that an overdose of chloroform injures the brain and causes insanity. A pound bottle of chloroform was used during the amputation and not touched until five weeks later. Swett was called to the witness stand and testified that he measured the bottle and almost two and one-half inches of chloroform was used during Wyant's surgery. That amount easily equals an overdose of chloroform; equivalent to 600 to 700 drops.

Swett's defense strategy and his use of six expert physician witnesses demonstrated his insightful research into the medical aspects of the harmful effects of chloroform.

Trying to depreciate the impressive accumulation of medical and lay testimony, Lincoln used folksy humor to rebut the insanity plea. In cross-examination of one defense expert physician witness, Lincoln remarked: "You say, doctor, that this man picks his head, and by that you infer that he is insane. Now, I sometimes pick my head and those joking fellows at Springfield tell me that there may be a living, moving cause for it, and that the trouble isn't at all on the inside. It's only a case for fine-tooth combs."

Testimony of the defense's six medical experts and the confirming observations by Wyant's family and friends impressed the jury. Believing so, Lincoln rebutted with sixteen witnesses to show that Wyant had ample reasons to kill Rusk and to discredit specific defense testimony, including the concept of chloroform induced insanity.

Rusk's family members testified about Wyant's motivation to kill Rusk. They reported Wyant's frequent bluntly stated threats toward Rusk, his fights with various Rusk family members, his bullying and whipping of Rusk and others, his using a bowie knife to intimidate Rusk and his obviously seeking vengeance for his amputated arm. A witness, Mr. Nixon, said that Wyant told him he craved revenge for his injury and "it was a damn hard thing for a man to be waylaid and have his arm shot off." Two witnesses, the Court Clerk McGraw and Constable Williams, said they did not hear Wyant say anything about killing his father or anybody else's father. Robert Lewis stated that Wyant "did not look strange when we saw him upstairs after the shooting."

Pertinent and impressive testimony about Wyant's feigning insanity came from a man named Taylor, Wyant's jailor for seventeen months. Since Wyant said he was a stranger and didn't know anyone, Taylor recommended Swett as a lawyer. Taylor testified: "Swett asked Dr. Lemon in jail in the presence of Wyant if the use of chloroform would affect the brain. Dr. Lemon replied in some cases it did. Afterwards on one occasion when I took food to Wyant, he put on foolish actions. I told him he need not feign to be insane to me and afterwards he did not; he acted then as usual."

Warner, who administered the chloroform to Wyant during the amputation, testified: "I didn't think Wyant inhaled double the ordinary dose ... chloroform evaporates quickly ... I suppose chloroform would lose its strength during ordinary usage."

Lincoln's last rebuttal witness responded to the proposition that a chloroform overdose induced insanity. Goodbrake, then President of the Illinois State Medical Society, was present at Wyant's amputation. He said that much of the chloroform was wasted because Wyant at first refused to take it. "An ordinary dose of chloroform was given to Wyant and a bit more when he awoke during surgery." While he was awake, Wyant cried and swore and said his friends ought to have killed Rusk. Symptoms of the type mentioned were not unusual when a man lost an arm and "might be present in a sane mind as well." Goodbrake did not consider the symptoms as a sign of permanent insanity caused by chloroform. In addition, he commented: "I have examined some books on the use of chloroform ... I have never found a case of permanent insanity made by chloroform." In summary, Goodbrake said that he had not seen much change in Wyant. "It impressed me that he was either a strange man or a crazy one. He was as much insane before the amputation as afterwards as it appeared to me." Lincoln s prosecution rebuttal concluded that afternoon.

  On Friday, April 4, Hogg delivered a three hour summation for the prosecution. Orme followed for the defense for almost three hours. Swett took the rest of the day starting his summation and finished on Saturday morning about noon. After lunch, Lincoln's speech began and went on until almost six o'clock.

  After the summations, Judge Davis gave instructions to the jury. He relied heavily in his directions on existing legal precedents regarding irresistible and uncontrollable impulses, the involuntary act determinations and the sound mind question. Defense pleas of irresistible impulse were previously upheld by the state supreme courts of Ohio, Massachusetts and Pennsylvania in 1834, 1844, and 1846. In the Massachusetts decision, Judge Lemuel Shaw declared that "One is not responsible for an act under an irresistible and uncontrollable impulse which is the result of mental diseases." Jury members were told that if the defendant's unsoundness overwhelmed his reason, conscience and judgment, he should be found not guilty. On the other hand, if Wyant had enough mental capacity to understand the nature and consequences of his act, the right and wrong of his action, he should be found guilty. Judge Davis admonished the jury that the law presumes a man is sane and that must be rebuffed by satisfactory proof to the contrary. After immediately taking supper, the jury retired to deliberate the case.

Judge Davis' wife, Sarah, accurately forecast the next step: "A trial for murder has engaged the attention of our people for five days past ... The jury are now locked up and I fear that they will send for my better half by the middle of the night." About one o'clock on Sunday morning, the jury came back to court with the result of their deliberations: "We the jurors duly sworn to try the cause of the People of the State of Illinois against Isaac Wyant, find on mature deliberation, that the said defendant, Isaac Wyant, is not guilty by reason of insanity. Our opinion being found principally under the fourth article of the instructions from the Court. Also the article touching evidence of medical witnesses, and we the jurors find that the aforesaid prisoner being of an unsound mind is unsafe to be at large, and therefore earnestly recommend that the Honorable Court take the necessary steps, to have him the said Isaac Wyant removed immediately to the State Lunatic Asylum at Jacksonville. [Court's response] "It is therefore ordered by the Court that the said defendant of the above indictment be discharged and go hence without delay."

With an acquittal verdict and a recommendation for the prisoner's confinement in a lunatic asylum, Swett immediately initiated legal procedures to assure that Wyant would be sent to the Illinois State Lunatic Asylum. In response, the court convened "a jury of six good and lawful men" to hear the evidence. After hearing the evidence, the jury was satisfied that Wyant was insane and should be sent to the Illinois State Hospital for the Insane. "That his age is about thirty-five years. That his disease is not of long duration, that the disease is with him probably hereditary, that he is not subject to epilepsy, and that he is free from vermin or any infectious disease and is not a pauper." A warrant was issued for Wyatt's removal to the Illinois State Hospital for the Insane.

In the McLean County Circuit Court docket of judgments and executions, the clerk recorded costs of $356.10 for the trial by jury in the case of the *People v. Isaac Wyant*.

Sarah Davis, the judge's wife, accurately reflected the public's dubious attitude toward the verdict in a letter to her brother: "The scamp who committed the murder is in the Insane Asylum at Jacksonville, the jury having acquitted him on the plea of insanity." Like the judge's wife, Lincoln was cognizant of the skeptical attitudes of professionals and the public toward the insanity plea. Based upon his own experiences in the courtroom, Lincoln was familiar with the abilities of skillful lawyers and expert witnesses to convince a jury and to persuade the public.

Popular feeling arose against Swett as rumors persisted that Wyant left the asylum and was at large in DeWitt county. On April 25, 1857, the *Clinton Transcript* published Swett's letter to the editor in which he responded to the public apprehension about Wyant. Swett reiterated his activities to securely confine Wyant in the Asylum. He included remarks by the Asylum superintendent Dr. McFarland:

---

**CLINTON TRANSCRIPT**         April 25, 1857

In passing through Clinton to my home, I frequently met the report that Wyant, since his acquittal, has been at large in your county. I believe this story to be wholly unfounded ... When acquitted, Wyant was at my request detained in custody. The second day afterwards I got the County Court to empanel a jury to pass again upon the question of his insanity. Upon the testimony of Drs. Hoover and Roe, and a statement of what happened in the Circuit Court, he was pronounced insane and William S. Brooks, his half-brother, was deputed by the Court to deliver him to the Superintendent of the Asylum at Jacksonville ... Dr. McFarland has written to me, and I take the liberty of making the following extract from his letter: "So far as Wyant's present appearance is of importance, it confirms the justice of the defence made for him He is moody and silent, save when spoken to, and has no idea apparently of the crime he committed, or at least of its criminal intent. He complains much of his head and wears the same fatuous expression of countenance that he did at Bloomington."

[from a letter to Judge Davis] "Under careful and exact surveillance we discover Wyant to be most unquestionably an insane man and the testimony from which opinions had to be gathered in the Court are abundantly corroborated by what we hourly see in the man now. By these facts the justice of his acquittal, it seems to me, is clearly established, and Wyant is shown to have been at Jacksonville as late as the 21st inst. It also shows, to which in justice to them I cheerfully bear testimony, that the relatives of Wyant, in their testimony and their conduct, have pursued a course honorable to themselves and conducive to humanity and truth."

---

After many years in the asylum, Wyant seemingly recovered. Upon an order from the Asylum's Board of Trustees, Wyant was released on the condition that he return to his native state, Indiana, and never return to Illinois. McFarland remarked about Wyant's confinement: "Strange as it may seem, the one at the hospital to whom he bore the most deadly hatred was the one whose opinion had saved him from the gallows. This is no paradox but only the universal experience in such cases."

After the murder trial ended, fellow Illinois attorney Joseph E. McDonald ran into Lincoln and Swett at a chance meeting in Danville, Illinois. He told them that he had defended Wyant from "every charge in the calendar of crimes ... he was a weak brother and could be led into almost everything." Intrigued, Lincoln listened intently as McDonald told all about Wyant. McDonald recounted his conversation with Lincoln the next day: "He told me that he had been greatly troubled over what I related about Wyant; that his sleep had been disturbed by the fear that he had been too bitter and unrelenting in his prosecution of him." Lincoln said: "I acted on the theory that he [Wyant] was 'possuming' insanity ... I fear I may have been too severe and that the poor fellow may be insane after all. If he cannot realize the wrong of his crime, then I was wrong in asking to punish him."

Holding true to his reputation, Lincoln put all his energy into the prosecution and presented the People's case with intensity and professional deftness. Lincoln drew up the indictment, made the opening and closing arguments to the jury and conducted most of the direct examination of the People's witnesses. He handled the cross-examination of the physicians who testified as to the effects of an overdose of chloroform and as to the insanity of the defendant. Considering the medical and scientific knowledge available at that time, this was a complex and perplexing assignment. Even with his extensive legal experience, Lincoln had little medical jurisprudence background. On the other hand, Swett did a much better job of medical investigation and research and emerged as a legal expert on insanity.

Lincoln recognized and emphasized the obvious legal facts. There was no doubt that Wyant murdered Rusk. However, Lincoln did not pursue the medical aspects of the chloroform induced insanity defense as relentlessly as possible. While medical literature existed to offer strong evidence of the safety of chloroform as an anesthetic, Lincoln didn't discover the material and bring it into court. Furthermore, there were other medical and asylum experts that Lincoln could have used to counter Swett's authorities on chloroform induced insanity.

Although Lincoln was "bitter and unrelenting" in the prosecution, he lost the case. His later conversation with lawyer McDonald about Wyant after the case was concluded bears evidence to his mixed emotions. Nevertheless, Lincoln applied his genius for simple, persuasive parlance, handy humor and deft depictions in this case as he did in all others.

Jurors, the judge and the lawyers would have benefitted from learning about the development of medical painkillers. During surgical procedures, physicians chose from a few accepted anesthetics to ease the patient's pain. Early on physicians used nitrous oxide and in the 1850s selected either ether or chloroform.

About the same time that Joseph Priestly found oxygen, in May 1772, he discovered nitrous oxide. Humphry Davy experimented with the effects of inhaling nitrous oxide when he was about seventeen. From May to June 1799, Davy inhaled the gas daily and named it "laughing gas." Davy noticed that the nitrous oxide diminished his pain from a toothache. In 1800, Davy published material about his research and suggested a possible use: "As nitrous oxide in its extensive operation appears capable of destroying physical pain, it may probably be used with advantage during surgical operations in which no great effusion of blood takes place."

Nitrous oxide was not used routinely as an anesthetic until some forty years later. Public demonstrations of laughing gas at entertainments and sideshows amused audiences. One enterprising showman, Gardner Q. Colton, administered nitrous oxide to dentist Horace Wells as his tooth was extracted by another dentist. Wells entered into a partnership in Boston with William T. G. Morton, who graduated dental school in 1842. Both of them experimented with nitrous oxide as an anesthetic agent in extracting teeth. In a widely advertised demonstration to prove the anesthetic value of nitrous oxide, Wells failed miserably, became a laughing stock, despaired and eventually committed suicide.

Morton abandoned nitrous oxide to experiment with ether. He administered sulfuric ether as an anesthetic in 1846 as Dr. John C. Warren removed a tumor from the neck of Gilbert Abbot at Boston's Massachusetts General Hospital. After the successful surgery, Warren exclaimed to those observing the surgery: "Gentlemen, this is no humbug."

Although better known for his initial use of ether, Dr. Crawford W. Long described his experience with nitrous oxide: "In the month of December 1841, or January 1842, the subject of the inhalation of nitrous oxide gas was introduced in a company of young men at night, in the village of Jefferson, Ga., and the party requested me to prepare some ..." Relevant to this murder trial, as early as 1842, Dr. F. Stanley reported on poisoning by the inhalation of impure nitrous oxide gas.

Another anesthetic discovery took about ten years to be utilized. Almost simultaneously, chemists Justus von Liebig in Germany and Eugène Soubeiran in France along with Dr. Samuel Guthrie in the United States discovered chloroform; a clear, colorless, heavy volatile liquid.

With scientific inquisitiveness, Dr. James Young Simpson, Professor of Midwifery at the University of Edinburgh and physician-accoucheur to the Queen of Scotland, inhaled chloroform at a dinner party at his Edinburgh home at 32 Queen Street. Some of his guests inhaled the gas as did his assistants, Drs. Matthew Duncan and George Keith. Simpson commented: "I have tried upon myself and others the inhalation of different other volatile fluids, with the hope that some one of them might be found to possess the advantages of ether, without its disadvantages." In a speech to the Medico-Chirurgical Society on November 10, 1847, Simpson described a new agent "for the purpose of producing insensibility to pain in surgical and obstetric practice." Seven advantages of chloroform over sulfuric ether were listed: the smaller dosage required; the much more rapid, complete and persistent action; "an agreeable, fragrant, fruit-like odor and a saccharine, pleasant taste;" the small quantity will be less expensive; odor does not remain on clothes or body; more portable and transmissible; and no need for a special inhaler. While Simpson's usual dose was one hundred to one hundred twenty drops, he found as little as thirty drops effective in some cases. Even at that minimal dosage, insensibility occurred in a few minutes with six or seven inhalations. Simpson promoted and encouraged the use of chloroform as an anesthetic: "I have exhibited the chloroform to about fifty individuals. In not a single instance has the slightest bad result of any kind whatever occurred from its [chloroform] employment."

Simpson reported on another application of the anesthetic: "I have employed it [chloroform] also in obstetric practice, with entire success." Reacting to Simpson's experiences, there were public outcries against administering chloroform as an anesthetic during childbirth. Religious adherents of bible teachings vociferated: "God intended childbirth to be painful; It was immoral to reduce women to unconsciousness at a critical point in their lives; and chloroform brought on erotic fantasies."

On September 3, 1850, Morton responded to Simpson's choice of chloroform and affirmed that ether was superior to chloroform. He alerted practitioners to the possibility of patient deaths, to the greater disturbance of the nervous system and to the increased strength of chloroform. Morton argued that chloroform is "very much more dangerous . . is a purer and superior article [in Britain] to that commonly used here [in U.S.] ... the brain and nervous system were affected to an alarming extent. Convulsions have frequently attended its use." In summary, Morton listed ten reasons for the superiority of sulfuric ether.

In a November 21, 1846 letter to Morton, Dr. Oliver Wendell Holmes suggested a name to be applied to the state produced by ether and to the agent: "The state should, I think, be called 'Anaesthesia.' This signifies insensibility ... The adjective will be 'Anaesthetic.'"

Heated medical differences about the choice of ether or chloroform as an anesthetic appeared in professional medical journals. These articles surfaced about 1847, ten years before Lincoln prosecuted this case.

Both lawyers overlooked potential evidence relative to anesthesiology. Medical textbooks advocating the use of anesthesia in surgical and obstetrical procedures did exist at the time of the trial. If Lincoln been more familiar with medical jurisprudence, he might have found relevant references.

Less than twenty months after Morton's ether demonstration, Fitzwilliam Sargent's book, *On Bandaging and Other Operations of Minor Surgery* appeared in 1848. One of the earliest American surgical texts, this volume described the use of both ether and chloroform as anesthetics. A revised edition was available in 1856. Joseph F. Flagg's 1851 book, *Ether and Chloroform: Their Employment in Surgery, Dentistry, Midwifery Therapeutics, etc.* included an entire chapter on "Chloroform as a Local Anaesthesia." Simpson's 1847 article in *Lancet* or his 1848 monograph declaring chloroform more efficient and superior to ether without harmful effects were powerful arguments for Lincoln's prosecution. Using Simpson's dosage data, Lincoln could have argued that the overdose indicated by the defense surely would have resulted in Wyant's death. Wyant himself told his sister that they gave him enough medicine to kill an elephant.

Dr. J. D. Gross described his experiences using chloroform since February 1848 in the *Transactions of the American Medical Association*. He stated that he abandoned the use of sulfuric ether altogether because chloroform "produces the desired effect in much shorter time, causes less excitement of the brain, is more persistent in its action and is more easily inhaled ... not noticed ... the use of chloroform exerted any injurious effect upon recovery of patients."

Writing about anesthetic agents, Dr. Washington L Atlee noted that he "employed chloroform very extensively ... never had unpleasant results ... produced so little mischief."

An 1850 report of the American Medical Association's Standing Committee on Surgery considered anesthesia. "Beyond comparison, the best anesthetic agent known," was Professor Richard L. Howard's enthusiastic endorsement of chloroform. Professor Joseph A. Eve declared that he had "uniform success with chloroform" and had "never seen the least injury." Dr. Amos Twitchell used "chloroform in all important surgical operations" and had "never seen any bad effects from it."

By 1857, the *American Journal of Insanity* was in existence for about thirteen years and later became the *Journal of the American Psychiatric Association*. If Lincoln had perused the journal, he could discover a number of articles relative to chloroform induced insanity and information about insanity generally. It's possible that Lincoln could have found the names of potential medical experts as witnesses.

Shortly after ether was introduced into surgical procedures, Dr. John P. Gray, Superintendent, Utica, New York Lunatic Asylum, experimented with sixteen insane patients and related that "to none has it [ether] proved the least injurious ... all improved ... continuing research." Ray also used Etherization in the treatment of insanity. While Ray reported that the ether treatment worked, the dosage was a bit higher than usual.

Dr. A. T. H. Waters employed chloroform in the treatment of puerperal insanity. After he described three case studies, Waters advocated chloroform as a safe and effective treatment of mental illness with no harmful effects.

Dr. James C. Bucknill advised that "feigned insanity is detected by the part being overacted in outrageousness and absurdity of conduct

... a person feigning madness will be overcome by its [chloroform's] influence." Describing an extraordinary case pretended insanity, Bucknill commented that the patient acted for five or six weeks by howling, raving, rolling his eyes, frothing from the mouth, biting people, tearing clothes, and refusing food.

Chloroform was generally accepted and utilized in British medical circles. A leading figure in anesthesia in London and in the world, Dr. John Snow, administered chloroform to more than four hundred fifty patients per year after 1852. On April 7, 1853, Snow administered chloroform to Britain's Queen Victoria as she gave birth to Prince Leopold. Snow's diaries revealed that he used fifteen minim [drop] doses on a handkerchief and inhalation lasted for fifty-three minutes. In all likelihood, Snow was preparing another royal chloroform application as Lincoln prosecuted this murder trial. When Princess Beatrice was born on April 14, 1857, Snow administered *chloroform à la reine*.

Perhaps, if the jury knew about the routine use of chloroform for the British Queen during childbirth, they may have thought differently about the defense assertions that the anesthetic caused insanity. Furthermore, the jury may have been impressed with the fact that Snow administered chloroform more than two thousand times by 1857, without a single mishap.

To rebut, Swett could have cited the "dire ... unfortunate and painful consequences" of using chloroform that included ten deaths. Dr. Warren, the eminent Boston surgeon, cited the untoward effects in his 1849 book on chloroform and strong chloric ether as narcotic agents.

*People v. Wyant* was erroneously cited as the first use of medical experts in an insanity plea in the Illinois courts. Probably, the unique chloroform causing insanity rationale heightened awareness of the case. However, Dr. Edward Mead of Boston, Massachusetts reported that defense attorney Isaac N. Arnold asked him to give his opinion in a murder trial in McHenry County, Illinois in 1847 or 1848. Arnold said "it was the first that had occurred in that state of that character." At first, Mead thought the accused feigned insanity. After the doctor concluded his examination, he found otherwise. Mead was cross-examined for two and one-half hours. Prosecution's rebuttal sources were two medical texts: Dr. Jean Etienne D. Esquirol's *Mental Maladies. A Treatise on Insanity* and Dr. Forbes Winslow's article on insanity in the *Cyclopedia of Practical Medicine*. A hung jury ensued with nine for willful murder, two for manslaughter and one for acquittal on insanity. At the second trial in Chicago, fifteen physicians testified; all said that the accused was insane. A jury verdict acquitted the defendant. Presiding Judge Hugh J. Dickey commented that the case was so clear that if the jury did not acquit, he would set the verdict aside. Without delay, the accused was placed under Mead's care. Three months later he was dead. A post-mortem revealed extensive organic changes in cerebral tissues.

Immediately following this Wyatt/Rusk murder trial with its volume of expert medical testimony, Lincoln and Swett reversed their legal positions and met again in a medical malpractice trial. In the same McLean County Circuit Court with the same Judge David Davis presiding, Lincoln defended two accused physicians while Swett represented the injured plaintiff. This medical malpractice case was settled out of court.

## UNCONTROLLABLE FRENZY AND A
## UNIQUE TEMPORARY INSANITY PLEA

In 1852, Teresa Bagioli, the daughter of a music teacher, married Daniel E. Sickles. He was almost thirty-three years old, and she was only sixteen years old and pregnant with his child. About one year later Sickles and his wife moved to England. He became the First Secretary of the American Legation in London when James Buchanan was the ambassador. While Sickles served at the post In London, his wife frequently acted as an official hostess for the bachelor Buchanan. After two years of service, Sickles returned to the United States and was elected as a Democratic U.S. Congressman from New York City's Third District. In Washington, D.C., he and Teresa lived in a fashionable house across from the White House.

Philip Barton Key became friends with the Sickles and frequently visited their home. It was not long before Key was involved in a protracted adulterous love affair with the now twenty-three year old Teresa. Thirty-seven year old Sickles was unaware of his wife's liaison for about one year. Teresa and Key's clandestine affair came to a tragic end early in 1859. Near the end of February of that year, Sickles' intense emotional compulsion to avenge himself resulted in Key's death. In April, the murder trial took place in Washington, D.C. "For the first time in American jurisprudence, the defense set up the plea of a brainstorm or temporary aberration of mind."

Two powerful and politically connected individuals were involved in this tragedy. Key, forty-two, was the U.S. Attorney for the District of Columbia, one of the eleven children of Francis Scott Key, the author of the poem that became *The Star Spangled Banner*. Francis Scott Key was himself a three time U.S. Attorney for the District of Columbia. Sickles was a career politician with friends in high places. At the time of the murder, Buchanan was the President of the United States and still a close personal friend of Sickles. When Sickles went to jail, Buchanan sent him a comforting note, but did not visit him. Evidently, George Templeton Strong learned differently and wrote in his diary: "Buchanan calling on Sickles in jail is rather exasperating." Teasingly, Strong commented on the relationship between Buchanan and Teresa Sickles: "Some people talk of relations between the lady and old Buck [Buchanan], of which Dan [Sickles] had full notice and in which he acquiesced, and which put that venerable sinner in Dan's power." Rumors circulated that Mrs. Sickles was "pleasant" to Buchanan to the point of dispensing her favors upon him.

Virtually every major newspaper in the nation reported about the sensational Sickles murder trial on their front pages. Typically, readers gossiped about testimony from witness John B. Haskin describing a visit he and his wife made on Mrs. Sickles when her husband was absent: "I found Mrs. Sickles and Mr. Key seated at a round table with a large bowl of salad on it; she was mixing it; there was a bottle of champagne and glasses on the table [laughter] ... Mrs. Sickles got up, blushed, and invited us to take a glass of wine with her ... on entering the carriage, my wife said that Mrs. Sickles was a bad woman."

Beginning early in 1858, Key secretly and regularly met Teresa at a rented house in Georgetown. Seemingly, everybody in Washington knew of the affair except Teresa's husband. Apparently, Sickles learned about his wife's infidelity from an anonymous letter delivered to him on February 24, 1859. Signed with the initials, R. P. G., the letter named Key, gave the address of the house where he met "your wife, Mrs. Sickles," and described the signal Key used to show that he was there. In closing, the letter writer was dramatic: "Sir, I do assure you he has as much use of your wife as you have. With these few hints I leave the rest for you to imagine." Confiding his distress to George B. Wooldridge, clerk of the U.S. House of Representatives, Sickles discovered that Wooldridge already knew about the affair. He told Sickles that Key and Teresa were seen entering the assignation house during the prior week. Wooldridge and Sickles made plans to investigate the allegations about Teresa's infidelity. After confirming the truth of the illicit affair, Sickles returned home, confronted and thoroughly frightened his wife. In a heated verbal altercation on February 26, 1859, the day before the murder, Teresa remorsefully admitted her infidelity. Sickles forced her to write a piteous and self-condemnatory confession: "I did what is usual for a wicked woman to do ... Have met half a dozen times or more ... The room is heated by a wood fire ... Went in the same bedroom, and there an improper interview was had. I undressed myself. Mr. Key undressed also. This occurred on Wednesday, 23d of February, 1859 ... I went in the front door ... undressed myself, and he also; went to bed together."

She signed the confession with her maiden name, Teresa Bagioli. In an added paragraph, she said that the "statement was written by myself without any inducement held out by Mr. Sickles of forgiveness or reward and without any menace from him." Not forgetting his legal training, Sickles had their two maids, Bridget Duffy and C.M. Ridgely, witness the signing of the confession. Teresa dropped exhausted on the floor in the guest room and slept there all night. Sickles retired to his bedroom, slept little, paced the floor and was in emotional distress all night.

After his tormenting night, Sickles was haggard and distraught the next morning. He sent for two close friends, Samuel T. Butterworth, a New York City Tammany politician and Superintendent of the Assay Office in that city, who happened to be in Washington, and Wooldridge. Repeatedly, Sickles sobbed and cried out loudly in front of them: "I am a dishonored and ruined man and cannot look you in the face." Sickles went upstairs to recover his composure while Wooldridge and Butterworth remained in the library. Suddenly, Sickles came rushing down the stairs into the library shouting that he had "seen the scoundrel making signals" to his wife. Butterworth tried to calm Sickles but he remained extremely riled. Finally, in accepting the fact of Teresa's infidelity, Butterworth told Sickles: "If that be so, there is but one course left for you, as a man of honor - you need no advice." Strong's diary records an astoundingly different version of the encounter: "[John Jay] Cisco says his friend Butterworth tells him he advised Sickles to challenge Key or else give him notice and kill him in a street 'collision' but that Sickles avowed his preference for an *ex parte* assassination."

Whether prearranged at Sickles' request or not, Butterworth went outside and walked slowly down the street. In perhaps laying a trap, he saw Key and engaged him in polite conversation for a few minutes until Sickles could secure his armaments and get there. As Butterworth turned to leave, he saw Sickles rapidly coming down the street toward Key. When Sickles quickly approached to within six feet of Key, Butterworth heard him exclaim in a loud infuriated voice: "Key, you scoundrel, you have dishonored my bed - you must die!" Butterworth stopped and leaned comfortably against a nearby iron railing while he casually witnessed Sickles' relentless mortal attack on Key. To avoid prosecution as an accessory to murder, Butterworth left town immediately after the shooting and failed to make an appearance at the trial.

This blatant, brutal confrontation between Key and Sickles took place on a Sunday afternoon in broad daylight in Lafayette Park, directly across from the White House. Allegedly, Sickles used two colts and a

Derringer to fire, or attempt to fire, three to five shots. After the first shot, Key fell to the ground, perhaps wounded, and tried to escape from Sickles' advances. He tried to hide behind a large tree shouting "Don't shoot me!" and "Murderer!" Savagely, Sickles followed Key waving a gun. As Key lay prostrate on the ground, Sickles continued to shoot at him. Standing over Key with his revolver in his hand, Sickles kept excitedly repeating that Key had dishonored his house. Hearing the commotion, several members from the Cosmos Club, which fronted the park, rushed out, led Sickles away, and carried the still breathing, but mortally wounded, Key into the Club. Soon after Key was laid on the floor in the club anteroom, he expired.

Calmly, Sickles walked away from the park to turn himself in at the nearby home of President Buchanan's Attorney-General, Jeremiah S. Black. Finding that Black was not at home, Sickles retired to his own house and waited for the police to arrest him. While Sickles waited he was visited by his friend, Robert J. Walker, who became the star witness to Sickles' emotional distress, his "brain-storm." Soon the police came and took Sickles to the jail at the corner of Fourth and G Street.

Called the "Blue Jug" because of the peculiar paint or wash of a bluish color of the wall, the old three story brick building, surmounted with a belfry, had high walls and was in a state of disrepair. It was dark, insanitary and poorly ventilated. Windows were iron-barred with shutters of heavy board. There were narrow slits in front of each of the upper windows. On Sundays, the prisoners could be clearly heard loudly singing familiar church hymns. Washingtonians considered the jail an eyesore, a disgrace to the community and a public nuisance. Iowa Senator James W. Grimes compared the jail to the French Bastille.

In deference to his position as a Congressman and at the intercession of his prominent friends, Sickles quickly was given special privileges and improved accommodations on his arrival in the jail. He was given his own room, allowed to keep his pet Italian greyhound, Dandy in his cell, and his young daughter was able to visit him.

Seven lawyers participated in defending Sickles: James T. Brady and John Graham of New York; Edwin McMasters Stanton, Samuel Chilton, A.B. Magruder and Daniel Ratcliffe of Washington; and Philip Phillips of Alabama. Brady, Graham and Stanton did the majority of the legal work during the trial. Key's assistant, Robert Ould, replaced Key as U.S. Attorney for the District and became the prosecutor. Mortified by the obvious imbalance of lawyers, the Washington Bar met, in an unprecedented move, and selected prominent and experienced lawyers, Joseph H. Bradley, Sr. and James M. Carlisle, to assist the prosecutor. Ould had studied law in Bradley's office. A *New York Herald* article reported that Bradley and Carlisle asked President Buchanan to allow them to assist the prosecutor. In as the President appointed the U.S. attorney, the President could also appoint others to assist, but Buchanan declined to interfere. At the last moment, friends of Key contributed enough funding to retain Carlisle to assist Ould. Unofficially, Bradley continued to confer with Ould and Carlisle about the case and even appeared in court several times to consult with the prosecution lawyers.

Individuals engrossed with the scandal paid two cents for the *New York Times* and read about the Grand Jury deliberations. On Thursday, March 24th, 1859, the murder indictment was handed up: "The jurors of the United States for the District of Columbia, County of Washington upon their oaths present, that Daniel E. Sickles late of the county of Washington aforesaid, gentleman, not having the fear of God before his eyes but being moved and seduced by the instigation of the devil, on the 27th day of February in the year of our Lord 1859, with force of arms at the county aforesaid, in and upon the body of one Philip Barton Key, in the peace of God and of the said United States then and being, feloniously and willfully and of malicious aforethought, did make an assault ... of which said mortal wound, he, the said Philip Barton Key, then and there instantly died ... that the said Daniel E. Sickles ... did kill and murder, against the form of the statute ... and against the peace and government of the United States."

An unprecedented proposed legal rationale added to the extraordinary atmosphere of the murder trial: "It was the aim of the defense to show that Sickles was rendered temporarily insane by rage and grief at the time of the slaying - the first time that defense appeared in American jurisprudence." Defense lawyers did not plan to rely upon only the temporary insanity argument. They bolstered their defense plea with the "unwritten law" that exonerated a husband who took mortal revenge upon a "defiler" of the marriage bed. However, a legal analyst declared that "there is no law in Anglo-American jurisprudence, written or unwritten, to support such a doctrine." As the defense lawyers presented their suppositions, a *New York Daily Tribune* editorial took a disparaging view of the propositions: "Absurd to talk of frenzy and insanity in this case ... insanity dodge can't bolster Sickles' defense ...It's a simple question - Does a husband have the right to kill the seducer of his wife?"

On Monday, April 4, 1859, the trial began in the courtroom in the old city hall. In size, the courtroom was forty feet square, dingy with age and neglect, dirty with much use and worn by many feet. In effect, the whole place was seedy and slovenly with dirty windows and ceilings festooned with cobwebs. About seventy-five persons could be seated within the bar with standing room for two to three hundred outside the bar. "The room was crowded to excess, nearly all the legal fraternity of Washington occupying the bar, the space without being filled by the citizens generally."

Judge Thomas Hartley Crawford presided in the Supreme Court of the District convening as a Criminal Court. Ominously for the prosecution, Crawford was the judge in two related cases where the insanity plea was used successfully. In *U.S. v Day,* Crawford's instructions to the jury indicated that Day killed his wife because he was driven insane from the mortification of his wife bearing someone else's child. In the other case, the judge allowed that Jarboe went insane and killed the seducer of his sister.

It took about three days to select a jury from a panel of more than one hundred citizens. Occupations of the twelve male jurors were given: four were grocers; two were farmers; plus a cabinet maker, a coach maker, a gent's furnishing owner, a merchant, a shoemaker, and a tinner.

Prosecution eyewitnesses vividly described what happened in the encounter between Key and Sickles. Eleven witnesses for the prosecution graphically detailed what they saw and heard on the day of the murder. There were variations in their accounts: Sickles fired two to three weapons; three to five shots were heard; Key retreated or threw something at Sickles; and Sickles kept advancing cold-bloodily shooting him again and again. Witnesses heard shouted words exchanged between Sickles and Key. Medical coroners described the wounds suffered by Key and identified the mortal bullet wound. There was little doubt about what happened and the defense lawyers did not deny that Sickles killed Key.

John Graham opened for the defense and delivered a grandiose and stirring speech of almost three days duration. He invoked the bible, literature, the law and prior cases. Graham impressed upon the jury that they were there "to decide whether the defender of the marriage bed is a murderer." Referring back to the prosecutor's opening remarks, Graham commented on the prosecution's "extraordinary expressions such as the prisoner coming to the carnival of blood, a walking magazine, adding mutilation to murder and bravely standing over his victim." Continuing, Graham defined the insanity question for the jury: "What was the mental condition of the defendant at the time he took the life of the deceased?" Jurors were asked to consider whether "the act of the husband who vindicates his marriage bed by slaying the man who dares to defile it is symptomatic of a wicked, depraved and malignant spirit." In contrast, Graham emphasized the "cunning" of Key in committing his acts of adultery and in betraying Sickles, who had befriended him. Following a lengthy exposition on the moral crime of adultery, Graham proceeded to delineate again the emotional insanity defense: "We mean not to say that Mr. Sickles labored under insanity in consequence of an established mental permanent disease, but that the condition of his mind at the time of the commission of the act in question was such as would render him legally unaccountable, as much as if the state of his mind had been produced by a mental disease. In other words, the proposition we argue to this Jury is this: It is no matter how a man becomes insane; Is he insane? That is the question ... Mr. Sickles, at the moment of the occurrence, was laboring under such a state of frenzy as deprived him of accountability for the act ... what must have been the frenzy of Mr. Sickles at the time he encountered Mr. Key ... there was no deliberation ... Is it possible that, under these circumstances, Mr. Sickles could have acted in cold blood?'

At the conclusion of Graham's speech, the defense called witnesses to attest to Sickles' emotional instability and uncontrollable frenzy. Of those testifying, Robert J. Walker most affected the jury with his impassioned and seemingly professional clinical testimony. Walker was a bosom friend of Sickles, a prominent Democratic politician, a northern-born Mississippi slaveholder, a former U.S. Senator from Mississippi, the governor of the Kansas territory, and one-time Secretary of the Treasury. Shortly after the murder, at about three-twenty in the afternoon, Walker depicted Sickles' mental condition when he visited him in his house: "his manner appeared excited ... something strange and unusual about it ... voice different ... He became very much convulsed ... broke into an agony of unnatural and unearthly sounds, the most remarkable I ever heard - something like a scream, interrupted by violent sobs. From his convulsed appearance he was in the act of writhing. His condition appeared to me very frightful ... I thought if it lasted much longer he must become insane ... turned to go for a physician ... The spasms became more violent till they ceased ... was there well over half an hour ... accompanied him to jail ... I was still alarmed at his condition, not knowing when the convulsions would recur."

During Walker's testimony, Sickles "was violently affected breaking out into sobs and profusely shedding tears." Many of the spectators were also moved to tears. At this point, the shrewd Stanton asked the judge to permit the defendant to retire for a few minutes to regain his composure. After Sickles returned, Walker continued his psychiatrist-like description of the defendant's condition under cross-examination: "It was the most terrible thing I ever saw in my life - an agony of despair. He was in a state of frenzy at the time, and I feared if it continued he would become permanently insane; his screams were of the most frightful character ... Sometimes he would start and scream in a very high key. He appeared in a state of perfect frenzy ... much stronger than grief ... I feared a recurrence of his paroxysms of grief and despair ... His person got rigid. His hands were to his head. He bent them down, and sobbed bitterly. He wept - wept and sobbed."

Having laid the groundwork for the temporary insanity defense, Brady set out to admit Teresa's confession as evidence of the provocation leading to Sickles' emotional distress. Prosecutor Ould objected to admitting the confession as evidence on the grounds that it was hearsay, that is was a spousal communication, and that it was aimed at proving that the confession "produced temporary insanity." Judge Crawford rejected the confession as evidence, strangely citing an injurious effect on the relations of husband and wife: "It would violate well-established principles and rules to admit it." However a few days later, *Harper's Weekly* exclusively published a facsimile of Mrs. Sickles' confession on the front page. This prompted a diary entry from Strong: "It is manifestly Dan Sickles' work, copied by his wife, and tells damagingly against him."

To circumvent the judge's ruling and inform the jury about Teresa's adultery, the defense called Wooldridge to the stand. Brady proceeded to ask him about his conversations with Sickles. As Wooldridge began to tell about Teresa's conduct, the prosecution objected declaring that the judge had ruled out communications between husband and wife. An angry exchange ensued between Stanton and Ould in which the prosecution was accused of having a "thirst for blood." Stanton continued: "Is this evidence to be shut against a free man who has vindicated the honor of the marriage relations ... [shall a man be punished] who, under the influence of passions excited by outraged honor, humanity, nature, feeling, has slain the corruptor of his wife, the adulterer, the violator of his bed, and the dishonorer of his home ... this evidence should not be excluded in order that vengeance might be obtain the blood of this prisoner, who was so fiercely hunted."

Jumping to his feet, Ould expressed his displeasure that Stanton "insinuated that the public prosecutor was actuated by thirst for blood, and that he hunted down the prisoner for vengeance." After Stanton disclaimed making such a charge, Ould referred anonymously to Stanton's role in the trial: "One of the counsel had carried out the part, whether assigned to him or not, of the bully and the bruiser." In resenting the implication, Stanton said that he knew his duty and would resist those who would "malignantly" lead his client to the gallows. Still stymied from presenting evidence of adultery, the defense called a string of witnesses to tell about allegedly intimate interactions between Key and Teresa.

In testimony, the witnesses reported seeing Key about the Sickles house, told about Key's signals, focused on the assignation house and reported about the door lock on the house Key rented. However, John A. Gray, who had rented the house to Key, was not permitted to testify on the ground that he was a Negro. Prosecutor Carlisle conceded: "It was one thing to seek to prove the insanity of Sickles; that was proper, but it was another matter to delve into the alleged cause of the insanity. To do so would be to introduce evidence of adultery by the back-door."

After considering the prosecution's arguments, on Monday, April 18, Judge Crawford ruled that the evidence of adultery was admissible because at the time of the shooting Sickles exclaimed that Key had dishonored his bed. He based his decision on his own precedent ruling in the prior Jarboe case that allowed evidence of the seduction. Accordingly, the anonymous letter was allowed into evidence and Wooldridge was recalled to recount his investigations of Teresa's adultery.

Mrs. Nancy Brown, who lived on the street where Key rented the trysting-house, testified to seeing the white string signal flutter on the upper shutters of the house, described Teresa's clothing and closed hood as she entered by the unlocked back door, and often saw Key unlock the door. Once she spoke to Key after he tied his horse to her tree: "I asked him whether he did not know that was against the law." There was laughter in the court since Key was the district attorney.

John Thompson, the Sickles coachman, titillated the courtroom spectators with his first-hand stories of Key's clandestine meetings with Teresa. In a broad Scotch accent and with evident relish, he stated that Key came to the Sickles house practically every night when Sickles was in New York. Thompson told of an early morning meeting between Key and Teresa in the Sickles house. As he was about to go to bed at one in the morning, Thompson heard them go into the study and lock the doors. "I stood a little while and heard them making this noise on the sofa for about two or three minutes ... I knew they 'was'nt' at no good work." Laughter erupted in the courtroom at his remark.

With the close of the defense's case allowing evidence on adultery, Ould now proposed that the prosecution would withdraw their objection to admitting Teresa's confession into evidence. Brady declined the offer and said the case of the accused was closed. Carlisle informed the court that the prosecution had new evidence to offer. This new evidence was intended to show that Sickles was not of good moral character. "It is surmised that this offer of evidence is connected with an inquiry into Mr. Sickles' own conduct and particularly into the matter of his visits with a lady to Barnum's Hotel in Baltimore. The proprietor of that hotel is in court." Hurriedly, Brady, Graham and Ould conferred with the judge about the offered evidence. Judge Crawford ruled: "For very obvious reasons the Court will do no more than merely state his opinion ... the evidence is not admissible."

After a late witness testified for the prosecution about what happened when Sickles showed up at the attorney-general's house, both sides closed their cases. Carlisle argued about the provocative actions delineated by the defense and referred to the acts of adultery such as Key's signals to Teresa: "Such provocation does not justify the act or reduce such killing from murder to manslaughter." In discussing the insanity issue, Carlisle belittled the impairment of Sickles' mind, the prisoner's lack of criminality and the transitory existence of the insanity. Carlisle ended his argument and the summations began.

Stanton began with a long passionate moral reckoning. With a thick crop of whiskers, black curly hair, and eyes set on a massive head, Stanton was known for his ferocious courtroom demeanor, frequently compared to an old testament prophet. He carefully explained the theories of the defense and stated that the cited points of law supported the doctrines. While he did this, Stanton heavily emphasized the sanctity of the family, the crime of adultery, the right of a husband to protect his family and felicitously indicated when murder is justifiable homicide. As the spectators cheered, Stanton's address to the jury was "a typical piece of Victorian rhetoric, an ingenuous thesaurus of aphorisms on the sanctity of the family." With a religious fervor, Stanton's remarks profoundly stressed the "unwritten law" protecting a cuckolded husband's right to revenge: "an adulterous intrigue ... homicide may be either with malice or without malice ... a third class of self-protection arising from the social relation - the law holding family chastity and the sanctity of the marriage bed, the matron's honor and the virgin's purity, to be more valuable and estimable in law than the property of any man. The present case belongs in that class ... [Key was] Received into his family, he debauched his house, violated the bed of his host, and dishonored his family. On this ground, alone, the deed of killing was committed ... counsel for the prisoner insist that the act is justified by the law ... [this adultery] presents a case surpassing all that has ever been written of cold, villainous, remorseless lust ...The death of Key was a cheap sacrifice to save one mother [Teresa] from the horrible fate ... The theory of our case is, that there was a man living in a constant state of adultery with the prisoner's wife ... [and the prisoner] meets him in that act and slays him, and we say that the right to slay him stands on the firmest principles of self-defence ... [according to] the principles of social law and jurisprudence."

As he took his seat, Stanton was saluted with an outburst of applause. Mrs. Olive Cole, attending in the courtroom, declared: "Brady did not half the services for Sickles that Stanton did." In actuality, Sickles was a serious drinker, an ardent gambler and a conspicuous philanderer. He was hardly a noble defender of American family virtue.

Brady followed and argued the defense's instructions to the jury. He reviewed the testimony and the facts as he focused on the questions of sanity, insanity and provocation.

In his ensuing closing, Ould pinpointed the prosecution's obvious contention "The question, however, is not of adultery, but one of murder ... A plea of insanity admits the charge." Referring to the legal time factors in Sickles' premeditation, Ould commented that the provocation existed in Sickles' mind longer than twenty-five minutes and even longer than twenty-five hours. Sickles did wring a confession from Teresa the evening before the murder. Pointedly, Ould concluded remarking about the "facility with which insanity may be simulated or feigned."

Earlier, both sides presented the judge with their Instructions to be given to the jury. In substance, the prosecution simply said the jury should find Sickles guilty of the willful and intentional murder of Key and that Sickles was not provoked into the act. In contrast, the defense offered eleven instructions, chief among them: "First, there is no presumption of malice in this case. Seventh, if, from the whole of the evidence, the jury believe that Mr. Sickles committed the act, but at the time of doing so was under the influence of a diseased mind, and was really unconscious that he was committing a crime, he is not in law guilty of murder. Eighth, if the jury believe that from any predisposing cause the prisoner's mind was impaired, and at the time of killing Mr. Key he became or was mentally incapable of governing himself in reference to Mr. Key, as the debauchee of his wife, and at the time of his committing said act, was, be reason of such cause, unconscious that he was committing a crime as to said Key, he is not guilty of any offence whatever. Ninth,, it is for the jury to say what was the state of the prisoner's mind as to the capacity to decide upon the criminality of the particular act in question - the homicide-at the moment it occurred, and what was the condition of the parties respectively as to being armed or not at the same moment. Tenth, the law does not require that the insanity which absolves from crime, should exist for any definite period, but only that it exists at the moment when the act occurred with which the accused stands charged."

Judge Crawford discussed each of the instructions submitted to him and ruled on each one as he instructed the jury prior to their deliberations: "If the prisoner was laboring under some controlling power within him which he could not resist, then he will not be responsible. The question is whether he was laboring under that species of insanity which satisfies you that he was quite unaware of the nature, character and consequences of the act he was committing ... under the influence of a diseased mind and was unconscious at the time he was committing the act that was a crime ... not to be excused if he has capacity and reason sufficient to distinguish between right and wrong ... partial insanity is not sufficient to exempt him ... if he still understands the nature and character of his act and its consequences ... If a day or half a day intervene between the conviction of the husband of the guilt of his wife [and the murder] the law considers that it was done deliberately, and declares that it is murder."

Moving to the question of Sickles' insanity, the judge responded: "It is for the jury to say what was the state of Mr. Sickles' mind as the capacity to decide upon the criminality of the homicide." Relative to temporary insanity, the judge agreed with the defense's instruction: "The time when the insanity is to operate is the moment when the crime charged upon the party was committed, if committed at all ... Whether a man is insane or not is a matter of fact; what degree of insanity will relieve him from responsibility is a matter of law, the Jury finding the fact of the degree too."

Both sides agreed to submit the case to the jury without further discussion. On Judge Crawford's order, the Marshall handed the indictment to the jury foreman, Reason Arnold, and the jurors retired to their consultation room. "After a most anxious suspense of seventy minutes the door is opened. The Deputy Marshall calls out to make room for the jury. In they come, one by one, and proceed to take their seats in the box" and spectators attentively followed the conversation: Daniel E. Sickles, stand up and look to the Jury. [Sickles stands]

| | |
|---|---|
| Clerk: | How say you gentlemen, have you agreed to your verdict? |
| Mr. Arnold: | We have. |
| Clerk: | How say you, do you find the prisoner at the bar guilty or not guilty? |
| Mr. Arnold: | NOT GUILTY. |
| Stanton: | I now move that Mr. Sickles be discharged from custody. |

Pandemonium broke out in the courtroom. To the cheers of the audience, Sickles was taken out of the dock by Captain Wiley and Mr. Brega. Sickles was paraded about on the crowd's shoulders. Spectators convened at a nearby tavern for several more hours of partying, singing and celebrating. Although usually austere, Stanton danced a victory jig upon the defense table.

Reactions to the verdict outside the courtroom were quite the opposite. "Strictly speaking the jury ruled against the proper interpretation of the law." A jury sworn to follow the law and the evidence should have convicted Sickles of manslaughter, at the least. This jury violated their oaths by finding him not guilty. In the New York *Evening Post*, Sickles was lambasted: "The man who makes no scruple to invade and destroy the domestic peace of others - a person of notorious profligacy of life ... a certain disgrace has for years attended the reputation of being one of his companions ... the man who in his own practice regards adultery as a joke and the matrimonial bond as no barrier against the utmost capricious licentiousness - has little right to complain when the mischief which he carries without scruple into other families enters his own."

On April 16 and 27, the *New York Daily Tribune* belittled the Sickles acquittal in two editorials: "Absurd that Sickles had sudden attack of insanity ... There does not appear to be a particle of evidence to support insanity ... Most mistaken and mischievous verdict ... can't justify verdict on that of insanity. Preposterous! ... Butterworth's testimony precludes insanity ... careful, cool, planning ... he acted eighteen hours later ... kept shooting an unarmed Key ... he killed Key purposely, deliberately, on calculation."

In Maryland, the *Baltimore Sun* discussed the jurors and the insanity plea: "the defense resorted to insanity as the plea. The jury must therefore have based their verdict upon the insanity of the prisoner, or the law has suffered violence, and twelve perjured men left the jury box upon rendition of their verdict ... [jurors ultimately] entitled to the benefit of an opinion that the prisoner was insane [but it is an opinion] which no other *sane* man out of the jury box will concur in."

During the trial, in a letter to the editor of the *New York Daily Herald*, a lawyer asked what law principles allowed Robert Walker to testify as to Sickles' mental status? After the verdict, the same newspaper editorially inquired: "Why was Walker's testimony admitted?" No medical expert testified as to Sickles' temporary insanity. In an analysis of the trial, legal experts concluded that prosecutor Ould did not do a good job. There was an insinuation that President Buchanan appointed Ould as "an acquiescent wheel horse" to put on a "futile performance" at the trial as was expected of him.

A special *New York Times* supplement reviewed the murder and subsequent events with manifest approbation. An editorial labeled the trial "one of the most remarkable cases in the whole history of criminal jurisprudence."

Strong's diary took Sickles to task: "Were he not an unmitigated blackguard and profligate, one could pardon any act of violence committed on such provocation. But Sickles is not the man to take the law into his own hands and constitute himself the avenger of sin ... One might as well try to spoil a rotten egg as to damage Dan's character."

About two months after the trial's end, by early July 1859, newspapers reported that Sickles reconciled with Teresa. Sickles responded to the public's disbelief with a letter to the editor in which he explained why he took his wife back: "I am not aware of any statute or code of morals which makes it infamous to forgive a woman." An article in the *London Saturday Review* presented a view of the Sickles case, enchanted by distance, and remarked that most were opposed to his taking his wife back. Eight years later, on February 5, 1867, Teresa Sickles died prematurely at thirty-one years of age. No cause of death was given.

More than 130 years after the murder, in 1991, the title of a book about Sickles bluntly reaffirmed the opinion of the public: *The Congressman Who Got Away with Murder*.

Two years after the acquittal, in 1861, Secretary of State William H. Seward introduced Sickles to President Lincoln. Soon Sickles became another of Mrs. Lincoln's "courtiers" and he frequently visited the White House. Both Lincolns found him "a diverting companion, a man of easy charm and ready conversation that rippled with theatrical allusion and humorous anecdote." When the Civil War erupted, Sickles became a Brigadier-General of New York's Excelsior Brigade in the Union Army. At the Battle of Gettysburg, he was badly wounded when a twelve pound shell crushed his lower right leg necessitating amputation. Surprisingly, Sickles remained conscious as he was carried from the field on a stretcher. With a calm presence, he smoked a cigar and coolly ordered the preservation of his amputated leg in a barrel of whiskey. Later, he had a miniature coffin constructed and packed the amputated leg in it. Sickles tacked his calling card to the coffin inscribed "with the compliments of Major General D.E.S., United States Volunteers." He sent the amputated leg to the newly created Army Medical Museum in Washington. Today, the bones can still be seen there.

From 1866 to 1868, Sickles was allegedly the "most hated" military governor of South Carolina. As Minister to Spain from 1869 to 1873, Sickles continued his usual ways and became romantically linked to the Spanish Queen. He was derisively labeled the "Yankee King of Spain." In 1893, he was elected again to the U.S. House of Representatives representing New York City's Tenth District. Despite the harsh criticism of Sickles' military actions during the battle of Gettysburg, he was awarded the Congressional Medal of Honor for that service on October 30, 1897, thirty-four years after the 1863 clash. On May 3, 1914, Sickles died at age ninety-four and was buried in Washington's Arlington National Cemetery.

## POLITICS AND THE MEDICAL EXPERT ON INSANITY

In the summer of 1863, a confederate civilian physician shot and killed a white Union officer who was training colored troops in Norfolk, Virginia. A military commission conducted a trial and the murderer was convicted. With no question as to guilt, President Abraham Lincoln responded to a rash of emotional clemency appeals. He chose a medical expert to conduct a professional examination to determine whether or not the murderer was sane or insane.

In this case, both legal and political factors conceivably influenced Lincoln's decision. Lincoln considered law and politics interrelated, mutually dependent, and wholly inclusive. Being an experienced and competent trial lawyer, Lincoln was cognizant of the legal precedents and of the public's skeptical attitudes toward the insanity plea. He was familiar with the abilities of skillful lawyers to use expert witnesses to convince a jury and to persuade the public. In addition to the legal aspects, Lincoln faced serious politically sensitive issues such as the deadly draft riots, the military necessity to recruit emancipated slaves into the Union army, the impact of Union Negro soldiers upon the troops from the border states, the morale and discipline of the army and the upcoming uncertain 1864 presidential election.

To comprehend Lincoln's decision-making process, the facts about the Lieutenant's murder must be considered along with the legal and political issues. These stressful events began shortly after the Union victory as the bloody, momentous Battle of Gettysburg in Pennsylvania ended during early July 1863. Reactions to the Lieutenant's murder came from both sides. Union adherents denounced the murder as an "undefended assassination." Confederates condemned the military commission's death verdict as the consequences of "abolition malice."

On Saturday, July 11, 1863, Dr. David Minton Wright celebrated two milestones; his wife's birthday and their thirtieth wedding anniversary. About 4:00 PM, a white officer, Second Lieutenant Alanson L. Sanborn, Company B, 1st Regiment, U.S. Colored Volunteers, marched at the head of his company as they drilled on the sidewalks of Main Street in Norfolk. Although the Lieutenant was sometimes called Anson, the official Army Register lists him as Alanson. Before joining the Army in May 1863, Sanborn was a school teacher from Whitford Centre, Vermont. He actively recruited blacks into the Union army during the prior two months as the regiment was organized in Washington, D.C. Wright, a tall erect man with long gray hair, a full beard and a moustache, stood on the street watching the Lieutenant drill the colored troops. He was emotionally overwrought by the spectacle of former slaves jostling Southern men, women and children off the sidewalk into the gutter. A vigorous secessionist, Wright owned six slaves; three females aged 60, 44 and 16; two males aged 60 and one male aged 46. He was incensed at seeing the former slaves, now soldiers clad in blue uniforms and armed with muskets and bayonets. Wright backed into a store doorway to avoid the marching troops.

Although witnesses differ on the exact scenario, heated and/or insulting words and gestures were exchanged between Wright and the Lieutenant. In one version, Wright clenched his fists and exclaimed: "Oh, you dastardly coward!" or called Sanborn "a son of a bitch." Approaching Wright, some said threateningly with sword raised as if to strike, Sanborn bellowed: "You are under arrest." Wright warned Sanborn to "stand off" but Sanborn continued advancing toward Wright. With emotions boiling over on all sides, a general mêlée ensued. Knowing that Wright was always unarmed, a friend in the crowd passed a gun to him to defend himself. As Sanborn approached him, Wright produced a five-chamber Colt revolver from behind his back and fired two shots, fatally wounding Sanborn. Staggering forward pursuing Wright, Sanborn stumbled into Foster and Moore's dry goods store and fell to the floor. As Sanborn lay on the floor, Wright struggled with the soldiers who captured him and yelled: "Let me go; let me do something to help this man." Sanborn died several minutes later. Immediately, Provost-Marshall Alexander E. Bovay sent a telegram to Major-General Dix: "Lieutenant Sanborn, of the colored regiment, was shot at the head of his company on Main Street this p.m. by Doctor Wright and died immediately. Doctor Wright is in jail heavily ironed."

During his trial, Wright revealed the intensity of his feelings toward the colored troops: "Is it to be supposed that a citizen of Norfolk, himself an owner of slaves, not knowing but what even one of my slaves was in that company, would submit to be arrested by Negroes and marched off to the guardhouse? No sir, I could not submit to that!"

Immediately after the shooting, Wright was jailed in the Customs House, not too far from his own home at 20 West Main Street, near the

Atlantic Hotel. As Wright was questioned, his eldest daughter, Miss Pence [Penelope] stood by him for about one hour without any of the Union guards gallantly offering her a seat.

Although a civil government existed and was able to try Wright, a special military commission was established for the trial. Lucius H. Chandler and Lemuel Bowden served as attorneys for Wright. Chandler was the U.S. Attorney for the Eastern District of Virginia. Bowden was a U.S. Senator representing Virginia. A bit later, Joseph Eggleston Segar joined the defense representing Wright. Segar was in the U.S. House of Representatives in the 37th Congress in 1862-1863. At the time, eastern Virginia was included in the Union and West Virginia became a state on June 20, 1863.

Two days after the shooting, on July 13, 1863, the Portsmouth [VA] City Council passed a resolution denouncing "the brutal murder of a Union officer by a rabid Secessionist." Military authorities were urged "to bring to speedy and condign punishment the author of this foul crime and treasonable act to his country and his God." Furthermore the Council sought "to remove from our midst the foul-mouthed traitors who infest the street corners and market-places of our city, plotting treason and even contemplating such deeds of bloodshed as we are now called to reflect on."

While in prison awaiting trial, Wright wrote to his wife: "I am to be tried by a military commission to-day or to-morrow. I suppose the verdict will be the same as that of the provost marshal, made before he had examined the first witness." Although the name of the court was different, the rules and regulations of a military court martial applied in a trial by a military commission. This trial distinction is consequential. Compared to civil courts, military commissions were often biased. Worse yet, military commissions could send the accused to the gallows while a conviction by a civilian jury generally resulted in imprisonment.

On July 20, 1863, the trial began in the Customs House. Wright's lawyers emphatically argued that Norfolk was under civil government and the military had no jurisdiction to try him. His lawyers protested that Wright was a noncombatant civilian and a March 3, 1863 Act of Congress prohibited a military trial. All the defense arguments failed to convince the military commission and the prosecution prepared to present their witnesses.

Personally, Lincoln felt that civil courts were powerless to deal with individual insurrectionary activity and trial by military commission was constitutional. That opinion was reinforced by Lincoln's experiences with the courts in Washington, D.C. shortly after he assumed the presidency. Secretary of the Navy, Gideon Welles, pinpointed the problem in his diary: "Unfortunately the hearts and sympathies of the present judges are with the Rebels." Massachusetts Senator Henry Wilson said that the chief judge's "heart is sweltering with treason." On May 23, 1862, the Congress introduced a bill to reorganize the District's courts. About three thousand citizens and almost all the lawyers in Washington, forty-nine, opposed the measure stating: "They believe that this measure is not called for by any public necessity, and that it would not be acceptable to the great mass of the people in the District." On February 20, 1863, Kentucky Senator Garrett Davis placed the opposition memorial before the Senate and the House. Lincoln supported the reorganization and the bill was passed on March 5, 1863 with nineteen Republican Senators in favor and sixteen opposed and in the House by 86 to 59. Promptly, Lincoln signed the bill and on March 23, 1863 appointed four-new judges loyal to the Union cause: David Kellogg Cartter from Ohio became Chief Justice. Cartter was a campaign manager when Lincoln gained the presidential nomination in Chicago; Associate Justices named were Abram B. Olin of New York; George P. Fisher of Delaware; and Andrew Wylie of Washington, D.C. Wylie was the only avowed Republican in Alexandria [VA] to vote for Lincoln in 1860 despite threats of violence if he did so. After Lincoln's election, Wylie was sitting on his porch relaxing in a rocking chair. A shot was fired that shattered the glass he was holding in his hand. Immediately thereafter, he moved to the District. Ohio Congressman Albert G. Riddle delivered a descriptive epilogue: "The Supreme Court of the District of Columbia was a court of *our* creation and for which we cleared the ground by sweeping the alleged disloyal Circuit Court from the boards." Lincoln had only one justification for his policy; necessity justified the exercise of arbitrary power by the president. While he was no dictator, Lincoln certainly did exercise the powers of the president boldly. However, Lincoln's friend David Davis, then an Associate Justice of the Supreme Court of the United States, apprized him during the war that military trials in areas where the federal courts were functioning freely were "unconstitutional and wrong." Furthermore, Davis told Lincoln that the Supreme Court of the United States should not uphold such trials. Davis firmly believed that military commissions had no jurisdiction over civilians. In a later disagreement, the 1866 Supreme Court of the United States decision in the *Ex Parte Milligan* case affirmed the illegality of military commissions to determine the guilt of civilians. In keeping with his own judicial opinion, Davis wrote the decision for the court.

When the military commission prosecution rested, defense lawyer Bowden began by cross-examining Provost Marshall Bovay. On the evening of the shooting, Bovay admitted that he interviewed Wright. Pointedly, Bowden asked Bovay to describe Wright's conduct and appearance during the conversation that evening. After a prosecution objection, the court ruled that no further evidence would be admitted as to Wright's conduct or appearance after his arrest. With court back in session, Wright's lawyers requested a half-hour for consultation. After the time expired, Bowden and Chandler, much to the surprise of everyone present, announced their withdrawal from the case and left the courtroom! With this tactic, the lawyers hoped to postpone the trial to gain time to plan to save Wright from the inevitable gallows. Immediately, the court asked Wright if he wished to obtain other counsel or if he prefer that his trial proceed. He responded by asking for a day to consider After agreeing, the court adjourned. Next day, Wright presented a written statement declaring that he could not and did not wish to obtain further counsel, nor did he wish to introduce any new evidence on his own behalf. Court adjourned to allow Wright to prepare a concluding statement. On the last day of the trial, Wednesday, July 29, 1863, Wright addressed the court.

Standing awkwardly before the five member military commission, Wright denied their jurisdiction, denounced the testimony of witnesses as erroneous, and stated that his actions were based upon self-defense. He questioned the "logic" of having colored troops in Norfolk, suggesting that the soldiers were there to provoke and harass white citizens. Furthermore, Wright puzzled aloud about Sanborn's motives and commented that Sanborn directed offensive remarks to him. Finally, Wright reminded the court that he immediately offered medical care to Sanborn after he was wounded.

In his closing, Judge Advocate John A. Bolles mentioned Wright's possible insanity. If that were so, he insisted that Wright should be confined in an asylum until cured. However, Bolles declared that the shooting of Sanborn was deliberate and unprovoked. Succinctly, Bolles advised the court that they were soldiers and knew what "the good of the service demanded."

Upon reaching a verdict, the court unanimously condemned Wright to be "hung by the neck until he be dead." Place and time of execution to be selected by the Fortress Monroe commander, Major-General John G. Foster, or by the president of the United States.

Hurriedly, defense lawyer Chandler met with Lincoln at the White House and appealed to him to suspend "a speedy enforcement of the judgement of the Military Commission" until he could "give the case a full examination." On August 3, 1863, Lincoln telegraphed Foster: "If Dr. Wright, on trial at Norfolk, has been, or shall be convicted, send me a transcript of his trial and conviction, and do not let execution be done upon him, until my further order." Foster replied: "Your orders will be strictly obeyed. The trial is concluded. General [Henry M] Naglee informs me that the proceedings, findings & sentence have been forwarded to you for your revision and approval." Reacting to the court's verdict, President Lincoln was beleaguered by "petitioners surpassing in number those of any other pardon appeal during the war for the privilege of a fair and impartial trial" for Wright. John S. Millson and ninety-four other citizens from Norfolk sent a telegram to "His Excellency ABRAHAM LINCOLN" on July 28, 1863: "The undersigned respectfully request that Dr. D.M. WRIGHT, of this city, charged with the murder of Lieutenant Sanborn, be restored to his home and family or be delivered over to civil authorities or some other tribunal where he can have the privilege of a fair and impartial trial, which right belongs to every human being."

More than 340 Norfolk citizens, including nine ministers, eleven physicians, five lawyers and consular representatives from Portugal and Austria, signed a petition to pardon or commute the death sentence. N.B. Webster, a New Hampshire native and then a Norfolk educator, delivered a clemency plea that stressed Wright's medical services to the community. Defense lawyers, Bowden, Chandler and Segar telegraphed the PRESIDENT OF THE UNITED STATES on August 7 from Norfolk: "I most respectfully request that so soon as the record in the case of Dr. D.M. Wright, charged with the murder of Lieutenant Sanborn, shall be laid before you, you will telegraph the Hon. L. H. Chandler and myself, fixing some day when we may appear before you and present the *mass of testimony* which has been taken to prove the insanity of Doctor Wright, and also to present such statements in regard to the manner of conducting his trial, and to the facilities afforded him for making anything like a fair defense, as the facts of the case will justify."

On August 7, 1863, Mrs. Stark A.W. Preighton of Edenton [NC], Wright's niece, wrote to the Confederate States of America President Jefferson Davis asking "if anything can be done by our Government for Doctor Wright." Her letter was endorsed by CSA Secretary of War J.A. Seddon who was doubtful the CSA could help and might "probably prejudice it [Wright's cause] with our brutal foes." President Davis responded to a similar letter from the former CSA Attorney General, Thomas Bragg, on September 1, 1863 stating: "I have been unable to devise any method which seemed likely to render him [Wright] effective service."

On August 15, 1863, "a committee of five gentlemen chosen by the Union League, Washington Council No. 4, had a very pleasant and impartial interview with his Excellency." They met with Lincoln in relation to Lieut. A.L. Sanborn, "a worthy member of the Union League, who was murdered in cold blood at Norfolk." A document was read to the President to argue for justice for the Sanborn shooting and for a warning to others. This document noted that the President had the sealed verdict to review and that Dr. Wright's friends were petitioning for a pardon. Committee members were instructed to "beseech you, for the sake of justice and humanity, and as a suitable warning to all future offenders against the majesty of the law." After listening to the sometimes bombastic phrases read by the draft club representatives, Lincoln commented: "An example would prove a great benefit to the cause."

Legislation passed on July 17, 1862 created the office of Judge Advocate General to provide supervision of proceedings of courts-martial and military commissions. Shortly after the legislation, Lincoln appointed Joseph Holt to the position. Judge Advocate General Holt sent Lincoln his review of the evidence in Wright's case on August 19, 1863. Holt asserted that the Military Commission followed proper legal procedure and conducted a fair trial. Testimony on Wright's conduct and appearance was disallowed because an insanity defense was never seriously proposed. After citing case references, Holt declared: "It will be seen, therefore, by this examination of his [Wright's] address that the accused himself not only disclaims the idea of insanity as an answer to his crime, but actually sets up another, that of self-defense." Holt concluded: "The crime then stands in the record as a homicide committed without just cause or provocation, an undefended assassination, and therefore fully meriting the sentence imposed by the court."

On August 28, 1863, Lincoln telegraphed General Foster: "Please notify, if you can, Senator Bowden, Mr. Segar, and Mr. Chandler, all, or any of them, that I now have the record in Dr. Wright's case, and am ready to hear them. When you shall have got the notice to them, please let me know." Foster replied the same day: "I have notified Mr. Chandler of your wishes & he will start for Washington this evening. I have also sent notice to Senator Bowden. Mr. Segar is not here but is understood to be in Washington." Lincoln gave a full hearing to Wright's lawyers, examined the trial transcript and considered Judge Advocate General Holt's report. His remarks illustrate his thought processes: "... being satisfied that no proper question remained open except as to the insanity of the accused, I caused a full examination to be made on that question ... by an expert of high reputation in that professional department."

Intriguing legal and political means and ends questions regarding how Lincoln caused a full insanity examination emanate from letters in the presidential papers. On September 2, 1863, Secretary of State Seward wrote to Lincoln: "Dr. Nicholl's surroundings are so disloyal as to shake public confidence in himself. Dr. Gray of Utica occurs to me as a very proper person."

A logical inference is that Lincoln was choosing between two physicians recommended by Seward, a Dr. Gray and a Dr. Nicholl. It is also reasonable to deduce that Lincoln had information about both doctors, that he and Seward discussed the matter and that Seward investigated and made a choice. However, it is not exactly clear what Seward meant when he wrote that Dr. Gray was "a very proper person?" Were Dr. Nichols' "surroundings so disloyal" as to interfere with his professional judgment?

In certainty, Seward's note must unquestionably refer to Dr. Charles H. Nichols, Superintendent of the Government Hospital for the Insane in Washington, D.C. Dr. John P. Gray was Superintendent of the

Utica [NY] Lunatic Asylum. Both, Gray and Nichols were specialists in the study of the mind and colleagues in the Association of Medical Superintendents of American Institutions for the Insane [AMSAII], the precursor to the American Psychiatric Association. Despite being colleagues, these two "experts of high reputation" could not have been more different in their professional and philosophical approach to the question of sanity or insanity.

Significantly, Lincoln's choice of a medical expert on insanity was likely influenced by his own prior legal experiences. On the day after Seward wrote to Lincoln recommending Gray as the medical expert, on September 3, 1863, Francis H. Pierpont, Union Governor of Eastern Virginia, wrote to Lincoln. He urged support for Wright's death sentence and claimed that his execution would aid in the recruitment of black soldiers for the Union army.

Besieged on all sides, Lincoln added a note to Seward's September 2, 1863 letter and sent it back to him to take action: "Please telegraph Dr. Gray asking him whether he could come and serve the government one month more or less, & how soon."

After learning of Gray's willingness to serve, on September 9, 1863, Seward endorsed his note to Lincoln "Introducing Dr. Gray of Utica" for his appointment with Lincoln on September 10, 1863. His note to "My dear President" said: "This will be handed to you by Dr. Gray of Utica." Lincoln had a lengthy interview with Gray at the White House. When they met the contrast between the two was striking. Gray was broad shouldered, short and stout, weighing 300 plus pounds. He was convivial, genial, kind and enjoyed criminal trials. Lincoln towered over Gray and looked like a sorrowful scarecrow as they sat and talked. After the meeting, Lincoln appointed Gray a Special Commissioner and gave him a letter of instruction dated September 10, 1863: "...The record is before me; and a question is made as to the sanity of the accused ... take in writing all evidence which may be offered on behalf of Dr. Wright, and against him ... All said evidence to be directed to the question of Dr. Wright's sanity or insanity, and not to any other questions ... you will report ... your own conclusions as to Dr. Wright's sanity both at the time of the homicide and the time of your examination .. If you deem it proper, you will examine Dr. Wright personally ..."

A few days later, on September 13, 1863, Lincoln telegraphed Gray who was already in Norfolk: "The names of those whose affidavits are left with me on the question of Dr. Wright's sanity are as follow: Mrs. Jane C. Bolsom, Mrs. M. E. Smiley, Moses Hudgin, J. D. Ghislin, Jr., Felix Logue, Robert B. Turnstall, M.D., Mrs. Elizabeth Rooks, Dr. E. D. Granier, Thomas K. Murray, William J. Holmes, Miss Margaret E. Wigeon, Mrs. Emily S. Frost." While Lincoln listed twelve names, Gray reported on testimony from thirteen witnesses for each side. Eventually, Gray dismissed the testimony for the accused because those witnesses were outside of Wright's social sphere and the statements were "too *few*, too *disconnected*, and too *insignificant*, to afford reasonable foundation upon which to establish the fact of insanity." Prosecution testimony found more favor with Gray: "On the contrary, those of the witnesses who knew him [Wright] intimately, and met him in the familiar intercourse of social life, testify to his sanity."

During his examination, Gray conducted two personal interviews with Wright. Each interview lasted about two hours and Gray recounted Wright's comments about his history and his attitudes: "Was born April 21, 1809 in Nansemond County, Virginia to David and Mary [Armistead] Wright ... attended Captain Patrick's military school in Middletown, Connecticut ... was there imbued more or less with Northern ideas in regard to slavery ... read medicine with Dr. William Warren in Edenton, North Carolina ... graduated from University of Philadelphia Medical School in 1833 ... practiced in Edenton for 18 years ... married Penelope Creecy of Edentown, [NC] in 1833 ... moved to Norfolk about 1854 ... rendered heroic service during the Yellow Fever epidemic of 1855 ... he changed his opinion on the subject of slavery and conscientiously believed it to be in accordance with the scriptures, and the true welfare of the negro, and that he looked upon the attempted destruction as a wrong to both races ... though at times he was depressed, he could not say the depression was frequent or great ... at the commencement [of the rebellion] he was a Union man, but gradually went into the current Southern feeling ... he voted for secession ... he thought the arming of slaves a great wrong ... he saw those colored troops, and this officer at their head, coming towards him, in an instant he felt the most unconquerable and desperate impulse to shoot him, and got a pistol ... immediately afterwards, he felt the most awful agony of mind ... In giving this account, he at times wept, and was greatly overcome by his emotions."

Gray found Wright to be "perfectly coherent, and presented no indications of aberration of mind in conversation, manner, or appearance." Furthermore, Gray carefully considered Wright's statement that he committed the murder under "a most unconquerable and desperate impulse." He decided: "It has been impossible for me to arrive at the conclusion that this impulse was an *insane* one, and uncontrollable in the sense in which an insane man's impulses are beyond his control." Earlier court decisions allowed for the "irresistible impulse" defense in a murder trail. In an 1844 Massachusetts trial, *Commonwealth v. Rogers*, Judge Lemuel Shaw ruled that: "One is not responsible for an act done under an uncontrollable impulse which is the result of mental disease." In contrast, Gray was dogmatic in his disbelief of the irresistible or uncontrollable impulse.

Based on all the testimony, his own interviews and his observations, Gray reported to Lincoln: "I am of the opinion that Doctor David M. Wright was not insane prior to the 11th day of July, 1863, the date of the homicide of Lieutenant Sanborn; that he has not been insane since, and is not insane now."

Gray concluded his examination on September 26, 1863 and General Foster notified Lincoln the next day. Foster gratuitously took the opportunity to state his own military biases: "I deem it a proper opportunity for me to forward to you my convictions in the case and my most respectful suggestions ... the homicide was a deliberate and cold-blooded murder ... looking to the nature and character of the troops of which Lieutenant Sanborn was an officer, I deem it essential to discipline and proper feelings of pride and self-respect among the officers of colored troops that Doctor Wright should pay the penalty to which he was sentenced by court-martial."

Foster's remarks reiterated the prosecution's closing comments. Judge Advocate Bolles admonished the military court members to do what "the good of the service demanded." Without the death sentence for Wright, white officers might decline to command colored troops. Former slaves and free men might be reluctant to volunteer to serve in the Union army. All told, the Union might flounder in its efforts to defeat the rebels. Even with the surge in new troops, it still took the Union more than eighteen months to win the war.

On October 7, 1863 Lincoln approved Dr. Wright's sentence. Lincoln noted that an "expert of high reputation in that professional department" reported to him that Wright was not insane prior to or on the day of the homicide and has not been insane since and is not insane now. He concluded: "I therefore approve the finding and sentence of the military commission, and direct that the major-general in command of the department including the place of the trial, and wherein the convict is now in custody, appoint time and place and carry said sentence into execution." Taking action, Foster ordered that Wright be hanged on Friday, October 16, 1863 at 10:00 AM. Learning of his fate, Wright designed his own coffin. Shaped like an immense wedge, there was a raised area near the head where Wright placed daguerreotypes of his whole family. Inspecting the coffin and expressing his satisfaction, Wright "wrote his name on the lid with a lead pencil in a good, bold hand."

Defense lawyer Bowden telegraphed the PRESIDENT on October 15: "Hon. L. H. Chandler has this moment informed me that Doctor Wright is ordered for execution in the morning, and that it is very desirable he should be granted a respite of one week in order to the arrangement of his private affairs and the making of provision for his afflicted family." Wright had a wife and eight children ranging in age from seven to twenty-three: Penelope [23], Minton [21], Elizabeth [19], Mary [17], John [15], Sarah [12], William [10] and Viola [7]. Lincoln immediately telegraphed General Foster: "Postpone the execution of Dr. Wright to Friday the 23rd Inst. [October]. This is intended for his preparation and is final."

As part of his preparations, Wright asked to witness the long planned marriage of his daughter, Elizabeth, who was engaged to William H. Talbott. Accordingly, on Saturday evening, October 17, 1863, the ceremony took place in the prison with Rev. Mark L. Cheevers, the Methodist chaplain from Fortress Monroe officiating. About thirty invited guests attended. "The sad circumstances ... drew tears from the eyes of even the Federal attendants."

On the same day as the wedding Foster telegraphed Lincoln: "The Hon. Mr. Chandler has made application for Mr. William Talbot and Mrs. Dr. Wright to proceed to Washington for the purpose of having an interview with you in behalf of her husband who is sentenced to be executed. My rules are not to allow any one to leave the Department who are not willing to take the oath of allegiance, but as you have postponed the execution one week I feel it my duty to forward the application to you for your decision." Wright's wife, accompanied by her new son-in-law, attempted to gain a personal audience with Lincoln to plead for her husband's life. Lincoln's reply was curt: "It would be useless for Mrs. Dr. Wright to come here. The subject is a very painful one, but the case is settled."

Wright's defenders argued that Lincoln's decision was prompted by his real concern that he might lose the upcoming presidential election. Reflecting upon the 1864 election, Lincoln said "I should not have been elected" if the Democrats waged a different campaign. It was possible for General George McCellan to be elected with a swing of only 31,500 votes in eight states. Lincoln's re-election jitters combined with his zealous nationalistic aim to preserve the Union at all costs.

Defense lawyers Bowden and Chandler remained steadfast up to the end. Bowden claimed a possible bias on the part of a member of the military commission. He had an October 22, 1863 dispatch from the Attorney General of Virginia which stated: "I have the signed certificate of a commissioned officer, U.S. Army, declaring that a member of the military commission which tried Doctor Wright expressed himself unfavorable to that individual before the prisoner was arraigned or he had heard any of the testimony. Answer immediately." In a letter to "His Excellency the President," dated October 22, 1863, Chandler enclosed a copy of the dispatch to Bowden with a urgent plea of his own: "To proceed with the execution when such doubt as to the fairness and impartiality of his trial ... would destroy the proceeding ... I received ... information ... which precluded the chances of an impartial trial, but was restrained by a pledge of secrecy and confidence from making any use of the information communicated to me ... I entertain the belief that proof can be exhibited ... the trial was not before such a tribunal as could be safely trusted with the liberties and lives of the people." It was reiterated that Wright was "of unsound mind" and urged that he be confined for life. They suggested that Wright be exchanged for a Northern physician, Dr. William P. Rucker, who was a Confederate prisoner in Richmond.

Penelope, Wright's eldest daughter, devised an audacious plan for her father's escape. On the evening of October 21, in the semidarkness of the cell and directly under the watchful eye of the guard, she used a master key to open his manacles. Penelope deftly draped some of her garments, including a face veil, over her father to transform him into a woman. She slipped on his boots and lay on the cot under the blanket with only her booted feet showing. In his disguise, Wright left with his other visitors and headed toward a waiting carriage. He managed to get about fifty feet away before a sentry became suspicious of the "tall woman" and "her gait." Lieutenant Cook, the officer of the guard, hurried after the "woman," lifted her veil and declared: "That's played out; I know you Dr. Wright." Without embarrassment, Wright replied: "Desperate means are pardonable under desperate circumstances." Numerous fires were reported in Norfolk that night. Possibly, the blazes were meant as a distraction for the escape.

Surreptitious efforts to free Wright continued. A Union war department telegrapher, Richard O'Brien, was supposedly offered a bribe to send a bogus telegram of reprieve to Fortress Monroe. He was offered $20,000 in gold and a free passage to England on a blockade runner. O'Brien refused the bribe.

During the morning of October 23, 1863, "soulless blacks, and senseless, vulgar whites, thronged Church Street as the cortege passed to the Federal gibbet" at the Fair Grounds at 18th Street. Norfolk newspapers described the thousands of spectators as "mostly Federals, white riff-raff and Negroes." Dressed in a dark coat, pants, buff vest and white necktie, Wright presented a dignified and self-processed appearance before the assembled clamorous crowd. Responding to rumored threats of a Confederate rescue attempt, a hollow square of massed Union troops surrounded the gallows in the center of the race track. Wright's final words consisted of a single sentence: "The deed I committed was done without malice." At 11:30 AM, General-in-Chief Henry W. Halleck received a telegram from General Foster: "Dr. Wright was executed this morning at Norfolk according to orders. Everything passed off very orderly."

Coincidentally, during his period of about four months pondering the death sentence for Wright, Lincoln frequently signed orders commuting death sentences for desertion, disobeying orders, mutiny, shootings, spying, stealing and assorted high crimes. When Lincoln reviewed the military courts-martial during the Civil War, he would usually give the man a second chance. On Saturday, July 18, 1863, Lincoln and Holt spent six hours going over courts martial verdicts. Lincoln's assistant secretary John Hay observed that the President "caught any fact" to justify saving a life. In addressing a meeting of the Union Veterans Club in Chicago, Lincoln's close friend and fellow lawyer, Leonard Swett recalled that he said that an approval of the death penalty tore his heart most. Lincoln told Swett that he went through the submitted papers to see "if I can't find something by which I can let them off." That sentiment is echoed in Samuel K. Jackson's 1893 letter to *The Landmark*, a Norfolk journal. Jackson was an intimate friend of Wright's until he moved in 1857. After correcting two minor errors in a prior article, Jackson recalled that "it was said at the time that Pres. Lincoln wanted an excuse to pardon him [Wright]." Lincoln's compassionate attitude is illustrated in his reply to a man who was weeping because his son's execution was merely suspended rather than receiving a pardon: "My dear man, if your son lives until I order him shot, he will live longer than ever Methuselah did."

There was a funeral service for Wright on October 24, 1863 at Christ Church, Freemason and Cumberland. His coffin was profusely decorated with white flowers and evergreens and the lid was open as hundreds viewed his face. Revs. E.M. Rodman, Parkman and M.A. Okeson performed the Episcopal solemnities. Wright was interred at Elmwood Cemetery

Ironically, on the same day as Wright's funeral a Major Crosby received a letter from Assistant- Adjunct General George H. Johnson, by command of Union General James Barnes. That letter ordered Wright's release upon his giving a bond of $1,000.00 to guarantee his appearance before Federal authorities as required. It is supposed that Wright was to be released to await a second trial.

General Barnes allowed Wright's family to leave Norfolk and they arrived within Confederate lines at Petersburg, Virginia. On March 10, 1864, legislator Richard H. Baker, Jr. proposed and the General Assembly of Virginia passed a resolution honoring Dr. D. M. Wright: "It is fit and proper that Virginia shall place upon permanent record her high appreciation of a son, whose courage, zeal and devotion marked with blood the first effort to establish upon her soil an equality of races, and introduce into our midst the leveling dogmas of a false and pretended civilization."

Mrs. Wright died on May 13, 1889 and was buried beside her husband in Norfolk. Wright's children remained in the south. Penelope [Pencie] married Alexander Watson Weddell of Petersburg. He was a Captain in the Confederate army, a lawyer, a journalist and finally the Rector of historic St. John's Church in Richmond. Their son, Alexander

Wilburne Weddell was the U.S. ambassador to Argentina and the president of the Virginia Historical Society. At 21, Minton Augustus Wright died in the Battle of Gettysburg but Wright's family decided not to tell him the sad news while he was in jail. Mary married Frederick A. Fetter. John [Joshua] C. Armistead was a midshipman on the CSS *Patrick Henry* in 1863 and in 1892 he was unmarried. Sallie [Sarah] married Thomas Warren. William married Sarah Coke.

Thirty-eight years after Wright's death, on May 8, 1901, the City Council of Portsmouth expunged from the records the earlier denunciations. "Aspersions by an official body of sycophants and scalawags on a heroic and spotless gentleman are forever blotted out." Nevertheless, a southern historian categorized Dr. Wright's execution as the "most agonizing tragedy of the occupation, the one that shocked Norfolk more than any other single incident, the one that has lived vividly in the memory of many Virginians."

A distinguished Norfolk physician, Dr. L.B. Anderson, reviewed Wright's case in 1892 and concluded he was unblemished: "Rest, our most worthy compatriot and professional brother, though abolition malice has striven to fix a stigma upon thy name and a blot upon thy character; it has only enshrined thy virtues more securely in the hearts of thy countrymen and engraved thy name more deeply upon their memories forever."

In retrospect, Lincoln plausibly considered a web of related circumstances and disparate factors beyond the "undefended assassination" and the sanity or insanity of Wright. A number of political interrelated events occurred before, during and after Wright's "undefended assassination" trial, guilty verdict, death sentence, sanity determination and public hanging. Emancipation was "a military necessity absolutely essential to the preservation of the Union." There were intensive efforts sought to enlist emancipated slaves and free blacks into the Union army as volunteers. A Confederate States of America Joint Resolution ordered that white commissioned officers commanding or training colored volunteers will be "deemed as inciting service insurrection, and shall, if captured, be put to death ..." There was continuous difficulties recruiting and/or drafting Union troops, and the growing conscription chaos including the spectacularly bloody carnage in the mid-July 1863 draft riots in New York City. On September 7, 1863, Major-General Henry M. Naglee reported that confederate guerrillas in Virginia blew up bridges and fired on Union soldiers. Military leaders advised that Wright's hanging was imperative to the morale and discipline of the white officers and the colored troops.

These interrelated events reflected the sensitive political climate at this point in the Civil War. Amid the turmoil, Lincoln remained tenaciously determined to preserve the Union and the nation. Lincoln's dilemma in the Wright case was deftly described by a *New York Times* book reviewer: "Nothing poses the question of justifiable ends and means in politics more poignantly than the problems Lincoln faced in suppressing a proslavery Southern rebellion by mobilizing a Northern constituency hostile to both slavery and black people."

Lincoln himself added a caveat to explain his legal and political means and ends actions: "A measure made expedient by a war is no precedent for times of peace."

Lincoln agreed with Seward's recommendation of Gray as the "very proper person' over Nichols whose "surroundings are so disloyal." In so doing, Lincoln's political choice bolstered military discipline and morale, calmed abolitionist Frederick Douglass, stimulated enlistments and allowed the Union to eventually recruit 179,985 colored troops.

Sanborn's public assassination severely damaged Union troop recruiting efforts in eastern Virginia for months. Between March and the end of August, 1863, comments to and from Lincoln proclaimed the concrete value of Negro troops to the Union cause and set a precedent for hanging verdicts.

At one point, colored troops constituted ten percent of the Union army and fought in 449 engagements, including 39 major battles. During the war, 37,300 black soldiers died. In addition, the Congressional Medal of Honor was awarded to twenty-one blacks serving the Union: seventeen soldiers and four sailors.

Two days before Wright was to be hanged, another "undefended assassination" occurred. On October 21, 1863, secessionist John H. Sothoron and his son shot and killed Second Lieutenant Eben White, 7th U.S. Colored Troops, at Benedict, Maryland.

## MURDERESS INSANE DUE TO BEING "CROSSED-IN-LOVE AND PAINFUL DYSMENORRHEA"

This murder dealt with all the ingredients to excite the public: disappointed love, feminism, honor, medicine, murder, painful dysmenorrhea, religion, sex, temporary insanity, virtue and even the possibility of child abuse. "Penny press" newspapers in the 1860s luridly printed anything that attracted paying readers. Today, "tabloid TV producers" would titillate television viewers to boost ratings. A reminder about a similar murder took the bodily form of General Daniel E. Sickles. He personally understood the tragedy because he was acquitted of murdering Philip Barton Key in 1859 on the grounds of temporary insanity caused by severe emotional distress. Sickles was warmly welcomed by President and Mrs. Lincoln into their social circle. He frequently hobbled about the White House on his crutches since his lower leg was blown off during the battle of Gettysburg in 1863. He probably encouraged Mrs. Mary Todd Lincoln to send a bouquet of flowers to the jail cell of the imprisoned murderess.

Coincidentally, this murder trial involved people Lincoln met during prior legal encounters: Dr. Charles H. Nichols and Dr. John P. Gray from the trial of Dr. David M. Wright; justice Andrew Wylie whom Lincoln appointed to the Washington Supreme Court; Joseph H. Bradley, Sr. from the trial of Sickles and as a prominent Washington lawyer who opposed the reorganization of the court; Edward C. Carrington, a Virginian whom Lincoln appointed U.S. Attorney for the District of Columbia; James Hughes whom Lincoln appointed as an Associate Justice to the U.S. Court of Claims; Charles Mason, who was the Commissioner of the U.S. Patent Office; Daniel W. Voorhees, who was a legal colleague and encountered Lincoln in the county circuit courts of Illinois; and even Dr. John Frederick May, who appealed to Lincoln for leniency for an imprisoned relative, testified in this trial about the murderess' insanity, and identified Booth's body after Lincoln's assassination.

At four o'clock on the afternoon of January 30th, 1865, Mary Harris stepped out from behind the floor-to-ceiling grandfather clock on the second floor of the Treasury Building in Washington, D.C. She aimed and fired two shots from her 1859 Sharps four-barreled .32-caliber derringer at Adoniram J. Burroughs as he walked down the hall toward her, leaving work for the day. Her first shot proved to be fatal while her second missed. Tearfully, she explained that Burroughs promised to marry her, ruined her, and then married someone else.

Burroughs began his relationship with Harris when they were both living in Burlington, Iowa. She was about twelve years old and he was about twenty-three. Harris was born in Ireland and her family were poor, immigrant Irish Catholics. She was the third child and had two sisters and three brothers. Her father was a stone mason and her mother a part-time dressmaker. Harris' parents opposed the relationship warning her that Burroughs, a Protestant, would never marry her because she was Catholic. Considering Harris' age, her family's poverty and their low social status, chief defense attorney Joseph H. Bradley, Sr. averred that Burroughs "formed, shaped, and molded her mind, feelings, habits, tastes, and her intellectual and moral character."

Burroughs held various jobs in Burlington. Once, he was even employed in the same millinery shop where Harris worked. Not succeeding in Burlington, Burroughs traveled to various Iowa locations seeking business opportunities. He moved from Burlington to Ottumwa to Eddyville to Des Moines. From November of 1858 to August of 1863, Burroughs wrote ninety-two letters to Harris mentioning stolen kisses, using many endearing terms, and expressing his love and admiration for "My dearest Mollie" and "My dear little Rosebud." After Burroughs relocated to Chicago, he persuaded Harris to move there. Harris did so against her family's wishes and lived with and worked for Jane and Louisa Devlin in their Clark Street millinery shop in Chicago. She was seen frequently in the company of Burroughs by a number of acquaintances. Late in 1863, Burroughs moved to Washington, D.C. when he secured a clerical job in the Treasury Department. Harris learned from a notice on the front page of the September 16, 1863 *Chicago Tribune* that Burroughs married Amelia L. Boggs, the daughter of a wealthy merchant. She firmly believed that he deserted her to insure his financial stability. Seeking revenge, Harris arranged for a bogus notice about her own marriage to Charles A. Devlin to appear on the front page of the November 12, 1863 issue of the *Chicago Tribune*. She made sure that Burroughs received a copy of that announcement. For two years after Burroughs' marriage notice, Harris became progressively distressed and exhibited bizarre behavior. She became silent, temperamental, melancholy, and emotionally unstable while still living with and working for the Devlin sisters. On a number of occasions, Harris exhibited unexplainable outbursts: she threw a covered brick pin cushion at a customer; she struck Jane with a heavy window brush; she tore apart a quilt, slashed clothing and rippled books; she slept on the bare floor; she chased Jane with a carving knife; and she wandered aimlessly outside in her nightclothes in the dead of winter. Harris sued Burroughs for a breach of a marriage contract but Burroughs could not be found to serve in Chicago. Finally, in early 1865, a desperate Harris decided to seek out Burroughs in Washington herself. She found him in the Treasury Department and shot him.

After Harris shot Burroughs, she was arrested and confined in the local jail and a coroner's inquest was held on January 31, 1865. A *New York Herald* investigative reporter interviewed her the next day and found that Harris "was visited by many prominent gentlemen and ladies to "ameliorate the sufferings of the unhappy woman." On the same day, the *Chicago Tribune's* Washington correspondent proclaimed that "the unfortunate girl has influential friends." Becoming very specific, Washington's *Daily National Intelligencer* reported that Mrs. Amelia Fales, a Washington socialite, was "unremitting in her attention to the prisoner since her incarceration."

A Grand Jury considered the murder on March 22, 1865 and found enough evidence for an indictment. Harris was arraigned on March 30, 1865, pled "not guilty," and the trial was scheduled to begin on April 24, 1865. There were several postponements for a variety of reasons. During June, the trial of the conspirators in Lincoln's assassination concluded and four of the accused were sentenced to death by hanging. Before the death sentence was carried out, Harris' trial began with jury selection on July 3, 1865. Court reporter James O. Clephane prepared the daily transcripts and the official report of the trial. However, the official report is not verbatim throughout. Clephane added comments and summarized information at various points in the transcript.

Worried defense lawyers felt that there was a direct relationship between the hanging of the conspirators involved in Lincoln's assassination and this murder trial. Brooding ill for the defense team, a woman, Mrs. Mary Surratt, was hanged along with three male conspirators in Lincoln's assassination almost immediately before the Harris trial began in earnest. Despite Lincoln being the President, and being killed before the murder trial, the events are still linked to Lincoln's legal career, to his wife and to legal concepts of insanity. In addition, the Harris case became a landmark of medical jurisprudence in the United States.

For the first time in a United States courtroom, expert medical testimony supported a defense of paroxysmal [temporary] insanity during the murder trial of Mary Harris. A forensic physician testified that the murderess was paroxysmally insane from the combination of "being crossed-in-love and suffering from painful dysmenorrhea" at the time of the shooting. Five "common-sense" physicians, prominent medical practitioners, testified on behalf of the prosecution that Harris was not insane, merely hysterical. A popular impression among the press and the public was that Harris was not insane. People surmised that "a cunningly devised fiction was being foisted on the jury regarding her mental condition." In part, that attitude related to the adversarial testimony of medical experts. Historical perceptions of psychiatric testimony are applicable in the Harris case. There are five major criticisms of such medical testimony: sin is excused; there is always disagreement; opinions turn into conclusions; the law is dictated; and the testimony is confusing, subjective, uniformed and jargon-ridden.

Public and professional perceptions of the legal defense of temporary insanity remain remarkably similar from 1865 to the present time. During the 1865 trial, medical experts constantly used the words "painful dysmenorrhea," despite the obvious tautology. Even today, dysmenorrhea and/or premenstrual syndrome, now classified as luteal-phase dysphoric disorder, are still alleged to cause antisocial acts.

Edward C. Carrington, United States Attorney for the District of Columbia, was the prosecutor in this case. He served in the Mexican War commanding Carrington's Rangers and the Virginia legislature honored his service by presenting him with a finely decorated sword. Stroking his full length beard, he addressed the twelve male jurors emphasizing that a verdict of "not guilty by reason of insanity" carried a special caveat. A verdict of that nature allows the judge "to certify the fact to the Secretary of the Interior and have the unfortunate accused confined within the walls of the insane asylum." Prosecution strategy appeared to be clear cut. There was no doubt that Harris shot and killed Burroughs; there were eye witnesses to the murder. Arguments focused on the evident facts, the premeditation since 1863, and the appropriate punishment for the crime. Knowing the defense attorneys so well, Carrington anticipated the interwoven medical and legal nature of their tactics.

Chief defense counsel Bradley had a reputation as the Father of the District of Columbia bar. He was instrumental in the reorganization of the District of Columbia courts after Lincoln became President. His renown as a skillful and successful legal practitioner was wide spread. In court, Bradley planned the legal strategy and was aggressive and knowledgeable in carrying out his tactics. Bradley declared that Harris suffered from paroxysmal insanity from moral causes when she shot Burroughs. To augment the legal foundation, Bradley read about uncontrollable impulses from Section 174, page 142 of Wharton and Stillé's treatise on medical jurisprudence. He told the jury that paroxysmal insanity from moral causes resulted in a "state of excitement of the mind" rendering Harris incapable of thinking and acting with discretion. With emotional emphasis, Bradley asserted that Harris was subject to irresistible impulses that controlled her will. He cited precedents where courts in Massachusetts, Ohio and Pennsylvania found irresistible impulse and temporary emotional distress predisposing factors in murder acquittals. In addition, Bradley cited the cases of John Day in 1852, the Devlins in 1858, and Daniel E. Sickles in 1859. Judge T. Hartley Crawford of the District of Columbia court presided over all of those cases. Judge Andrew Wylie, presiding in the *People v. Harris* trial, indicated his deep respect for his fellow Justice in the same court.

In the 1859 *People v. Sickles* case, Bradley assisted his former student, Robert Ould, the U.S. Attorney for the District of Columbia. There was an apparent carry-over to the Harris trial. In broad daylight, a cuckolded Sickles brutally fired several shots chasing and killing his wife's lover, Philip Barton Key, as he lay wounded on the ground in the District's Lafayette Square. After being charged with murder, Sickles' lawyers, including Edwin M. Stanton, advanced the defense of moral mania [temporary insanity]. Significantly, there was no supporting expert medical testimony presented at the Sickles trial. Only lay witnesses testified as to Sickles' uncontrollable emotional outrage causing temporary insanity. Despite evidence of premeditation, the jury found the defendant not guilty. While the "irresistible and uncontrollable impulse" resulting from Sickles' emotional outrage was accepted by the jurors, the verdict did not mention temporary insanity.

That decision was probably abetted because of the "unwritten law" allowing husbands to protect their households. It may have helped that Sickles was politically connected, being a Congressman from New York City and a confidant of then President James Buchanan. On the other hand, Philip Barton Key was the U.S. Attorney for the District of Columbia and the son of the author of *The Star Spangled Banner*. Francis Scott Key had also been the U.S. Attorney for the District of Columbia three times.

Despite the extenuating circumstances and the political overtones of the Sickles case, defense attorney Bradley related specific points about the Sickles defense and the trial that took place in "this very same court house" to the Harris case. Precedents from the Sickles case were cited as rationales for admitting non-medical testimony from lay people relative to Harris' insanity.

Former United States Court of Claims Associate Justice, James Hughes, was a member of Harris' five-man volunteer legal team. He was a principal in the Washington law firm of Hughes, Denver and Peck with an office on Delaware Avenue opposite the Capitol. According to an expert, "Judge Hughes was a profound lawyer. It is doubtful if there is a better one in this part of the State [Indiana]." A historian described his legal and personal mannerisms: "He was a master of invective and sarcasm, a powerful speaker ... His legal rationales were able and exhaustively logical ... When speaking in court, Hughes was deliberate and usually toyed with a pencil, paper, or book, passing the object from hand to hand ... No one ever called him Jim to his face, slapped him on the shoulder, or took liberties with his person and he always carried a chip on his shoulder."

Hughes cited liberally from Dr. Isaac Ray's *A Treatise on the Medical Jurisprudence of Insanity*, which was first published in 1838. He discussed the insane impulse and informed the jury of the eight indicators of insanity delineated by Ray. Among others, these indicators included the following: prior illness; access to murderous weapons; either a loved or hated victim; a voluntary confession; and the rational appearance or strange behavior of the murderer. Because Ray was a physician specializing in mental illness, the quotations from his widely respected *Treatise* bolstered the defense's allegations of "moral insanity."

Referring to the *People v Sickles* case and Bradley's earlier pleadings, Hughes petitioned judge Wylie to allow lay people to express opinions as to the sanity of Harris. Over prosecution objections, judge Wylie ruled in favor of the defense. Particularly impressive to the jury was the testimony of the then Comptroller, and later Secretary of the Treasury, Hugh McCulloch. He observed and spoke with Harris in the treasury building immediately after the shooting and later when he and his wife visited her in jail. McCulloch described in vivid detail her intense emotional distress, her wild looks and her uncontrollable behavior.

In an innovative twist, Bradley was allowed to testify as to his observations on his own visits to Harris in jail. At that time it was infrequent, but not uncommon, for defense attorneys to testify. Today, it is unethical for participating attorneys to take the witness stand. In opening his testimony, Bradley noted that his interest in moral insanity, paroxysmal insanity, and paroxysmal insanity from moral causes went back some twenty years and continued to the day of his testimony. He described a number of incidents to illustrate clearly to the jury Harris' "paroxysmal insanity." In concluding his testimony, Bradley said that there were 'three occasions in which she was undoubtedly insane. She was insane from moral causes aggravated by disease of the body."

Judge Wylie permitted the defense to enter into evidence the letters written to Harris by Burroughs. In doing so, the judge stated that the letters were admitted not to prove insanity, but to show that causes existed for Harris' behavior. Parts of thirty-four letters were read to the jurors, mainly by William Y. Fendall, another volunteer member of the defense team and the son of a lawyer Bradley knew quite well. Apparently, these "love letters" left a decided impact upon the jury and the spectators. There appeared to be no doubt that Burroughs was a cad who had despoiled a young and virtuous girl.

In addition to Bradley, Hughes, and Fendall, the jury was impressed with the presence of Indiana Congressman Daniel W. Voorhees and judge Charles Mason at the defense table. Voorhees was well known for his powerful and emotional courtroom cratory as a jury pleader in criminal cases. "Others gathered the evidence and planned the fight; he [Voorhees] made the speech." Everybody called him "Dan." Mason had been United States Commissioner of Patents and the first chief judge of Iowa. He was in private patent law practice in Washington and took the lead in securing legal representation for Harris, who came from his home state of Iowa. Significantly, Mason graduated number one in his class from West Point in 1829, ahead of Robert E. Lee who was number two. Paradoxically, all five of the prominent Northern defense attorneys were alleged to be sympathetic to the confederate cause while Carrington, the Virginian born prosecutor, was a staunch Union man.

Presented with that sterling array of legal talent, Carrington utilized Greek mythology to identify the actors in his courtroom allegory: Bradley was the Ajax Telemon of the defense; Mason became the sweetly speaking Nestor of the Grecian camp; Hughes was the wise, the prudent, the cautious Ulysses; Voorhees assumed the mantle of the fierce, implacable, irresistible Achilles; and Fendall served as the young, the ardent, the amorous Tydides. For good measure, Carrington labeled judge Wylie as the sympathetic old Agamemnon and described Harris as "the lovely Helen, bathed in tears, surrounded by her female attendants, urging on these sturdy warriors to deeds of superhuman valor." This star-studded legal defense team made sure that the jury was exposed to testimony that clearly led them toward a conclusion that Burroughs took advantage of Harris from early childhood up to budding womanhood.

In contrast to the illustrious defense legal team, Carrington modestly pointed out to the jury that he was aided only by Assistant District Attorney Nathaniel Wilson. Faced with the fame and reputations of the defense attorneys, Carrington forcefully attacked. He pontificated his position about Harris and her insanity:"this is a case of murder, and this woman is not scientifically insane; she is not legally insane; she is not practically insane; she is not generally insane; she is not periodically insane; she is not spasmodically insane; she is not even hypothetically insane; but she is as sound today as she was before the murder; and this idea of insane impulses is a modern humbug."

Jurors may have read Nichols' expert medical testimony in the local Washington newspapers when he was called as a defense expert regarding the insanity of Lewis Thornton Powell [alias Paine or Payne] at the trial of Lincoln's assassins in June 1865. In the questions and answers printed in the newspapers, Nichols defined and gave the symptoms of moral insanity and responded to hypothetical examples. Defense lawyer William E. Doster told Nichols that Payne shouted, "I'm mad. I'm mad," after attacking and almost killing Secretary of State Seward. Answering, Nichols stated that madmen seldom say that they are mad and therefore he would suppose the attacker to be feigning madness. Owing to his wife's death on June 12, 1865, Nichols was not able to complete his examination and to be present for the defense's efforts to introduce an insanity plea for Payne. Nichols' reputation as a medical expert on insanity was certainly enhanced by the numerous newspaper stories about the assassination trial.

Defense attorneys endeavored to persuade the jury that after Harris read the notice of Burroughs' marriage, her disposition changed drastically. She became melancholy and emotionally unstable. Repeatedly, Harris bemoaned the fact that Burroughs had deserted her to marry the daughter of a wealthy Chicago merchant.

As Harris' condition worsened, Dr. Calvin M. Fitch was called to treat her toward the end of September 1863. As a defense witness under Bradley's questioning at the trial, Fitch testified that Harris suffered from severe congestive dysmenorrhea due to irritability of the uterus and that such uterine irritation always affects the nervous system. "In some instances it develops into insanity, and indeed a disturbance of the uterus -- uterine irritability -- is with females one of the most frequent causes of insanity." He gave her anodyne to quiet the nervous system and to induce sleep. Fitch stated: "We know that among the moral causes of insanity, disappointed affection is one of the most frequent." Furthermore, Fitch stated that the combination of "uterine irritation" and "disappointed affection" produced "a very much greater effect than either one would induce alone." He told the jurors that "there are many cases on record of paroxysmal insanity." On cross-examination by Assistant District Attorney Wilson, Fitch admitted that he was not an expert on the subject of insanity other than as an educated physician. Wilson queried Fitch regarding the severity of Harris' symptoms of hysteria and dysmenorrhea, his treatments, and his observations of her behavior. He declared that her symptoms were common, but severe; his remedies were not extraordinary; and "she seemed to be very despondent and melancholy." Fitch responded to questions about Harris' ability to distinguish right from wrong and his opinion as to her sanity when she shot Burroughs. He said that he merely saw Harris professionally "perhaps for five minutes at a time" and none of his visits extended beyond fifteen minutes. His suspicion that Harris was insane was based on the testimony of other witnesses that Bradley had read to him when he questioned Fitch.

In medical practice for twenty-two years with a specialty of the study of the mind for eighteen years, Nichols was the only witness that judge Wylie advised the jurors to recognize as a medical expert. Nichols visited Harris in jail four or five times and assessed her condition. So as not to offend Harris' sensitivity, Nichols asked her in writing whether she was having her period at the time of the shooting. In writing, Harris replied "yes" to the question.

Nichols was present for most of the trial testimony, especially when eye-witnesses spoke about Harris' state of mind immediately after the shooting and on their visits to her in jail. Based on his interviews and the testimony, Nichols concluded: "Mary Harris' brain and nervous system are large and active." Her painful dysmenorrhea had existed since Autumn 1863 up to July 1865. He said that she had her menstrual period at the time of the murder. In his opinion, she was "unusually susceptible to either a physical or moral cause of insanity." Nichols stated that Harris' "disappointment in love" shocked her delicate moral sensibilities and that she was "unquestionably insane at times." He cited her fearing harm from Lincoln's assassins while in jail as an example of her delusions.

Continuing, Nichols referred to the M'Naghten rule. There are, at least, sixteen different spelling variations of M'Naghten, but the rule is the same regardless. Briefly, the M'Naghten rule declares that a person is to be found not guilty, on grounds of insanity, if that person was laboring under such a defect of reason, from disease of the mind, as not to know the nature and quality of the act the person was doing. Generally, that person did not know right from wrong.

Nichols stated: "I do not consider a knowledge of right and wrong, in the abstract, as a test of insanity." He diagnosed Harris' condition as "periodical or paroxysmal mania." Furthermore, Nichols defined "insane impulse" as an inability to restrain the committing of a sudden act. "In some instances there is probably a consciousness of the nature of the act; but in most instances I think there is not."

To rebut the expert testimony of Nichols and the conclusions of attending physician Fitch, the prosecution called upon five prominent physicians in the District of Columbia area. None of the prosecution physicians had practical experience in the treatment of patients with mental illness, but all five were highly respected physicians. Carrington stressed to the jury that any educated physician was a proper witness on a question of insanity. Prosecutor Carrington sought to have his defense physicians testify that Harris' behavior was routine and could be explained by ordinary medical conditions relating to diseases of women, particularly symptomology in cases of hysteria or dysmenorrhea. He anticipated that his medical witnesses would discuss the specific symptoms and infer that the patient was not insane. These five prosecution "common-sense" physician witnesses were in contrast to Nichols, the "mad" doctor.

In the practice of surgery and general medicine since 1834, Dr. John Frederick May was called as a witness for the prosecution. He was the first to do an ovariotomy and did most of the major surgery in the District of Columbia. At one time, May was a Professor at Columbia College holding the Chair in Principle and Practice of Surgery. Shortly before this trial, in April 1865, May was summoned to the Navy Yard to identify the body of John Wilkes Booth on the deck of the ironclad monitor *Montauk*. Two years earlier, during April 1863, May surgically removed a carbuncle from Booth's neck and was familiar with the resultant scar.

Prosecutor Carrington presented a brief hypothetical case detailing the physical symptoms and behavior resulting from hysteria, dysmenorrhea and disappointment in love. He then posed three questions for his medical expert to answer: " (1) State how frequently you have noticed in your practice such symptoms in cases of hysteria or dysmenorrhea, and whether upon such symptoms you would infer the insanity of the patient? (2) Considering the actual premeditated events involved in the murder, state whether the act of homicide could be attributed to an insane impulse or whether the accused was sane and was compelled by another motive? (3) In view of the alleged provocation and desire for revenge, state whether the act of homicide could be attributed to an insane impulse or whether the accused was sane and was compelled by another motive?"

May testified as to the conditions labeled "hysteria" and "dysmenorrhea" and said: "I consider hysteria as a disease emanating from the uterus." In discussing both conditions, May commented that he had seen many cases with and without the symptoms mentioned and attributed the symptoms to nervous excitement dependent upon uterine irritability. Based on the information in the second and third questions, May concluded: "The simple abstract question, as stated here, would not satisfy me that the patient was insane at the time of committing that act."

Bradley cross-examined May. Although not an expert on mental diseases, May categorized insanity into four types: mania; monomania; dementia; and idiocy. Under questioning, May admitted the distinctions between intellectual insanity and moral insanity and stated that moral insanity is included in his four types. Following-up, Bradley's asked: "Among the exciting causes of mental disturbance, is or is not disappointment in love set down as one of the prominent causes?" May responded: "Unquestionably, I should say a very powerful cause." Getting May to agree that he would need the whole past history of the patient to make a diagnosis, Bradley presented a much more detailed and sympathetic hypothetical case concerning a little girl and a man twice her age covering the broad scope of their relations over a period of about ten years. When the hypothetical case is presented, the medical expert testifies on facts assumed to be proven by the defense or prosecution. There is no direct testimony as to the mental condition of the defendant, although everybody knows that the expert's testimony refers to the defendant.

After describing the facts in the case for more than thirty minutes, Bradley questioned: "I will now ask you whether you think she has been, at any time up to this period, the subject of mental or moral insanity?" May answered: "I have no hesitation in saying that, having reference simply to the hypothetical case so minutely detailed by the counsel, Mr. Bradley, that the person labored under a deranged intellect, paroxysmally deranged, produced by moral causes, and assisted or increased by a physical cause, derangement of the uterus."

Carrington's rebuttal examination put questions to May as a "scientific gentleman" and "positively as a physician." May stood steadfast in his reaction to Bradley's hypothetical case. Acknowledging deference to Carrington, he repeated that the person "labored at the time under paroxysmal insanity" and "under mental derangement."

Looking for a hands-on physician/patient experience with Harris, Carrington called Dr. Noble Young to testify. His credentials included being the Chair of Theory and Practice of Medicine at Georgetown Medical College for twenty-five years and the President of that Faculty. Young was the physician at the prison where he observed Harris daily during her confinement. He testified that he prescribed porter for her sleeplessness. Porter is a heavy, dark-brown beer brewed from brown or charred malt. Physicians prescribed it to calm patients, to produce a sound sleep and as a general nutrient. While Young prescribed for Harris' other symptoms, he did not see any indication of insanity or of dysmenorrhea. He stated that her last period was June 16 to 19, 1865. Bradley did not elicit any supportive testimony during his cross-examination.

Next, the prosecution called Dr. William P. Johnston to the witness dock. Johnston was Professor of Obstetrics and Diseases of Women and Children at Columbia University since 1845 and a founder of the Pathological Society of Washington. He was the first physician in the District of Columbia to devote special attention to diseases of women and had the reputation of being the most successful and popular obstetrician in the District. Under Carrington's questioning, Johnston clarified the symptomatic differences between hysteria and dysmenorrhea. He concluded from the prosecution's hypothetical case that the patient suffered from dysmenorrhea attended with marked symptoms of hysteria but declared that he would need much more information to make a diagnosis. On cross-examination by Bradley and reacting to his hypothetical case, Johnston said: "By the term, as used medically, we consider an individual suffering from hysteria as irresponsible for any act which she might commit."

Continuing with "common-sense" medical testimony and also seeking to establish mental illness experience, Carrington called Dr. Thomas Miller to testify. Miller was a Professor of Anatomy at Columbia College and an attending surgeon at the Washington Infirmary. He had been President of the Board of Health and was a founder of the Washington Medical Institute in 1830. Many years ago, Miller provided care for the insane and helped to establish the Government Hospital for the Insane. Defense attorney Bradley asked for Miller's reaction to the defense's hypothetical case. In his brief testimony, Miller stated that he agreed completely with Dr. May.

Finally, Dr. Flodoardo Howard was called for the prosecution. Howard was Professor of Obstetrics and Diseases of Women at Georgetown Medical College and was a pharmacist before graduating in medicine at age thirty. Assistant District Attorney Wilson asked Howard about the symptoms and detection of the illnesses. Howard commented on the extreme mood changes in hysteria and whether or not a diagnosis could be made at the initial medical visit. Again, defense attorney Bradley asked for Howard's reaction to the defense's hypothetical case. Howard stated: "I would suppose the patient thus described to be subject to mental alienation, and that she was subject to insane impulses -- possibly suicidal or homicidal mania."

Despite Carrington's effort to label insane impulses as modern medical humbug, his "common-sense" expert medical testimony did not support his contention. Clearly, the District Attorney's "common-sense" physicians did not destroy the temporary insanity proposition advanced by the defense. Carrington's medical witnesses testified about hysteria and dysmenorrhea symptomology emphasizing various probabilities and rationales. However, in their reactions to the defense's hypothetical case, all the physicians seemed to agree on the medical possibility of Harris' derangement. Defense attorneys commented that even the testimony of the "common-sense" doctors supported their assertion that Harris was insane at the time of the murder.

Following the expert testimony in the case, Carrington referred to judge Wylie's instructions to the jury that Dr. Nichols was an expert medical witness and they should be bound by his opinions, only if they believed him credible. Prosecutor Carrington was quite harsh in his personal characterization of Nichols' theory as the defense's expert medical witness: "this propagator of the new and dangerous doctrine -- this modern philosopher of the humbug of paroxysmal insanity." Carrington did not accord Fitch in the same expert status.

To attack Nichols' credibility, Carrington contended that the doctor relied upon false assumptions in arriving at his opinions. These four assumptions and responses were enumerated by the District Attorney: "(1) A marriage contract existed between Mary Harris and Adoniram J. Burroughs. (2) Mary Harris was melancholy due to disappointed love. (3) A. J. Burroughs made a dishonorable proposition in the letters signed by J.P. Greenwood. (4) Mary Harris suffered from dysmenorrhea at the time of the shooting."

Responding to each of the false assumptions, Carrington bolstered the supposition of a rational deliberate murder: "(1) There was no evidence that a marriage contract existed and even if a contract existed, it was violated by Mary Harris. (2) Mary Harris went to parties, played cards and engaged in actions that did not indicate a melancholy mood because Mary Harris never loved Adoniram J. Burroughs. (3) Rev. John C. Burroughs, brother of the murdered man, an ordained Baptist minister and the President of the University of Chicago, said that the J.P. Greenwood letters were not in his brother's handwriting; they were not written by A.J. Burroughs. (4) Mrs. Flemming, Harris' landlady when she stayed over in Baltimore, said that Mary was not sick when she left for D.C. that morning."

Harris received two letters signed by a J.P. Greenwood requesting a meeting at an address in Chicago. Upon investigation, Harris and the Devlin sisters discovered that a "house of ill repute" was located at that address. Hughes implied that Burroughs wrote the letters in an effort to disgrace Harris.

Rev. Burroughs was a key prosecution witness and sat at the prosecution table actively interacting with Carrington and Wilson throughout the trial. To assist the prosecution, Rev, Burroughs sought out and arranged for witnesses to testify, initiated his own information quest through personal visits, interrogated his network of clergymen, and even hired private detectives to uncover information. Hughes and Voorhees sharply attacked Rev, Burroughs in their cross-examination and in closing arguments. They insinuated that Rev. Burroughs paid a key witness to disappear. Hughes said that he meant to attack Rev. Burroughs "and if I failed to do so, I would be recreant to the duty that I owe to my client in this case." Voorhees stated that Rev, Burroughs stood "in contempt of the teachings of the merciful Master on the Mount, by coming here with deceit and treachery in his heart to strike this helpless, feeble, sick, and lonely being [Harris], to whom his name is an unendurable misery." During the trial, on July 14, Rev, Burroughs complained that the prosecution against Harris was very feebly conducted with the defense having everything their own way.

Carrington's effort hardly dented the defense's case that had been presented in a three-hour long theatrical, emotional, passionate, and colorful argument by Congressman Voorhees, an outstanding court room orator. He painted an eloquent picture of the growth of a pure girl's first affection, confidence and love. Voorhees held the audience spellbound as he interwove biblical passages, literary quotations, historical allusions, scientific evidence and pure poetry to manifest his persuasive powers, pathos and sympathy. At the one o'clock recess, "the ladies drew their lunches from satchels and water was distributed." Espousing that no murder was committed, Voorhees' summation produced tears and intense emotional reactions from the spectators crowded into the courtroom. A number of times, spectators interrupted his summation with shouts of "Bully for you!" as he drew bursts of applause for eloquent passages. A note in the trial transcript from the court reporter stated that Mrs. Abraham Lincoln sent flowers to Harris; a beautiful bouquet whose center flower signified, in botanical language, *Trust in me*. While not mentioning the name, Voorhees alluded to the flowers sent to Harris while she was in jail: "Her prison abode has been brightened by the presence of the noblest and purest of her own sex, and delicate flowers from the loftiest station in the world have mingled their odors with the breath of her captivity."

In closing, Voorhees appealed to the jury: "Unlock the door of her prison, and bid her bathe her throbbing brow once more in the healing air of liberty. Let your verdict be the champion of law, morality, of science. Let it vindicate civilization and humanity, justice and mercy."

In his strident two hour "tersely stated argument, without the least attempt at eloquence," Hughes told the jury to "let this poor, blighted, afflicted, ruined, and persecuted girl go. The law has no claim on her ... Let Washington justice travel to Chicago, and unmask there, before a confiding and trusting congregation and people, a man who wears the livery of Heaven to serve the devil under."

Aware of the reactions of the spectators and the jurors, prosecutor Carrington acknowledged the popular sentiment existing within the courthouse. "If you acquit her upon the ground of insanity, it will be a pretext only. Now, gentlemen, if you wish to acquit her, do it because you want to do it; but do not render yourselves ridiculous by listening to this nonsense of insane impulse."

Apparently, the District Attorney's arguments fell upon deaf ears. Judge Wylie told the jury that he would wait for their decision indicating his belief that they had already made up their minds. Defense counsel Mason predicted in his diary that the jury would not leave their seats to find Harris not guilty. That belief was confirmed when the jurors later said that they only went out of the jury-box out of deference to the District Attorney. On July 19th, 1865, the jury took only five minutes to acquit Harris. She was set free without any restrictions. Jury foreman, John Scrivener, did not say "not guilty by reason of insanity." He merely faced Harris and rendered a "not guilty" verdict.

In a courtroom crowded with empathetic women spectators and sympathetic men, the not guilty verdict was greeted with cheers, handkerchief waving and hats tossed into the air. There was a stampede to congratulate the darling girl. Outside the courtroom, newspaper and magazine reactions to the verdict were quite different.

During the trial, press coverage was intense and continuous. Each day, the court reporter's transcript was published verbatim in several newspapers in each city, notably Washington, Chicago, and New York, with abridged versions in many other papers. There were large crowds in attendance daily in the court room, with tickets of admission being required at times and crowd control a necessity. In support of Harris, many women attended regularly. Dr. Mary Edwards Walker, a well known dress reformer, attended wearing a frock coat and pants under her skirt. In November 1865, Dr. Walker became the only woman to ever be awarded the Congressional Medal of Honor for her battlefield valor during the Civil War.

There were changes in the attitudes expressed in the newspapers immediately after the murder and during the trial. Immediate press reaction in Washington's *Evening Star* after the murder portrayed Burroughs as a cad or scoundrel and Harris as a "the injured and maddened woman - his victim." A *Chicago Tribune* article reported on the "domestic tragedy" that "brought swift doom to a seducer." Harris was depicted as "above all suspicion or reproach until her unfortunate relations with her destroyer ... She fell a victim to his deliberate wiles ... We cannot find it in our heart to pronounce against the justice of the retribution "

Washington's *Daily National Intelligencer* revealed that Burroughs' friends "claimed for him an unblemished reputation for morality and true gentlemanly conduct." In contrast after the trial, *Harper's Weekly, A Journal of Civilization*, labeled Burroughs' conduct as "inexcusable," but "the provocation was insufficient for the justification of murder."

Acknowledging the public's sympathy during the trial for Harris, the "despoiled woman," the *Chicago Tribune* agreed that if that was so, Burroughs' fate would be appropriate. However, the paper said that there was no evidence of Burroughs' guilt; not an "iota of proof that he ever committed an impropriety with her." About the same time, support came from the *Albany Argus* stating that Burroughs was a victim of a "jealous, revengeful, vindictive woman incited by female conspirators." A week later, Israel, the *Chicago Tribune's* Washington reporter, wrote about

"Meddlesome Interference in Love Affairs ... Mary Harris met the wrath of doom in the form of Louisa and Jane Devlin in Chicago."

At the verdict, the *Evening Star* vividly described the courtroom scene: "A tremendous shout rent the air, some ladies waved their handkerchiefs, others cried for joy, while a number crowded around Miss Harris and kissed her, and many gentlemen came pell mell over the benches and tables to greet her." Harris fainted and her chief counsel applied an "extraordinary restorative," a "labial salutation" according to the *New York Daily Tribune* headline. A large crowd gathered to greet Harris as she exited and *The Saturday Review* observed that "Even the judge, together with his wife, waited on the opposite corner of the street to see her pass."

After the not guilty verdict, the newspapers soundly denounced the outcome in editorials, in copy-cat stories, with puns and with satiric comments. Reporters fanned the public's feelings about suspecting fraud in defendant's pleas of paroxysmal insanity. As a defense, paroxysmal insanity was, and continues to be, denigrated as "getting away with murder" or "copping a plea."

"The Acquittal of Miss Harris - Killing No Murder" was the editorial headline in the *Brooklyn Daily Eagle*. That three cent newspaper said that Harris walked out of court "free as air" even though "a more deliberate murder never was committed." If the insanity theory was followed, "half the women in the land would be liable to incarceration in an insane asylum."

Commenting on the state of things, the Washington *Evening Star* felt the verdict was backed by public sentiment and custom illustrating American law: "That any women who considers herself aggrieved in any way by a member of the other sex, may kill him with impunity, and with an assured impunity from the prescribed penalties of law ... It is useless to find fault with this state of things ... It is peculiar to America." In "A Warning to Young Men," the paper told men to keep the facts in mind and comport themselves so as to never give women "a real or fanciful pretext for taking them off untimely."

"What right was there to presume that twelve intelligent men should declare a deliberate murderess to be not guilty of a proven crime!" was the question posed by the *Baltimore American*. This editorial acknowledged that Burroughs engaged in a shameful betrayal "but women have been deceived and betrayed in all generations ... The rupture of plighted troth is an old story that deserves a penalty - but not murder." People are not convinced of "insanity," "insane impulse" and the "moral justification."

In its editorial, the *New York Tribune* commented: "Burroughs jilted Mary Harris and she shot him ... If the situation were reversed, nobody would adjudge him guilty of insanity ... Women are treated differently."

Taking a legal tack, the *Chicago Tribune* suggested: "It's practically impossible to hang a woman for crime ... there should be an alternative to hanging such as sending a person to prison for life. Then, the plea of insanity will be taken at its worth."

An article from the *New York Tribune* called the verdict "A Queer Kind of Insanity." "We don't see it," was the last line of the editorial.

*Harper's Weekly* said the murder appears to be deliberate and the insanity plea should be set aside. "We have had enough of dalliance with murder on such whimsical pleas."

Reacting to the verdict, the English journal, *The Nation* commented on the deferential treatment of women. "We believe ... that it is simply another illustration of the barbarous state of public opinion with regard to a certain class of offenses." A follow-up editorial headlined "Killing No Murder" said that it is "fearful to contemplate the social consequences of this legal precedent ... A dainty jeweled revolver may become an essential part of full dress or demi-toilette."

In an editorial about "An Interesting Criminal," the British journal, *The Saturday Review*, advised women "to practice pistol-shooting as assiduously as possible" since "any young lady who puts a bullet into a treacherous lover may do so with impunity, with the certainty of winning the sympathy of all free American citizens to the bargain." It can be surmised that Burroughs "had been a scoundrel and Mary Harris shot him, and it served him right." In view of the long premeditation, this editorial made light of "the rubbish which medical experts talk in our own Courts." An enthusiastic American reporter was quoted as saying that "*The whole thing was beautifully managed*."

After the verdict, the *Washington Republican* reported that Harris attended a celebration at the home of Mrs. Amelia Fales. Afterwards, the *New York World* commented: "Miss Harris will go West, it is said, instead of to an insane asylum, where it was proved she belonged."

In England, *The Nation* editorialized that the jury didn't want Harris "to exchange a lace collar for one of hemp around her lovely neck for this slight exaggeration in her notions of the feminine proprieties."

Taking everybody into consideration, the February 17 issue of the *Albany Argus* found "the judge, jury and counsel seem to have enlisted fully in the veiled murderess' favor." Harris wore a heavy black opaque veil throughout the trial.

Summing up, the *Chicago Tribune's* Israel characterized the trial: "It has been so wholly exceptional and withal; so farcical, that it must forever stand by itself - a glaring instance of disregard of justice and common sense .. Paroxysmal insanity - the phrase is already a by word of mockery and will soon be a bitter jest." Jurors were labeled as "professionals who regularly served" and "courthouse loafers" having "little intelligence."

Questions, puns, and copy-cat examples appeared in the press for some time after the trial ended. After a survey, the *New York World* puzzled about all women likely to be insane once a month. "If Mary Harris be insane, then are nine-tenths of all women crazy? Is there a madness of the whole sex?"

"A Question", in the *Petersburg Express* asked: "Did the kiss of Joseph H. Bradley, Sr. demonstrate affection? Will Mary Harris be justified in shooting Mr. Bradley if he refused to marry her?"

An *Albany Argus* column punned: "A bachelor suggests that in view of the recent verdict in Washington, young men should be circumspect and careful in their attention to young ladies, or they may be *Harris-ed* to death."

An editorial in the *New York Times* put the extensive and spectacular press coverage of the Harris-Burroughs tragedy into the perspective of the times: ... the "crime was not extraordinary; the counsel not distinguished; and the principle not new." Why then the interest? "The popular interest manifested in this case mainly, we suppose, form the fact that the times are rather dull, and an episode of this kind furnishes a lively subject of gossip amid the grave public questions before the country."

Almost one month after the end of the trial, the Rev. Dr. John C. Burroughs, brother of the diseased and a prosecution witness at the trial, wrote a long letter to the editor of the *Christian Times* : "Not that I find fault with the judgement which the public has passed. On the contrary,

I have been impressed with the correct moral discernment and the high sense of justice which the judgment evinces ... The press of every portion of the country has shown a remarkably correct estimate of the case, especially considering the meager known facts and the distortions of the defense lawyers."

However, Rev. Burroughs then raised questions about the marriage intentions of his brother, the antics of the defense lawyers, the missing love letters, the mutilated letters read in court, the veracity of "those two Irish girls" [the Devlin sisters] and the authorship of the infamous Greenwood letters. Harris received two letters signed J.P. Greenwood inviting her to meet him at what turned out to be a "house of ill repute." Defense lawyers alleged that the letters were written by Burroughs to compromise Harris.

At a May 25, 1867 meeting of the Association of Medical Superintendents of American Institutions for the Insane (AMSAII), Nichols summed up that sentiment: "The public press pretty universally condemned the verdict in this case, and in a few instances, the medical press united in that condemnation."

Professionally, Ray commented that Nichols presented the psychological and pathological aspects in the Harris case with a force and clearness seldom exhibited on the witness stand. Ray also impugned the community's feelings that the insanity plea was merely "a dodge whereby a villain is saved from merited punishment."

On the other hand, Gray, editor of the *American Journal of Insanity* and Superintendent of the Utica (NY) Lunatic Asylum, was decidedly opposed to the diagnosis of moral insanity. He stated that, in the medical-legal sense of the term, no delusion was exhibited by Harris at any time in her history. Her temporary visual and aural hallucinations in Chicago and in jail were the "natural result of excitement and not worthy to be mentioned. ... Any degree of mental enfeeblement is also disclaimed for her. There remains, then, the plea of moral insanity, which we maintain has not, and cannot have, any place in the sciences of law or medicine."

Gray claimed that periodical or paroxysmal insanity are two species of disease and not a single entity. Furthermore, Gray stated that neither dysmenorrhea nor disappointed affection causes homicidal insanity; that cause and effect was merely a popular error of attribution. In fact, Gray said that Fitch described hysteria alone during the trial.

Gray concluded that there was no grounds for a diagnosis of insanity for Harris. With a flourish, Gray commented that moral insanity is indistinguishable from moral depravity.

In response to the reading of Ray's article on the insanity of women at a meeting of asylum Superintendents in July of 1866, Gray commented: "Mary Harris, though belonging to the general class discussed, does not come within the category of typical cases described, and certainly is not such a case as the one detailed. ... I can hardly conceive the phrases 'paroxysmal fury' and 'uncontrollable criminal impulse' as the result of disease, applicable to the Mary Harris case."

In those same AMSAII Proceedings, Dr. Thomas S. Kirkbride, Superintendent of the Pennsylvania Hospital for the Insane and then President of the Association, took the argument one step further while trying to pacify the divided physician audience: "In regard to the Mary Harris case, as much as we may differ in respect to her condition of mind, I am very sure we shall not differ in the fact that a great outrage was committed upon community when she was acquitted on the ground of insanity and then immediately discharged. It seems to me a perfect farce of judicial proceeding."

In an article in the *Quarterly Journal of Psychological Medicine and Medical Jurisprudence* in 1867, Dr. Ralph L. Parsons, Superintendent of the New York City Lunatic Asylum, enumerated the eight principal points to consider regarding the insanity of Mary Harris including the defendant's conduct, physical and mental characteristics, affective disturbances, and insane acts of the defendant. By the time Parsons wrote his article, he was able to say that Nichols was proven correct in his conviction about Harris' insanity because she was now a patient in the District of Columbia Government Hospital for the Insane.

What happened to Mary Harris after the trial? On May 25, 1867, the 21st Annual Meeting of the AMSAII convened in Philadelphia, Pennsylvania. Nichols responded to inquiries from attendees and brought the membership up to date about the Mary Harris case.

Using another name, Harris moved to Richmond, Virginia shortly after the trial and continued to live and work for Jane and Louisa Devlin, the sisters who were her employers ever since Harris moved to Chicago. Frequently, Harris expressed her bitter dislike and hostility toward Mr. Collins, the man who wanted to marry Louisa Devlin. Finally, for no apparent reason, Harris attempted to stab him. While Harris did no serious harm, she did actually cut his clothes. Harris was taken to the District of Columbia by Louisa Collins [Devlin] to meet with Bradley, her former chief defense attorney. Bradley asked Nichols to examine Harris as to her mental condition.

As in the past, Harris "denied distinctly, as she had always, that she was insane, and that she needed any such treatment as insane persons require; or, in fact, that she needed any treatment at all, on account of ill health."

At the end of the examination, Nichols told Bradley that "she [Harris] was insane, and unless she was put under restraint, she would commit a homicide or suicide. I [Nichols] regarded her insanity as dangerous to herself and others."

After persuasion by her attorney, Harris reluctantly came to the Government Hospital for the Insane with Bradley. Dr. Thomas Miller, a prosecution expert medical witness, and Bradley made out the necessary certificate, under oath, for her admission as a free District patient.

On February 1, 1867, Harris was admitted to the Government Hospital for the Insane in the District of Columbia with a diagnosis of Periodic Homicidal Mania. In May of 1867, Nichols reported that Harris' health was considerably improved with her sleeping and eating and even gaining weight.

From 1867 to 1881, Harris had three admissions and discharges from the Government Hospital for the Insane. Additionally, the patient Register noted that Harris was born in Ireland, had a common education, resided in the District, she was single and white, and her station in life was civil and indigent. While Harris was known to be Catholic, her second and third admissions listed her religion as Protestant. Furthermore, a penciled notation said the patient was named Harris or Harrison.

Harris also enjoyed a brief escape from July 5 to July 26, 1873, until recaptured in Philadelphia and returned to the Hospital in the District. Nichols immediately discharged the attendant who helped Harris get over the wall.

Harris spent more than nine years out of the 14 years between 1867 and 1881 as a patient at the Government Hospital for the Insane. Between her admissions, Harris worked as a clerk in the Philadelphia post office using the name Mary Harrison. In addition, Harris worked in the District of Columbia law office of Judge Charles Mason, one of her former defense attorneys and a resident of Burlington, Iowa. Mason may have also helped Harris to get a job in the Patent Office at one time.

In Philadelphia, Pennsylvania on October 31, 1883, after working for about two years after her last discharge, Mary Harris married Joseph H. Bradley, Sr., the attorney who defended her in 1865. He was over 80, and Harris was about 40. Bradley died four years later from natural causes. Amazingly, the newspapers still reported these events.

In 1865, Harris' defense attorneys successfully argued that moral insanity resulting from "disappointment in love and painful dysmenorrhea" caused her to commit murder. Currently, there still appears to be no consensus that symptoms related to the menstrual cycle are responsible for criminal insanity pleas contending that society is responsible for causing their clients' behavior.

Have the legal and medical rationales regarding temporary insanity changed since this 1865 murder trial? Have attitudes and behaviors been drastically altered? How does the public react to a plea of temporary insanity?

There appears to be an undercurrent of public disbelief when the insanity defense is used in criminal proceedings. People still think that killers are "getting away with murder" as defendants are sentenced to psychiatric institutions instead of to the death chamber. Defense arguments still rationalize murder, assault and criminal behavior with a plea of temporary insanity. Physicians in general, and psychiatrists in particular, become entangled in intense conflicts by expertly testifying for either the defense or for the prosecution. Neither side escapes derogatory comments. It is possible that merely changing the sentimental and flowery antebellum language of the 1865 Victorian period might allow the same legal and medical arguments to be resurrected with minimal loss of impact in today's legal system. As the French proverb goes - *Plus ça change, plus c'est la même chose* [The more things change, the more they remain the same].

## JOHN WILKES BOOTH
## DIAGNOSED AS A MONOMANIAC

On April 13, 1863, a "fashionably dressed and remarkably handsome young man" visited Dr. John Frederick May's Washington, D.C. office. This young man sought his professional services for an irritating and growing lump on the back of his neck. A lawyer, who knew him, glowingly described this patient: "He was a man of polished exterior, pleasing address, highly respected in every regard, received into the best circles of society; his company sought after; exceedingly bold, courteous, and considered generous to a fault; a warm and liberal-hearted friend, a man who had obtained a reputation upon the stage."

An April 18, 1863 review in Washington's *Daily National Republican* complimented this patient's benefit appearance as Shylock in *The Merchant of Venice* and pinpointed the date of his medical visit: "Mr. Booth is a young man of rare abilities, and considering his experience, really wonderful in his impersonations. His representations, notwithstanding the severe surgical operation of Monday last [April 13], entitle him to the admiration of the public."

Introducing himself to May as "Mr. Booth," John Wilkes Booth may have been accompanied by his former manager, Matthew Canning. Another source finds that Booth may have been accompanied by David E. Herold. Booth purchased drugs to treat the growth on his neck at Thompson's drugstore where Herold worked. Herold's interrogation as one of the assassination conspirators in 1865 revealed their relationship and confirmed the date of Booth's medical visit:

**Q:** When, if at all, did you first become acquainted with J. Wilkes Booth?

**A:** I do not remember exactly. I think I was a clerk with Wm. S. Thompson, Druggist, corner of 15th St. and New York Avenue, two years ago this spring. It was the night Booth played *The Marble Heart* - about two years ago, the time when Booth had a ball taken from his neck by some Surgeon in Washington.

It is most likely that government investigators learned about May during their interrogation of Herold. Coincidentally, President Abraham Lincoln saw and applauded John Wilkes Booth's performance in *The Marble Heart* on November 9, 1863 at Ford's Theatre in Washington.

Booth complained that the lump was gradually increasing in size and showed above the collar line of his costumes. After asking May to cut out the lump, Booth urged the doctor to say the surgery was for the removal of a bullet, if anybody questioned him about the operation. Without agreeing to label the growth as the result of a bullet wound, May examined his neck and found "quite a large fibroid tumor," commonly called a wen, on the left side. After advising surgical excision of the tumor, May cautioned Booth that absolute rest was necessary for the wound to heal properly and leave a hardly noticeable cicatrix (scar). However, the adhesion could be easily broken by undue violence. If that happened, a large ugly scar could result. May suggested that Booth suspend his engagement at the theatre. Booth listened to the explanation quietly but he told May he could not possibly stop playing his engagement. He did say that he would be careful and moderate in his movements to avoid straining the adhesion.

Realizing that was the best that he could expect, May proceeded with the operation: "I took the tumor out and united the wound very closely [April 13] ... Booth played his engagement, and came regularly to my office for some two weeks afterward to have the wound dressed [April 26]. He came some four or five days after the wound united, with it all torn open [April 30]. In some part of the play, in which he said Miss Cushman (who he remarked was a strong, powerful woman) bore a part, she either had to throw her arms around his neck - perhaps to strike him a blow; and she struck him on the tender cicatrix, tearing it completely open, and making a gaping wound, which had to fill up by the process of granulation."

May's teenage son, William, who became a physician, recalled the operation on Booth in a letter written May 18, 1925, when he was about 76 years old: "I distinctly remember the operation he performed on John Wilkes Booth. In fact, I assisted him (although only a boy of fourteen years of age) by holding the basin to receive the blood from the wound. We did not have trained nurses in those days. The operation was a minor one ... it was done without any anesthetic of any kind ... she [Cushman] tore out the stitches and tore open the wound ... healed by what we call second intention ... left a scar that looked like the scar made by a burn."

On April 19, 1863, Booth wrote to his business manager, Joseph H. Simonds: "And am far from well. Have a hole in my neck you could run your fist in. The doctor had a hunt for my bullet." When his fellow actors asked Booth about his neck wound, he explained that a pistol ball he received from desperate gun-play down South before the war had worked its way out and had to be removed.

May wrote his account of the incident about 24 years later, in 1887, and his son wrote his letter about 60 years later. They may have confused the names of actors and actresses. Probably, Booth deliberately and melodramatically mispoke Cushman's name with his usual braggadocio. With his concern with glorification and dramatic effect, Booth constantly spread myths about himself.

Factually, Charlotte Cushman was living in Europe throughout April 1863. At the time, she was 47 years old and Booth was 24. Booth and Cushman had not appeared together since he had minor parts in her theatre company in 1858 using the name, J. Wilks. Cushman was more suited to playing the manly Romeo rather than the feminine Juliet. In July 1860, Edwin Booth's wife, Mary Devlin, played Juliet to Cushman's Romeo. Her fellow actor, Edwin Forrest said that Cushman was "not a woman, let alone womanly." Following May's timetable, Booth was leasing and managing the Washington Theatre while starring in *Romeo and Juliet* on April 30, 1863. However, Juliet was being played by Miss Alice Gray, not Charlotte Cushman! Gray starred with Booth again at Ford's Theatre in *The Apostate*, a month before the assassination. Furthermore, it is surprising that May was unaware that Cushman was not playing with Booth in Washington since he said: "I have seen all the best [actors] that ever trod our stage."

In 1863, Booth had a strenuous acting schedule and earned incredible sums, ranging from $500 to $1,000 a week. "His cashbook, for one single season, showed earnings deposited in bank of twenty-two odd thousand dollars" plus his investments [in Pennsylvania oil fields]. In contrast, senior federal government administrators earned about $2,000 per year and presidential Cabinet secretaries about $8,000. Patrons purchased parquette and dress circle seats for 50¢, orchestra seats for 75¢, private boxes for $5.00 and the colored gallery cost 25¢. Booth was appearing at Grover's National Theatre, Pennsylvania Avenue between 13th and 14th Streets, Washington, D.C. Grover's playbill grandiloquently proclaimed Booth's star engagement: "First appearance in Washington of J. Wilkes Booth, the pride of the American people, the youngest tragedian in the world! Who is entitled to be denominated a star of the first magnitude! Son of the great Junius Brutus Booth. And brother and artistic rival of Edwin Booth."

He starred in *Richard III* [April 11], *The Marble Heart* [April 13], *Hamlet* [April 14], *The Lady of Lyons* [April 15], *Money* [April 16], *The Merchant of Venice* [April 17], and *The Marble Heart* [April 18]. Susan Denin and Effie Germon were his leading ladies in the ensemble company during the week he performed at Grover's theatre. Alice Gray was his leading lady in his following engagement at the Washington Theatre at the corner of 11th and C Streets. Booth had photos of Germon and Gray in his possession when he was killed.

Booth was a gymnastic and athletic actor who displayed boundless energy, superior skill and extraordinary gusto in combat and dueling scenes. Routinely, he was carried away seeking fierce realism and suffered bruises, sword nicks and cuts. Reviews of Booth's performances were floweringly complimentary: "without a rival ... masterly achievement ... impressive, grand and startling ...with boldness and originality ...genius is wonderful ...to repeated and rapturous applause ... among very finest actors in our country, unquestionably." His more famous brother, Edwin Booth, saw him play Pescara in *The Apostate* at the Boston Museum on January 21, 1863 and commented to a friend: "A bloody villain of the deepest red and my brother presented him rare enough for the most fastidious `beef-eater.' He is full of true grit." After seeing John Wilkes Booth in *Richard III* at Mrs. John Drew's Arch Theatre in Philadelphia, the newspaper reviewer compared him to Edwin Booth: "Mr. [JW] Booth has far more action, more life, and, we are inclined to think, more natural genius."

A son of a physician, John Frederick May was born in Washington on May 19, 1812. He earned his medical degree from Columbian College [DC], Medical Department in 1834. Following graduation, he augmented his education with a year long visit to leading hospitals in London and Paris to learn the latest in medicine and surgery. Upon returning, he was respectively a Professor of Anatomy and Physiology, Professor of Surgery (both at Columbian College), a Professor of Surgery at Shelby Medical College (TN) and also at the University of Maryland. In 1865, May went into private practice in New York City until he returned to Washington in 1880. He died on May 1, 1891 of pneumonia at his Washington home at 2022 G Street NW at 75 years of age.

May's brilliant reputation attracted most of the surgical work in the D.C. area. In the United States, he was the first to do a successful amputation at the hip joint. His son claimed that his father did this surgery in thirty seconds. In the Washington area, he was the first to do an ovariotomy. He also succeeding in a ligation of the popliteal artery, previously considered only a feat for the dissection room. These surgical procedures were previously considered disastrous.

Medical education left much to be desired. An 1846 book by a physician derided the "half-baked graduates in medicine" who practiced the "rifest and rankest quackery." In 1860, a *New York Times* editorial lamented that "any ignorant clown may enter a medical school by paying five dollars and without ever having read a medical book ... be transformed into a student of the most recondite and abstruse sciences."

About 10:15 PM on April 14, 1865, President Lincoln attended Ford's Theatre to see the farce, *Our American Cousin*. As Lincoln sat in his rocking chair enjoying the play, John Wilkes Booth easily gained access to the box and fired a .44-caliber lead ball from a single-shot derringer into the back of the President's head just behind his left ear. According to the autopsy report, the lead ball traveled through Lincoln's head and lodged behind his right eye. Along with other prominent physicians, May was called to Lincoln's bedside to examine the assassinated President.

May and Lincoln knew each other. He had a personal interview with Lincoln in 1861 before he petitioned the President on October 10, 1861, about the declining health of Maryland Congressman Henry May. His relative was in a Union prison on a charge of holding "criminal intercourse and correspondence with rebels.' Henry May was arrested on September 13, 1861 and paroled on December 2, 1861.

After May probed the head wound, he agreed with the other physicians that nothing could be done to save Lincoln's life. Lincoln lingered through the night and died the next morning. Booth fled the theatre, mounted a horse and was made his way south out of Washington.

Booth disguised himself by trimming his hair, cutting off his mustache with a scissors, and allowing his beard to grow. A massive manhunt tracked him to Garrett's tobacco farm near Port Royal, Virginia where he was shot in the neck and died on April 26, 1865. During Booth's final hours, a local physician, Dr. Charles Urquhart, probed the wound for the ball, examined him, shook his head sagely, talked learnedly, diagnosed the punctured spinal cord wound as fatal, and left. There was no record and no death certificate. With blood dripping, Booth's body was transported about thirty miles in a one horse rickety cart to a waterway. There, the body was transferred to the river steamer, *John S. Ide*, to deliver to the ironclad monitor, *Montauk*, anchored outside the Washington Navy Yard. Crowds rushed to the Navy Yard to see Booth's body but heavy guards were posted to prevent the body from becoming "a subject of glorification by disloyal persons." An entry in the *Montauk's* log gives details: "April 27 [1865] At 1:45 [a.m.] the steamer "Ide" came alongside bringing the dead body of J.W. Booth ... At 11 [a.m.] a number of government officers came on board and took charge of the body of Booth. Surgeon Genl. Barnes & assistant performed an autopsy on it. Judge Holt took depositions of a number of persons who identified the body."

With Booth's body on the ship, a special commission directed by Surgeon General Joseph K. Barnes, his assistant John A. Bingham, Judge Advocate General Joseph Holt and Special Judge Advocate Major Thomas T. Eckert, summoned and questioned witnesses to make a postmortem identification of the remains. May explained that "a commission of high functionaries of the government was formed to obtain evidence as to its [Booth's body] identification, and I received a summons to appear before it." Through the information supplied by Herold, May's name may have come up as somebody capable of making a positive and scientific identification of the body. May did not respond the first time he was summoned to identify the body. A "second and more peremptory message" came when a soldier arrived at his house at 312 C Street NW. This time, he "deemed it prudent to obey" since the "*inter arma silent leges*" [laws are silent in the midst of arms] power was in full force. Driving his father's doctor's buggy, May's son took him to the Navy Yard and the chief of the detective corps met them and conducted May and his son on board the ship.

A lengthy article on the assassin's end in *Harper's Weekly* included a drawing of the inquest and vividly described the scene under a protective canvas awning on the deck of the monitor *Montauk*: "Booth's body was laid out on a carpenter's bench between the stern and turret, wrapped in a gray blanket, and a guard placed over it. The lips of the corpse were tightly compressed, and the blood had settled in the lower part of the face and neck. Otherwise his face was pale, and wore a wild, haggard look, indicating exposure to the elements and a rough time generally in his sulking flight. His hair was disarranged and dirty, and apparently had not been combed since he took flight. The head and breast alone were exposed to view, the lower portion of the body, including the hands and feet, being covered with a tarpaulin. This shot which terminated his life entered on the left side, at the back of the neck, a point not distant from that which his victim, our lamented President, was shot."

Barnes ordered the tarpaulin cover removed for May to examine the body. "To my great astonishment revealed a body in whose lineaments there was to me no resemblance of the man I had known in life! [addressing Barnes] There is no resemblance in that corpse to Booth, nor can I believe it to be that of him." After a moment's reflection, there was a conversation between Barnes and May:

**M:** Is there a scar upon the back of the neck?
**B:** Yes.
**M:** If that is the body of Booth, let me describe the scar before it is seen by me. [May did so as to position, size and general appearance.]
**B:** You have described the scar as well as if you were looking at it; and it looks, as you have described it, more like the cicatrix of a burn than that made by a surgical operation.

When the body was turned around, May examined the neck and "my mark was unmistakably found by me upon it." In addition, May looked at the body propped up in a sitting position and "I was finally enabled to imperfectly recognize the features of Booth." He described the body: "a haggard corpse with yellow and discolored skin; unkempt and matted hair; and a facial expression sunken and sharpened by the exposure and starvation. The right lower limb was greatly contused and perfectly black from a fracture." May was questioned by Judge Holt of the investigative commission:

**Q:** Were you acquainted with J. Wilkes Booth; if so, how long and under what circumstances?
**A:** I was acquainted with him - I cannot with exactness give the date, but I should say eighteen months or two years ago. I could specify the time by reference to my books ... I told the Surgeon General these facts this morning, before I looked at the cicatrix at all, and said that he would probably find a large ugly looking

scar, instead of a neat line. He said it corresponded exactly with my description.

Q: Have you since you came on board this vessel, examined the dead body which is alleged to be that of J. Wilkes Booth?
A: I have, sir.
Q: Will you state whether or not, in your opinion, it is the body of J. Wilkes Booth?
A: I believe it to be, sir; I have no doubt that it is. I believe I have only seen Booth once since the time to which I have referred. I have no doubt that is the person from whom I took the tumor, and that is the body of J. Wilkes Booth.

Readers paid four cents for the *New York Herald* and read the newspaper's Washington correspondent's report about the postmortem examination: "After it [Booth's body] was deposited there it was identified by Dr. May, of this city, who had on one occasion cut a tumor from Booth's neck and recognized the scar thus made." Continuing the *Herald* said that "it was also identified by some thirty [sic] others, who were familiar with Booth during his lifetime." A *New York Times* article stated that "the body of Booth has just been formally identified by prominent surgeons ... A surgical operation performed upon him several weeks [sic] ago rendered identification easy." In the *Daily National Intelligencer*, it was noted that "Surgeon General Barnes, assisted by eminent medical practitioners, yesterday made an autopsy of the body of the criminal."

In his testimony at the trial of the assassination conspirators, Barnes only mentioned May's identification of Booth: "He had a scar upon the large muscle on the left side of his neck, three inches below the ear, occasioned by an operation performed by Dr. May of this city for the removal of a tumor some months previous [sic] to Booth's death. It looked like the scar of a burn instead of an incision, which Dr, May explained by the fact that the wound was torn open on the stage when nearly well."

Several inconsistencies marred May's identification: May said the *right* leg was broken; Booth broke his *left* leg. He said the corpse was freckled; Booth was not. Booth was shot through the neck; May does not mention any bullet holes. Although the body was much altered; May positively identified a man he had not seen in two years. Additionally, the newspapers contradicted each other about the condition of the body: "The body was somewhat bruised on the back and shoulders by the ride in the cart from Garrett's farm to Belle Plain, but the features were intact and perfectly recognizable ... appearance altered, lower part of face is discolored by extravasation of blood ... not in a rapid state of decomposition ... From long exposure it has changed very much." Extravasation creates "post-mortem lividity," a freckling caused by the settling of blood that no longer circulates.

Barnes said that he and nine others identified the body as J. Wilkes Booth. A number of the witnesses, not that familiar with Booth, testified making positive identifications.

Washington photographer Alexander Gardner and his assistant Timothy O'Sullivan came aboard the *Montauk* to take a picture of the body. A *New York Daily Tribune* article reported that "Yesterday a photographic view of the body was taken before it was removed from the Monitor." Although a detective reported seeing the photograph, both the photographic plate and the single print disappeared.

At 2:00 PM on April 27, 1865, Barnes and Assistant Surgeon General Dr. Joseph Janvier Woodward conduced a postmortem examination of the body. A letter to Secretary of War Edwin M. Stanton reported their autopsy findings: "left leg had fracture of the fibula 3 inches above the ankle joint ... cause of death was a gun-shot wound in the neck - the ball entering just behind the sterno-cleido muscle - 2½ inches above the clavicle - passing through the bony bridge of fourth and fifth cervical vertebrae - severing the spinal chord and passing out through the body of the sterno-cleido of right side - 3 inches above the clavicle. Paralysis of the entire body was immediate, and all the horrors of consciousness of suffering and death must have been present to the assassin during the two hours he lingered."

Immediately after the autopsy, Barnes removed two spinal spools from Booth's neck wound, wrapped them in brown paper, and sent them to the Army Medical Museum and Library that he had established. During a Congressional debate in 1866, Senator Henry B. Anthony of Rhode Island commented that "a small part of the skeleton of Booth is in the anatomical museum of the Surgeon General." Those spinal spools were delivered to the Army Medical Museum in Washington and still remain there today. A 1993 reexamination of the anatomical specimens claimed that the posterior and anterior views did not wholly support the reliability of the autopsy.

Due to the combination of the cryptic War Department records, the dazzling speed of events, and the shrouding of many facts in wartime secrecy, a mystique arose regarding whether or not Booth was actually killed at the Garrett farm. In an 1866 debate about the distribution of the reward money in the U.S. Congress, Senator Garret Davis of Kentucky stated that he had not seen "any satisfactory evidence that Booth was killed ... It may be that he is dead; but there is a mystery and a most inexplicable mystery to my mind about the whole affair." With suspicion still thriving by July 1867, May felt compelled to issue an emphatic denial that he could have been wrong in his identification of Booth. Notwithstanding all the innuendos and rumors, May remained certain of his identification.

Doubts, rumors and myths continued to persevere. In 1907 a book detailed *The Escape and Suicide of John Wilkes Booth, or The First True Account of Lincoln's Assassination, Containing a Complete Confession by Booth, Many Years after His Crime.* Finis L. Bates' book was replete with "evidence" including anatomical identification, personal identification, photos, handwriting and personal interviews. He concluded that David E. George, who committed suicide in the Oklahoma Territory on January 13, 1903, had confessed on his deathbed that he was John Wilkes Booth. This book created a sensation and 70,000 copies were sold. George's body was mummified and exhibited on the circus side show circuit. In 1937, the alleged mummified remains of John Wilkes Booth earned more than $100,000. This mummy remained on tour throughout the nation until at least 1942, when it disappeared.

Even after all this time, the legend still survives. Ken Hawkes of the Pathology Department at the University of Tennessee used the computer Internet on August 28, 1995 to search for the mummified remains to demonstrate that forensic medicine could now prove if the mummy was John Wilkes Booth. In 1997, an Internet message asked: "What's new on the John Wilkes Booth front?" Even May raised another aspect of the case relating to the mental condition of the assassin.

After May described his positive identification of John Wilkes Booth, his 1887 account continued and he devoted about double the number of pages concerned with identifying Booth to a discussion of his mental condition. May never believed that Booth was of sane mind when he assassinated Lincoln. He read intensive newspaper coverage of a host of expert medical testimony on insanity that discussed current diagnostic theories and practices. May focused on heredity, physical appearance, insensitivity to heat and cold, insanity with a lack of organic disease and self-glorification.

"Insanity through inheritance is so well recognized by all men of common sense, as to need no support from expert evidence." May cited the probability of insanity through inheritance among the "Mad Booths of Maryland." There was "a family trait of melancholia." Booth's father "was subject to occasional or periodical attacks ... characterized as aberrations or eccentricities of genius." Like his father, Booth became so "madly excited" and "madly frenzied" during his performances that "his fellow actors feared to encounter him; for his onslaught on them was more real than feigned." Booth's alleged granddaughter emphasized the heredity factor as she titled her book *This One Mad Act*. John M. Barron, a veteran Baltimore actor, knew all four Booth brothers and commented about the family: "The strain of potent and determined will power reached the borderland of eccentricity, not to say of mild insanity ... As Edwin said, Insanity was in the makeup of the entire family ... For all who know the history of the Booths for two generations know that mental extravagance was hereditary in the family ... It was more pronounced and firmly fixed in John than in any of the others ... which to the minds of those, like myself, who knew him best, only confirmed the fact of the inheritance of the unfortunate strain which Nature gave him."

Booth's sister, Aisa Booth Clarke, protested that "Wilkes Booth was not insane" but grudgingly proposed in the same book that "If Wilkes Booth was mad, his mind lost its balance between the fall of Richmond and the terrific end." His brother Edwin labeled him " a poor, crazy boy." Actress Clara Morris recalled that Booth had "an exaggeration of spirit -- almost a wildness ... Who shall draw a line and say: here genius ends and madness begins?" A fellow actor, Sir Charles Wyndham felt that Booth "suffered from progressive insanity" and delivered a poignant characterization: "There was but one John Wilkes - sad, mad, bad John Wilkes."

May concluded that "most writers on mental disease have noticed the insensibility of many maniacs to pain and extremes of temperature ... Many of those afflicted without appearing to suffer, support the most intense degrees of heat and cold as well as pain." He used several case studies to bolster his conviction "of this insensibility to both local and general pain and extremes of temperature by maniacs. ...I firmly believe it was the indifference, both to the elements and to pain, from this *tempest in the mind*, which enabled Booth to elude his enemies so long ... How else can we account for the indomitable spirit?" May quoted from the King's lines in the storm scene in *King Lear* to demonstrate his point: "Thou think'st 'tis much that this contentious storm invades us to the skin; so 'tis to thee; But where the *greater malady is fix'd The lesser is scarce felt* - When the mind's free the body's delicate: the tempest in my mind doth from my senses take all feeling else save what beats there."

"In shape and form, and feature, the son strongly resembled the father." Booth had a familial wild expression in his eyes; at the time a common symptom of madness. May referred to Booth's "vengeance gleaming in his eyes ... With a maniac's look and rage, [Booth] hurled defiance at his foes, while enveloped in flames and standing on the very verge of death." May cited an account by one of Booth's captors and found that "the appearance of a maniac at that moment cannot better be described: His eyes were lustrous, like from fever, and swelled and rolled in terrible beauty, while his teeth were fixed, and he wore the expression of one in the calmness before frenzy."

In his widely known book on the on the medical jurisprudence of insanity, Dr. Isaac Ray theorized that monomania or moral insanity does not affect one's intellect or ability to distinguish right from wrong. An individual could be an incurable monomaniac deranged only on one or two subjects and sane on all others. Referring to Booth and monomania, May noted that experts contended that chronic insanity of the brain often gives no physical evidence of the disease. Such was the case with Booth.

Booth's murderous action to achieve fame actually made Lincoln into a sacred symbol. Prior to his death, "most people held Lincoln in mixed or low regard." "Only in death did Lincoln win universal approval." Booth would have been mortified by Lincoln's martyrdom emanating from his own quest for self-glorification. Would any sane man have shot the President "publicly, in the sight of every one without the slightest attempt at concealment?" Booth was an actor and knew how to disguise himself. Why didn't he? Was he "driven to it by another impulse than solely the gratification of personal malice or revenge?"

May avers that Booth shot Lincoln believing he was performing a heroic deed for public acclaim, "solely to immortalize himself." According to May, Booth "believed he had done a deed which would place his name upon the scroll of future fame." That motive could only have originated in "a mind diseased, a *madman's brain*!" Booth "proclaimed his infamy to the world as if *acting a part upon the stage*." A quote from *Richard III*, a role often played by Booth, was used to illustrate his glorification rationale: "The aspiring youth that fired the Ephesian dome, outlive in fame the pious fool that rais'd it."

When surrounded at the farm, Booth hurled defiance at his foes and challenged his captors to a series of man-to-man combats: "Draw off your men and I will fight them singly and each one in his turn." That proposition was labeled by May as "so absurd and wild that it could only have proceeded from a crazed and bewildered brain."

May concluded that Booth was a monomaniac when he assassinated Lincoln and that "for the credit of our country none but *madmen* have assailed with murderous intent the Chief Magistrate of the Nation since the foundation of the Republic."

Analysts of Booth's behavior considered the influence of his theatrical roles and psychiatrical rationales for his assassination of Lincoln. "The verdict of the period in which this tragedy occurred was that John Wilkes Booth was deranged ... Credit our grandfathers with the evaluation that the *mad* Booth wanted primarily to become famous." Interestingly, May wrote about the influence of Booth's acting roles upon his behavior and actions, identified Booth's obsession and touched upon additional psychiatric manifestations. John Deery, owner of a saloon that Booth frequented daily for two weeks before the assassination, credited alcohol with making Booth insane: "I believe that Booth was as much crazed by the liquor he drank that week as by any motive when he shot Lincoln ... He drank a quart of brandy each night ... He was crazy but he didn't show it."

May utilized quotes from Shakespeare's *Richard III* to illustrate Booth's self-glorification and from *King Lear* to explain his insensibility to the elements. A fellow actor declared that 'John's madness has been ascribed to the environment in which he lived - to his reading, studying and acting the Roman plays in which assassination runs riot." *Julius Caesar* and *Hamlet* are "profound meditations on the art of political murder ... There remains the possibility that John Wilkes Booth, too, could have been mad in craft." A number of his fellow performers remarked that he got carried away with the fierce realism of his portrayals. In his diary, Booth wrote that he was being hunted like a dog "And why? For doing what Brutus was honored for."

According to a medical reconstruction of John Wilkes Booth's personality, he was known as a moody, aggressive, unpredictable man who was a strict vegetarian and consumed large quantities of alcohol. He was "his mother's darling" becoming a pampered, spoiled child. He developed an Oedipal conflict creating a repressed homicidal hatred for his father. From a psychiatric viewpoint, he was suffering from paranoia [when] this murder was compulsively committed and represented the physical expression of an overwhelming, repressed patricidal impulse. Booth's act not only constituted unconscious father-murder, but represented unconscious suicide as well.

Junius Brutus Booth was a stern, aggressive, domineering father and Booth hated him unconsciously. He was not accepted as a man and an actor by his father. Booth repressed his envy and hatred of his father and brothers, particularly Edwin. This father/brother hatred was transferred to Lincoln who became a father substitute. Lincoln was called Father Abraham in newspapers and in song. Booth was obsessed with the idea that Lincoln was a tyrant who would become a king and destroy the South. In assassinating Lincoln, Booth unconsciously murdered his own father/brother. In his diary, Booth wrote "I think I have done well. Though I am abandoned, with the curse of Cain upon me." Could that refer to the act of a brother who kills a brother unconsciously? When he jumped to the stage after shooting Lincoln, Booth uttered the same Latin phrase used by Brutus when he stabbed Caesar, *Sic semper tyrannis*. He made no attempt to disguise his identity. Booth had a pathological need for fame and had openly stated: "I want fame, fame, fame!" Analysts concluded that he wanted to be seen, identified and eventually caught and killed; unconsciously committing suicide. Final words uttered by Booth can be translated into psychiatric terms. "Tell Mother, I die for my country" becomes "Mother, I killed my father because of you." Booth asked to have his hands raised and shown to him. His following comment, "Useless, utterly useless," demonstrates his complete failure to adjust his unconscious to reality. When a strong compulsive sadistic impulse is physically expressed in reality, an equally strong self-destructive impulse manifests itself in the same act.

This same author declared: "Booth was not a madman; he believed he had good reason to take Lincoln's life. He was not alone." Upon publicly expressing joy at Lincoln's death, several people, including a clergyman, were tarred and feathered and/or threatened with that ignominy or hanging. If Booth had lived to be tried with the other conspirators, there is no doubt about the outcome within that societal environment.

May wrote his insightful psychohistorical account in 1887 diagnosing Booth as insane. In conclusion, May contended that Booth was a monomaniac when he assassinated Lincoln. He cited assassination examples involving a failed attempt "by a foreign lunatic named Lawrence" to kill President Andrew Jackson and a successful assassination of President James Garfield by a disappointed office seeker, Charles J. Guiteau. An obviously insane Guiteau, was declared sane by a host of forensic alienists, legally tried and executed by hanging for assassinating Garfield in 1881. Perhaps that enduring environment explained May's trepidation in declaring Booth insane and his article not being published until 1910.

Even though John Wilkes Booth was shot and killed more than 140 years ago, the mystery surrounding his death and/or escape remains with us today. Despite the inconsistencies in May's testimony, he is still cited as *the* medical expert witness providing a scientific identification of the body. Even Booth's alleged mummified and unlocatable remains still attracts the attention of forensic scientists. Even the high technology of the computer Internet is probing into the current status of John Wilkes Booth. Notwithstanding the tenacious skepticism, reliable historical researchers appear to agree that John Wilkes Booth's body was "identified beyond any possibility of a mix-up."

William H. Seward

Chart on the faculties of the mind used by Dr. Thomas Spencer in his expert testimony for the prosecution

Dr. Amariah Brigham

New York State Lunatic Asylum at Utica

Abraham Lincoln

Leonard Swett

McLean County Courthouse, Bloomington, Illinois

Dr. Andrew McFarland

Teresa (Bagioli) Sickles

Philip Barton Key

Daniel E. Sickles

Sickles shooting Key with Samuel T. Butterworth leaning on fence watching

President Abraham Lincoln

Dr. David Minton Wright

Dr. John P. Gray

Government Hospital for the Insane, Washington, D.C.

Mary Harris

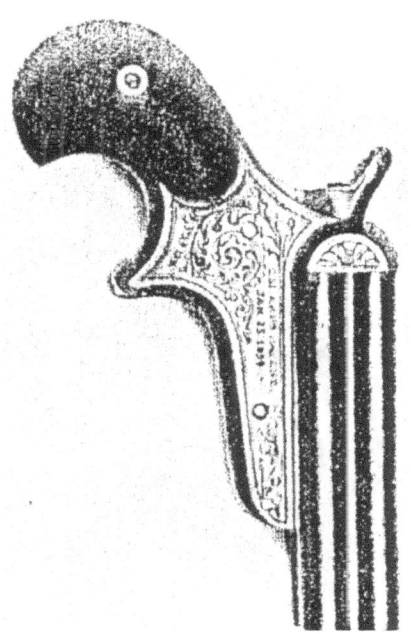

1859 Sharps .32-caliber four barreled Derringer used in the murder

Joseph H. Bradley, Sr.

Dr. Charles H. Nichols

Dr. John Frederick May

John Wilkes Booth

Booth brothers in their only joint appearance in *Julius Caesar* in 1864
*left to right:* John Wilkes (Marc Anthony), Edwin (Brutus) and Junius (Cassius)

Post-mortem on *USS Montauk* to identify Booth's body

Dr. James McHenry

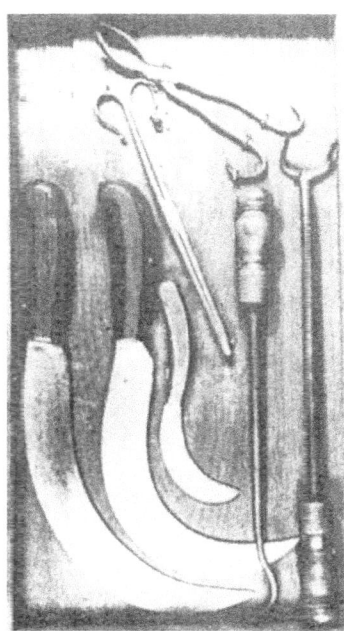

Revolutionary War Surgeon's field case for probing,
extracting bullets and amputations

Dr. Benjamin Rush

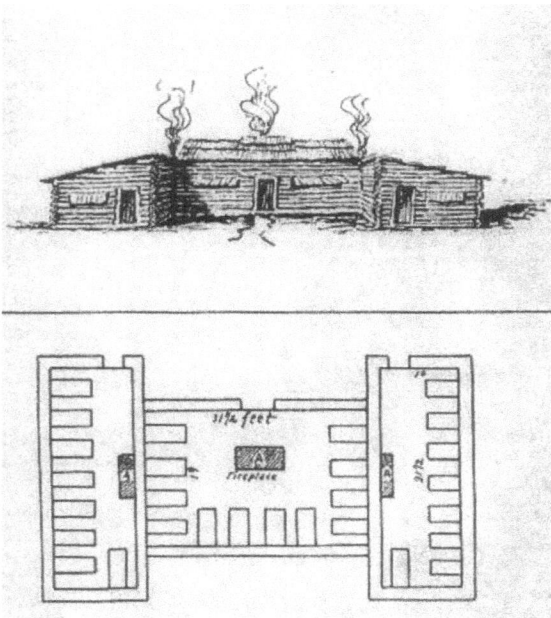

Plans for a Revolutionary War flying hospital

Francis Scott Key

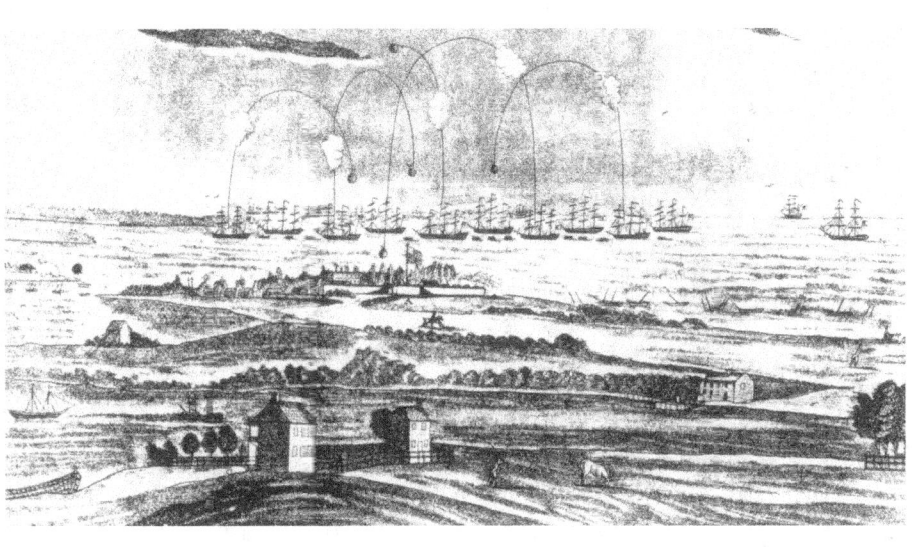

British fleet attacking Fort McHenry with rockets and bombs

Rear Admiral George Cockburn, the Red Devil

Francis Scott Key, Dr. William Beanes and John S. Skinner watch a bombardment of Fort McHenry from their truce boat

Dr. Bernard J. D. Irwin, U.S. Army Captain

Cochise, Chief of the Apaches

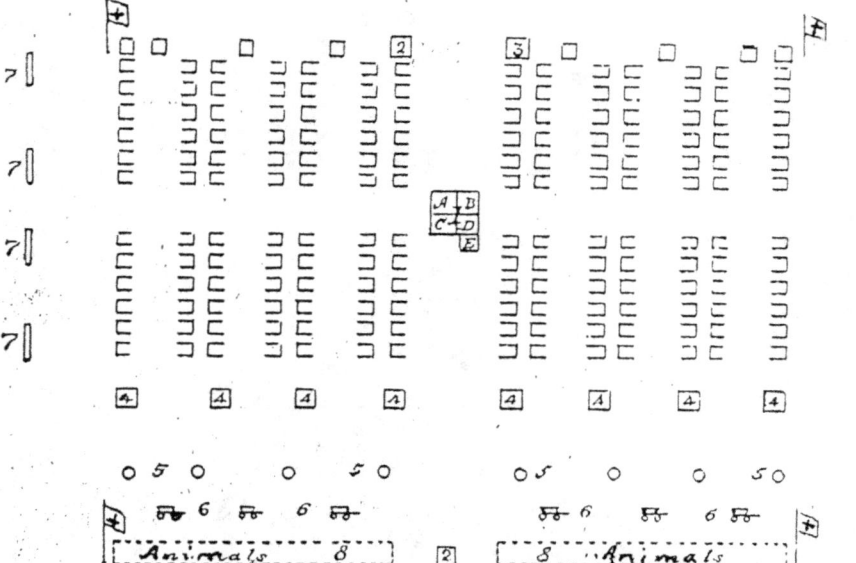

Plan of the tent field hospital, Shiloh, Tennessee
[A] office, [B] operating room, [C] dispensary, [D] officers dining room, [E] kitchen,
[2] guard, [3] stores, [4] officers and sick officers, [5] teamsters,
[6] ambulances and wagons, [7] latrines and [8] picket lines

Brigadier General Bernard J. D. Irwin

Clara Barton

U.S. Patent Office, Washington, D.C.

# LECTURE!

## MISS CLARA BARTON,
OF WASHINGTON,

## THE HEROINE OF ANDERSONVILLE,

The Soldier's Friend, who gave her time and fortune during the war to the Union cause, and who is now engaged in searching for the missing soldiers of the Union army, will address the people of

### LAMBERTVILLE, in

### HOLCOMBE HALL,

### THIS EVENING,

APRIL 7TH, AT 7½ O'CLOCK.

SUBJECT:

## SCENES ON THE BATTLE-FIELD.

ADMISSION,     25 CENTS.

Poster advertising a Clara Barton lecture

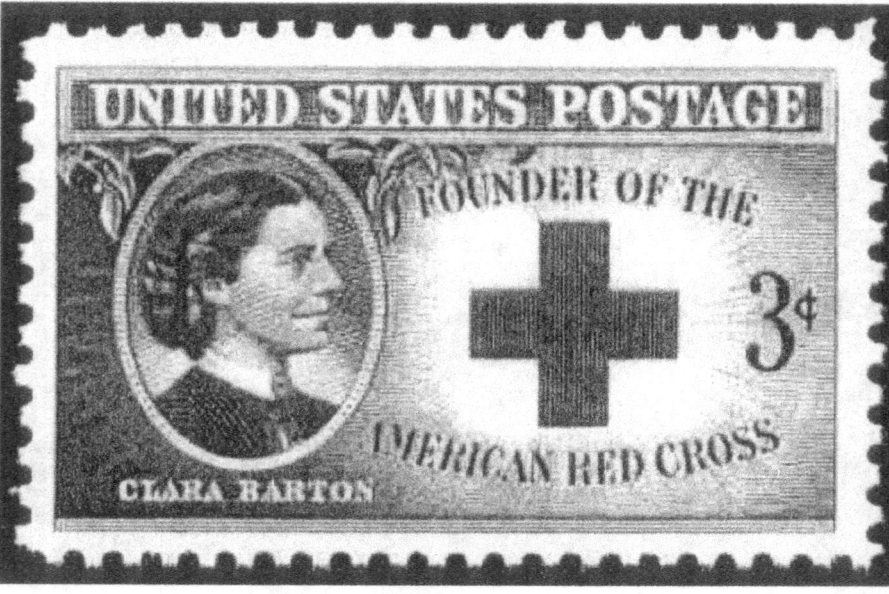

U.S. postage stamp honoring Clara Barton

Dr. Mary Edwards Walker in "bloomer" outfit

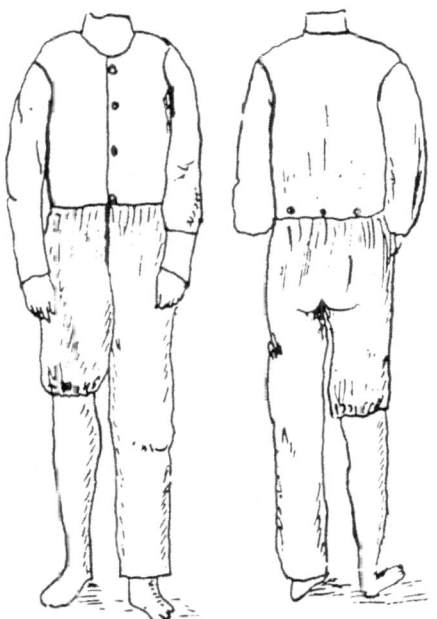

Front and back view of the "dress reform undersuit"

Dr. Mary E. Walker's two Congressional Medals of Honor

Dr. Mary E. Walker in full formal dress (male attire)

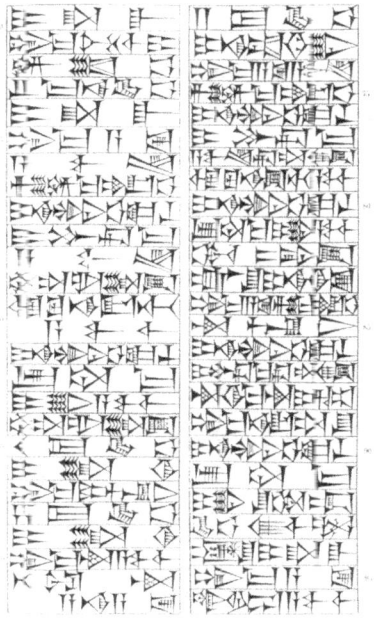

Cuneiform writing from Codex Hammurabi

King Hammurabi receiving ring and scepter from the god, Shamash

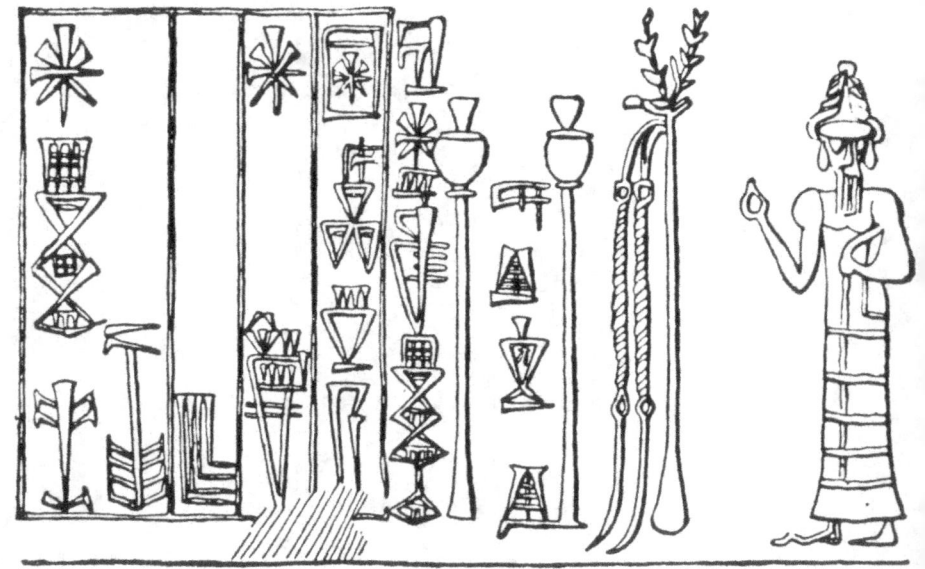

Seal of a Babylonian physician

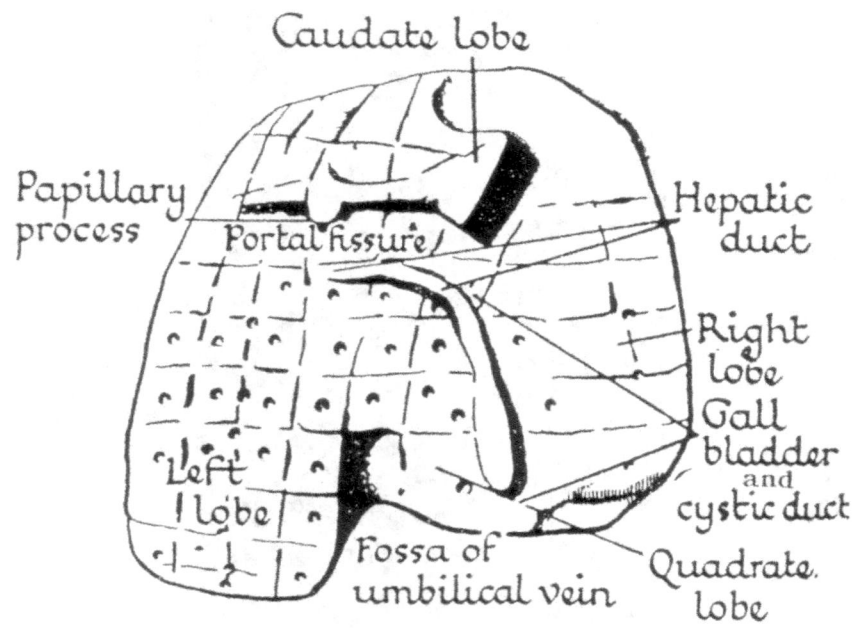

Clay model of a sheep's liver used for divination

John J. Elwell, physician and lawyer

Medical advertisements in the newspaper

Dr. Frank H. Hamilton

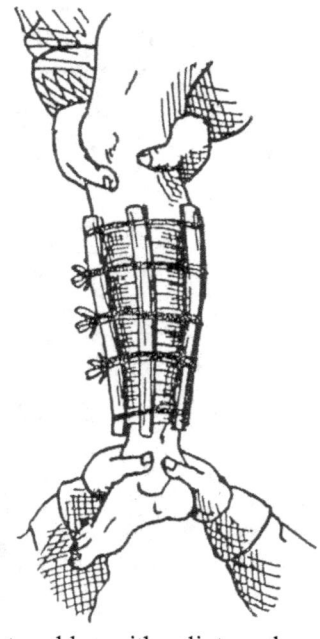

Fractured leg with splints and packing

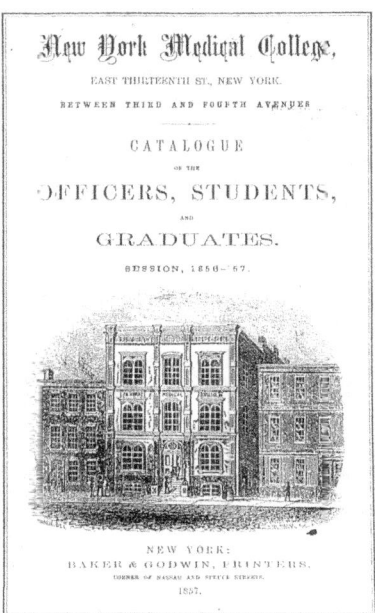

Front view of New York Medical College Catalogue

Dr. B. Fordyce Barker

Dr. Edmund Randolph Peaslee

Dr. Robert Ogden Doremus

| SECTION TWO | MILITARY MATTERS |

These military matters relate to a number of American battles: the Revolutionary War, the Indian Wars, the War of 1812, and the Civil War. There are numerous memorable milestones and moments occurring that go beyond strictly military matters. However, the individuals concerned are the people still creating the milestone or the moment.

James McHenry studied medicine as an apprentice to Dr. Benjamin Rush, America's most eminent physician. He participated in the Revolutionary War rendering care to the American soldiers. Later, he served on the staff of General George Washington and also for the Marquis de Lafayette. Washington appointed McHenry his Secretary of War when he became the President of the United States. As Secretary, McHenry ordered the construction of the battleship, *Constitution*. Continuing as Secretary under President John Adams, McHenry initiated plans for a military academy at West Point. In 1798, Fort McHenry was named in his honor During the War of 1812, Fort McHenry was the focus of a horrific bombardment as the British warships attacked the bastion guarding the harbor.

Francis Scott Key was a Federalist who opposed the U.S. entry into the War of 1812. However, he is indelibly linked to the 1814 attack on Fort McHenry by the British. Friends prevailed upon Key to attempt to get the British to release a civilian non-combatant physician held in prison aboard a battleship. While Key did win freedom for the doctor, the British refused to allow them to leave because Key heard about their plans to attack Fort McHenry. Key and his party were detained on a sloop and guarded by British marines. He watched the brutal attack from the small American boat. During this detention, Key wrote the poem that turned into the national anthem, *The Star Spangled Banner*.

Chronologically, the first person to be awarded the Congressional Medal of Honor was Dr. Bernard J. D. Irwin. He received the Medal for heroism in 1861 as he battled Chief Cochise and his Apache Indians in Arizona. At the time, Irwin was an assistant surgeon with the U.S. Army's New York Seventh Infantry Regiment. During the Civil War, Irwin created the first Army field tent hospital before the battle of Shiloh in Tennessee in 1862. This precursor to the MASH [Mobile Army Surgical Hospital] units in later wars could handle up to 2,500 patients.

Irwin discovered the remains of the great Tucson Meteorite in Arizona and sent it to the Smithsonian Institute in Washington, D.C.

Although not widely known, Clara Barton created a free public school in Bordentown, New Jersey in 1852. She was the first female federal government employee to receive pay equal to that of a man in a similar position. She was not a nurse, but she provided care to Union soldiers at ten battlefields during the Civil War. At age 55, Barton began her quest to establish the American Red Cross. In 1881, Barton gained fame for incorporating the American Red Cross. As President of the Red Cross for 23 years, she served through a host of disasters.

Dr Mary E. Walker was, and still is, the only female ever awarded the Congressional Medal of Honor for heroism during war. She was an advocate for female dress reform and wore male attire for most of her life. In addition, she invented a Dress Reform Undersuit to discourage rape and seduction. Furthermore, Walker was a suffrage activist, an inventor and an author of sensational books.

## JAMES McHENRY: A FORT NAMED IN HIS HONOR

Fort McHenry in Baltimore, Maryland is celebrated for being the birthplace of the national anthem of the United States. During the War of 1812, Francis Scott key and prisoner exchange agent, Colonel John S. Skinner, met the British fleet in Chesapeake Bay in September 1814. Under a flag of truce, they argued for the release of a civilian prisoner, physician William Beanes. After agreeing to release Beanes, the British detained Key's party to prevent them from revealing their plans to attack Fort McHenry. Key, Skinner and Beanes were transferred to a small American boat and four British marines stood guard over them. About six o'clock on the morning of September 13, 1814, the British began a furious bombardment of the star-shaped bastion. Cannons and mortars fired between 1,500 to 1,800 shells weighing 200 pounds and measuring 13 inches in diameter. Deafening rockets eerily punctuated the bombardment. All through the cloudy, rainy day and night the bombs exploded in the air continuously amid the red glare of the rockets. In the morning, Key peered through the hanging haze of murky battle smoke and saw the large American flag still flying over the ramparts. Inspired, he wrote on the back of an old letter composing a poem to *The Defence of Fort M'Henry*. About two months later, Thomas Carr published sheet music and the poem was renamed as *The Star Spangled Banner* using the melody of an existing composition. Surprisingly, the melody was an old British drinking tune, *To Anacereon in Heaven*.

While most people know the story of Francis Scott Key and the national anthem, few people know that the renowned fort was named for a physician, James McHenry.

During his lifetime, McHenry became a physician, rendered medical care as a surgeon in the Colonial army, functioned as an aide to George Washington and afterward to the Marquis de Lafayette, was active in Maryland state and federal politics and dabbled in composing verse for family occasions.

McHenry was born in Ballymena, County Antrim, Ireland on November 16, 1753. His parents were wealthy enough to send him to Trinity College in Dublin to receive a classical education including the study of Latin and Greek. However, McHenry's health was not strong and he sought to improve his well-being by emigration to the American colonies in 1771 at the age of eighteen. Upon arrival, he settled in

Baltimore. Impressed with the promise of this new country, McHenry persuaded his parents and younger brother to emigrate to the American colonies. They did so a year later. In 1772, his father established an importing business which prospered in the busy Baltimore harbor area.

Later that year, McHenry enrolled at the Newark Academy to continue his classical education. This school was well known for its educational program and Newark was labeled the "Athens of Delaware." He studied logic, mathematics, moral and natural philosophy, political science and the liberal arts. At the Academy, McHenry developed a life-long interest in composing poetry. After a short stay at the Academy, he decided to study medicine.

There were only two medical schools in the colonies when McHenry set out to become a physician. In 1765, the University of Pennsylvania in Philadelphia initiated "anatomical lectures" and a course on "the theory and practice of physik." Two years later, Kings College in New York City became the first medical school to award an MD degree. Of the 3,500 physicians practicing in the colonies in 1775, only 400 had degrees from medical colleges. Of the 1,200 medical practitioners serving with the Continental Army during the Revolutionary War, only 100 had MD degrees. Almost 90 percent of the colonial physicians were either self-taught or educated through apprenticeships.

Training by apprenticeship was a highly individualized process with a wide range of experiences within a traditional three to seven year instructional period. At this time, few physicians had either equipment or factual knowledge to aid in distinguishing one specific disease from another. Perhaps with good reason, ill people in colonial America sought the help of the Lord, not the physician. A handwritten 1770 medical text stated the first rule for health: "Fear God and follow a calm moderate life, and with the blessing of Providence, you will preserve your health."

McHenry did not enroll at either medical school. Instead, he became an apprentice to Dr. Benjamin Rush during the second year of Rush's already busy and flourishing practice in Philadelphia. Rush studied with Drs. John Morgan and William Shippen, Jr. in Philadelphia and earned his medical degree from the University of Edinburgh in Scotland. After graduation, he spent a year in France before returning home. As a student of Rush, McHenry joined his fellow apprentices

James Dunlap, Elisha Hall, Andrew Leiper, Abel Morgan, John Stevenson and James Tate. Rush's apprentices lived as part of his family in his house. It is estimated that Rush taught more than 1,000 medical students during his forty-five year career.

While teaching medicine to his apprentices, Rush mixed in a continuous heavy dose of patriotic fervor for the emerging aspirations of the colonists to be independent of Great Britain. Being Irish, McHenry had no problem wanting to be rid of the British. Within a short time, he included himself among the "sons of freedom" seeking absolute independence from Britain.

Rush's theory of pathology, or the "proximate cause" of disease, identified three reasons for fevers: (1) a predisposing debility; (2) a stimulus evoking the immediate cause upon the debilitated body; and (3) production of a convulsive excitement or "excessive action" in the walls of the blood vessels. In his medical lectures, Rush stated "that there was but one fever in the world ... and I will say there is but one disease in the world. The proximate cause is irregular convulsive or wrong action in the system affected. This is ... a concise view of my theory of diseases."

To treat the convulsive action, Rush taught McHenry depletion therapy, an application of copious blood letting together with purgation. Blood letting as a treatment dates from antiquity. Greek physicians in the fourth century BCE commonly used the practice for almost every condition. In Rush's essay *A Defence of Blood Letting,* he said: "Blood letting should be repeated ... should it be until four-fifths of the blood contained in the body are drawn away ... It reduces the uncommon frequency of the pulse ... It renders the pulse more frequent when it is preternaturally slow." If the amount of blood in a normal sized man was about six quarts, Rush did not hesitate to remove a quart at a time and to repeat the procedure two or three times within two to three days. Rush's teachings on blood letting were blamed for the death of George Washington in 1799. Within twenty hours, Washington was bled an estimated gallon and a pint by Drs. James Craik and Elisha Dick. Dick was an apprentice of Rush's in 1780.

To ensure results from purging, Rush advised his students to administer a powder of ten grains of calomel (mercurous chloride) and fifteen grains of jalap bindweed, a Mexican plant. Today, that would seem like an massive dose. Referring to calomel, Rush called it the "Samson of medicine."

Rush was in the forefront of enthusiasts using mercury to treat inflammatory diseases, especially pleurisy, pneumonia and rheumatism. Eventually, physicians used mercury for dropsy, dysentery, hydrocephalus, liver disease, smallpox, tuberculosis, typhus, and yellow fever. According to Dr. David Ramsay, a noted American physician of the colonial period, mercury set up an artificial illness "transferring diseases of the head, of the eyes, and of the bowels to the mouth, where they are less dangerous and more manageable."

McHenry learned from Rush that a miasma, a poisonous vapor or mist, was responsible for spreading infection. Along with many others, Rush believed that putrefaction or organic decomposition from the earth discharged into the air to form gases or miasms. In the process, the decayed matter produced a noxious odor that identified the miasma. This was a widespread theory and the word, malaria, is derived from the words, *mal aire*, bad air. Believers in this theory also felt that cholera and yellow fever were caused by miasmas. As a remedy in addition to blood letting, Rush advised the firing of numerous cannons to break up the clouds of deadly miasma.

McHenry's medical instructor earned the pre-eminent ranking among American physicians and greatly influenced his students.. Rush was hailed as "the American (Thomas) Sydenham", "the Pennsylvania Hippocrates," the "father of modern psychiatry" and the founder of American medicine. He was a member of the Continental Congress, a signer of the Declaration of Independence, the greatest American physician of his time and an adamant believer in miasmas and bloodletting. In addition, Rush was an author, a caustic critic, a passionate evangelist, a lecturer, a patriot, a philosopher, a politician, a devoted social reformer, and a teacher. Despite his scathing humorless, disputatious and satirical nature, Rush had a talent for friendship. He wrote a great deal and others wrote much about him.

Opinions about Rush's medical theories and ability are conflicting in the extreme. A contemporary critic observed that Rush's work was utter nonsense and unqualified absurdity. Another found that Rush combined judgement and sagacity. These contrasting viewpoints continued well into the twentieth century. One latter day evaluator declared that Rush's works were not worthy of perusal. Another found that Rush was extraordinarily successful in his treatments and that he anticipated modern medicine in many ways.

While McHenry was still studying with his medical mentor, hostilities broke out in Lexington, Massachusetts. On April 18, 1775, the colonials fired the shot that was heard around the world. Still a civilian, McHenry immediately joined the American forces in the Boston area. He rushed to put into practical use the medical skills he had acquired from Rush.

John Jones, Professor of Surgery at Kings College Medical School in New York City, wrote the first medical book published in America in 1775. His discourse on the treatment of wounds and fractures as well as diseases of Armies was primarily designed for use by young military surgeons.

However, wounds or deaths from military encounters were not the major problem for medical personnel. Investigations of battlefield mortality concluded "that ten men died of disease for every one whose life was taken by the enemy." In a similar vein in 1777, Rush condemned military medicine: "Hospitals are the sinks of human life in an army ... a greater proportion of men have perished with sickness in our armies than have fallen by the sword." Although the number of battle casualties were similar, there was much less sickness and mortality from disease among the British and the Hessians, their hired German mercenaries. A tabulation compared the casualties between the colonial, British and Hessian troops.

**A Comparison of Death Rates from Battle and Disease Among Colonial, British and Hessian Troops**

Death Rates per 1,000 per Year

|  | Battle | Disease | Total |
|---|---|---|---|
| Colonials | 20 | 180 | 200 |
| British | 18 | 100 | 118 |
| Hessians | 18.75 | 62.5 | 81.25 |

Source: Duncan LC. Medical Men in the American Revolution 1775-1783 Army Medical Bulletin No. 25, Carlisle Barracks, PA: Medical Field Service School, 1931, 29.

A portion of the difference is due to the relatively more efficient British medical department and seasoned, well organized, well equipped and disciplined professional army personnel. In contrast, the medical department of the colonials was not well organized, indifferently administered, torn with dissensions, and inadequately equipped and staffed. This Continental army consisted of a poorly managed inexperienced militia with soldiers who were partially disciplined, if at all. Often, the troops were badly fed and frequently improperly clothed.

Obviously, the American army presented favorable conditions for the spread of a variety of deadly conditions, mainly infectious diseases. Bloody flux (dysentery), jail, hospital, malignant or putrid fevers (typhus or typhoid), and smallpox ( prior to inoculation of the Army) were the most severe. Less conspicuous were measles, meningitis, pleurisy and peri-pneumonia (pneumonia). Mainly in the South, intermittent and remittent fevers (malaria) were common and yellow fever was a threat. Venereal disease occurred frequently. Syphilis and gonorrhea were thought to be one disease, namely different forms of gonorrhea. Scurvy was a danger on both land and sea. Scabies, known as the itch, was more than an ordinary nuisance for the military forces.

Regardless of the symptoms, Rush taught McHenry that treatment usually consisted of vigorous purges with calomel and jalap, bleeding until the patient fainted and a moderate diet.

Based on the experiences of the military with illnesses and death, there was a concerted effort to preserve the health of soldiers by applying preventive measures.

As McHenry arrived in Massachusetts to attend soldiers at the American Hospital in Cambridge, he was alerted to one of Washington's first general orders of 1775. This general order addressed the line officers responsible for the health of their men. Washington wrote that officers should keep their men neat and clean and "inculcate upon them the necessity of cleanliness." He said that officers should see that the soldiers had dry straw to lay on. Regarding necessaries (latrines), Washington ordered their provision and frequent filling in "to prevent their being offensive and unhealthy." At the end of the winter of 1777-1778 at Valley Forge, Washington routinely inspected the camp. He found the quarters filthy with carcasses of dead horses and much offal in the streets. "Nastiness, is spread amongst ye Hutts, which will soon be reduc'd to a state of putrefaction and cause a Sickly Camp." On March 13, 1778, Washington emphasized and reiterated his "orders & commands in ye most positive terms" to clean up the camp.

In 1776, an English translation of Baron Gerhard van Swieten's

*The Diseases Incident to Armies, With the Method of Cure* was published in Philadelphia. In the preface, Swieten remarked: "It may not be amiss to premise some observations, by means of which, sickness may in some degree be prevented and the health of the soldier preserved." His eleven observations included a regard for clothing, dry campsites, heat exposure, personal hygiene, shoes, ventilation, and water. To prevent scurvy, he recommended eating "garden stuff and fruit." Additionally, Sweiten stressed that overcrowding of soldiers should be avoided and the air be renewed frequently. Otherwise, there could arise "the most dangerous and even contagious distempers." Swieten recognized the need to attend to the problems of morale, recreation and nostalgia or homesickness among the troops.

  Rush entered the Continental Army medical service in December 1776. About four months later, Rush was assigned to the Middle Department as a surgeon and physician. Acting on a request from Richard Peters, Secretary, Rush published a small pamphlet: *DIRECTIONS FOR PRESERVING THE HEALTH OF SOLDIERS. RECOMMENDED TO THE CONSIDERATION OF THE OFFICERS OF THE ARMY OF THE UNITED STATES. PUBLISHED BY ORDER OF THE BOARD OF WAR.* His pamphlet comprehensively covered five areas: dress, diet, cleanliness, encampments and exercise. His advice reflected the prevailing medical theories that he had taught McHenry: "Perspiration of the body ... is disposed to form miasmata which produce fevers ... intermitting fever staid ... by nothing else but the use of flannel shirts." Regarding food, Rush advocated a diet mainly of well cooked vegetables and the use of wheat for bread instead of flour. "The use of rum ... lays the foundation of fevers ... plentiful draughts of milk and water ... (result in ) fewer inconveniences to their health." After stating that "Too much can not be said in favor of cleanliness," Rush recommended that soldiers wash their hands and face at least once every day and wash their whole body at least twice or three times a week. "Frequent changes of linen are indispensably necessary ... vessels ( for cooking) should be carefully washed after each (meal)." To avoid "gaol fever," Rush urged no crowding in tents, frequent changing of straw for beds and no sleeping in wet clothes or on damp straw. "Environs should be kept perfectly clean of the offals of animals and filth of all kinds." In considering encampments, Rush warned that "marshes and mill-ponds let loose intermitting fevers ... if winds pass across the river (to reach the army, they) probably bring the feeds of bilious and intermitting fevers." He proposed a frequent changing of encampments to contribute to the army's health. Commanding officers were told to avoid exposing troops to unnecessary fatigue, to march in the cool morning or evening and to have sentries eat a hearty meal before going on duty. "Exercise should be regular and performed at fixed periods." Commenting on the side effects of fire, smoke from gunpowder and the burning of sulphur, Rush noted "a singular efficiency in preserving and restoring the purity of the air." He cited a battle encounter in which putrid fever was stopped by the "explosion and effluvia of the gunpowder." In closing, Rush admonished the officers "that an attention to the health of your soldiers is absolutely necessary." Most of Rush's content was adapted from a 1752 book on *Observation on the Diseases of the Army* by a British physician, John Pringle. Furthermore, Rush corresponded with Congressman John Adams in the Winter of 1777 to express these views and to praise the medical department of the British army for its attention to preserving the health of their troops.

During the winter of 1778-1779, Baron Friedrich von Steuben prepared his *Regulations for the Order and Discipline of the Troops of the United States*. Chapter 23 dealt with the treatment of the sick and focused on the principles and practices of military hygiene. Specifically, von Steuben addressed cleanliness, manner of living, the laying out of latrines and the immediate referral of soldiers with any infectious disorder to the hospital.

All of these recommendations and suggestions to preserve the health of the troops were expounded and observed in varying degrees. A number of preventive principles emerged: commanders were responsible for the preservation of the health of the troops; medical officers advised line officers; personal hygiene and cleanliness were stressed; advice was rendered on diet and nutrition; attention was paid to clothing and shoes; extremes in heat, cold, fatigue and prolonged wetness were to be avoided; morale and recreation had to be considered; smallpox inoculation was urged; isolation or quarantine of ill soldiers could prevent contagion; and attention to environmental hygiene - campsite selection, crowding, sanitation, waste disposal, water supplies - was absolutely vital.

As a volunteer assistant surgeon, McHenry rendered medical care in a military hospital in Cambridge, Massachusetts. Rush continued to intercede on behalf of his former student. He sent McHenry a copy of an August 26, 1776 Congressional resolution: "Resolved that Congress have a proper sense of the merit and service of Doctor McHenry and recommend it to the Directors of the different hospitals belonging to the United States to appoint Doctor McHenry to the first vacancy that shall happen of a surgeon's berth in any of the said hospitals."

Shortly thereafter, McHenry was asked to report to a hospital in northern New York in anticipation of caring for soldiers wounded in an American attack on Canada. Needing medical supplies, McHenry was directed to proceed to Philadelphia to purchase the necessary material for the hospitals in the Northern Department. In a jurisdictional dispute about appointments among the various Department medical directors, McHenry was promptly dismissed in Philadelphia. In a letter to Dr. Jonathan Potts, his former superior, McHenry wondered who was to pay the expenses he incurred in providing the medicines Potts requested that he procure.

Before the Continental Congress confirmed his appointment to the New York hospital, Pennsylvania officials appointed McHenry to serve as a surgeon to the $5^{th}$ Pennsylvania Battalion commanded by Colonel Robert Magaw. His surgeon's field case contained equipment for probing wounds, extracting bullets and knives for amputations.

This battalion was ordered to New York to defend Fort Washington at the northern end of Manhattan Island. Their assignment was to deny the British access to the city and to the Hudson River. On November 16, 1776, an overwhelming British and Hessian force attacked the fort from three directions. While the Americans fiercely resisted, the outnumbered garrison was forced to surrender. McHenry was one of five physicians and 2,000 soldiers captured by the British. After spending some time caring for the sick and wounded colonials being held prisoner by the British, McHenry was paroled to his home on January 27, 1777 to await his formal exchange. In the interim, he attended to "the sick privates and those who remained of the well who were ordered off on parole under my care as Doctor, and the conduct of a British Officer." McHenry reported to General Washington four days later and asked to be freed from his parole restrictions as soon as possible. This took some time. About fifteen months later, on March 5, 1778, McHenry received a letter from Alexander Hamilton: "It gave me pleasure to inform you that Mr. Bondinotte has been able to effect your exchange for a Doctor Mentzes. Allow me to congratulate you on the event."

With his parole, McHenry was free to join the Continental Army at Valley Forge, Pennsylvania. He was assigned as a Senior Surgeon to the flying hospital at this camp. Washington had ordered a flying hospital for his army in the field. Hospital Department directors considered the flying hospital a necessity to provide care quickly to the wounded to prevent infections. It was a type of revolutionary Mobile Army Surgical Hospital (MASH). Personnel for a flying hospital included a director, who on occasion acted as a surgeon and physician; two surgeons; four surgeon's mates; a steward; and male or female nurses. In 1777, Congress passed regulatory measures for the Hospital Department providing one physician and surgeon general for each separate army to head a flying hospital. In reality, the flying hospitals remained a kind of separate department until the end of the war.

Located about twenty miles from Philadelphia, the campsite at Valley Forge had inadequate food, forage or shelter. By February 1, 1778, almost 4,000 of the 11,000 soldiers at Valley Forge were unfit for duty. In March 1778, Rush commented on the serious sanitation problem at the camp: "The encampment dirty & stinking ... the men dirty & ragged." General Anthony Wayne wrote: "The whole Army is sick and crawling with vermin." Alarmed by "finding the small pox to be spreading," on January 6, 1777 Washington "determined that the Troops shall be inoculated." All the troops were inoculated "and Dr. (William) Shippen will inoculate all the recruits, that have not had the disorder, as fast as they come in to Philadelphia." With these wretched conditions, McHenry had a difficult task rendering effective medical care during his abbreviated assignment at the flying hospital at Valley Forge.

After only two months with the flying hospital, on May 15, 1778, Washington selected McHenry to serve as an assistant secretary on his staff. With his appointment as secretary to Washington, McHenry gave up the practice of medicine for the rest of his life with one notable exception. On September 21, 1778, he wrote a detailed prescription for Hamilton who was experiencing stomach trouble. McHenry delineated a diet for breakfast and dinner that included brown sugar for tea "because it is more laxative." He forbid the use of milk "until your stomach recovers its natural powers." His dinner advice suggested six ounces of beef "because it contains more of a natural animal stimulus than mutton

... Your best condiment will be salt ... You must not eat as many vegetables as you please ... Water is the most general solvent, the kindliest and the best assistance in the process of digestion ... I strictly forbid all eatables which I do not mention." In conclusion, McHenry forecast that following this diet would result in recovery. "But in case you should fall into a debauch - you must next day have recourse to the pills."

For two and one-half years, McHenry remained as a volunteer on Washington's staff without rank or pay. On Washington's staff, he interacted with Hamilton, Henry Knox and the Marquis de Lafayette. As Washington's aide, McHenry saw action at the battles of Monmouth and Springfield in New Jersey. To correct misleading impressions, McHenry described the battle of Monmouth in a series of letters intended for publication.

In August 1780, McHenry was transferred to Lafayette's staff to serve as his aide. In late September 1780, McHenry went to General Benedict Arnold's headquarters to make Washington's apologies to Mrs. Arnold for delaying breakfast. As they were still eating, Arnold received a sudden communiqué. After reading the message, an agitated Arnold spoke quietly to his wife, quickly mounted his horse and rode off avoiding capture for treason. Arnold was plotting to turn over the West Point fortifications to the British.

Finally, McHenry's commission as a Major took effect as of October 1780. While serving as an aide to Lafayette, McHenry participated in the climactic battles in Virginia leading to the surrender of General Charles Cornwallis in Yorktown, Virginia.

McHenry resigned his commission at the end of 1781 to enter Maryland politics. He had already been elected to the Maryland Senate while still serving with Lafayette. A year later his father died leaving him substantial funds. With this money, McHenry could afford to live the life of an independent gentleman.

For thirteen years McHenry served in the Maryland state legislature. He was in the Senate from 1781-1786 and 1791-1795 and in the Assembly from 1789-1791. Being a staunch or High Federalist, he was anti-French, pro-British and looked to Hamilton for political leadership. Between 1783 and 1786, he sat in the Continental Congress and in 1787 he represented Maryland at the Constitutional Convention in Philadelphia. William Pierce, a delegate from Georgia, prepared character sketches of the delegates to the convention: "Mr. McHenry was bred a physician, but he afterwards turned Soldier and acted as Aid to Genl. Washington and the Marquis de la Fayette. He is a Man of specious talents, with nothing of genious to improve them. As a politician there is nothing remarkable in him, nor has he any of the graces of the Orator. He is however, a very respectable young Gentleman, and deserves the honor which his Country has bestowed on him. Mr, McHenry is about 32 years of age."

Although McHenry was a consistent and responsible attendant at the Convention, he did not participate frequently in debates and deliberations. However, he took meticulous notes of the proceedings of the Convention from the opening day on May 25 until September 18, the closing day. However on June 1, a family emergency caused McHenry to leave the deliberations: "Recd. An express from home that my brother lay dangerously sick in consequence of which I set out immediately for Baltimore." He was back in his seat on August 4 and reported: "Returned to Philada. The Committee of Constitution ready to report. Their report is in the hands of Dunlap the printer to strike off copies for the members." After revisions, the Constitution was signed by the delegates on September 17. Elbridge Gerry of Massachusetts along with George Mason and Edmund Randolph, both representing Virginia, were the only delegates who refused to sign the Constitution. On the next day the gentlemen of the Convention dined together at the City Tavern.

In 1789, when Washington assumed his presidency as provided in the Constitution, McHenry sent him a flattering congratulatory letter: "You are now a King, under a different name; and, I am well satisfied, that sovereign prerogatives have in no age or country been more honorably obtained; or that, at any time they will be more prudently or wisely exercised ... That you may rein long and happy over us, and never for a moment cease to be the public favorite is a wish that I can truly say is congenial to my heart."

Although Hamilton was an advisor and mentor to McHenry, he did not think highly of McHenry's abilities. Regarding considerations for the Secretary of War, he cautioned Washington that "McHenry you know. He would give no strength to the administration, but he would not disgrace the office." Nobody seemed to want the position. Consequently, as a last resort President Washington called upon his wartime aide to serve his country again. On January 20, 1796, he wrote to McHenry: "It would now give me sincere pleasure if you will fill the office of Secretary of War ... Let this letter be received with the same friendship and frankness with which it is written; - nothing would add more to the satisfaction this would give me than your acceptance of the offer."

With surprising candor, Washington informed McHenry that three others had already turned down the position. A relative of McHenry reported that he felt Washington's letter was "an injunction that he could not refuse and most reluctantly accepted the appointment leaving his pleasant retirement to embark in the led sea of politics." About a week after McHenry accepted the offer, he was promptly confirmed by the Senate. He received a salary of $4,000.00 per year which later rose to $4,500.00. At the time, the War Department budget was $1.3 million, about 23 percent of the total U.S. budget.

Washington's letter also asked McHenry to confidentially sound out Samuel Chase about his willingness to be appointed to the Supreme Court of the United States. Acting as intermediary, McHenry was gratified to see Chase appointed to the high court.

On July 29, 1796, Hamilton was severely critical of McHenry's abilities as Secretary of War: "My friend McHenry is wholly insufficient for his place, with the additional misfortune of not having himself the least suspicion of the fact." In a letter, Washington informed Hamilton that his "opinion respecting the unfitness of a certain Gentleman ... accords with mine ... I early discovered after he entered upon the duties of his Office that his talents were unequal" to the task. "For the fact is, it was a Hobson's choice (between men like McHenry, Pickering and Wolcott). But such is the case, and what is to be done?" A "Hobson's choice" is an apparently free choice that offers no alternative.

Until 1798, the Secretary of War also administered naval affairs. To bolster the naval forces, McHenry proposed adding three 32 gun frigates and six 16 gun sloops of war. McHenry ordered the construction of the war ships *Constitution* and *Constellation* to protect American property on the high seas from the Barbary pirates. During his War Department tenure, McHenry handled Indian affairs, worked on organizing the military supply system, erected armories, stocked arsenals, and acted on subordinating the military structure to the authority of a civilian Secretary. When McHenry sought to establish regular military procedures, he relied upon Hamilton to revise the regulations of military service. In June 1799, McHenry utilized Hamilton's detailed plan to propose the establishment of a military academy to President Adams. At the same time, he requested that Congress establish a military academy at West Point. Specifically, McHenry wanted instructors in arithmetic, designing, geometry, hydraulics, and mechanics to prepare artillerists and engineers for the art of fortifications. Early in January 1800, Adams recommended to Congress the creation of a formal military school. Two months later, McHenry asked Hamilton to prepare legislation for the military academy. However, the United States Military Academy at West Point, New York was not established until Congress passed legislation that President Thomas Jefferson signed on March 16, 1802.

With the possibility of a war with France arising in 1798, McHenry sought to set up a professional standing army of 20,000 men to meet the immediate threat. Despite opposition, McHenry's arguments prevailed and Congress approved the creation of twelve new regiments of regulars. In agreement with prevailing opinions, McHenry commented that Washington should be the "genius in command of it." Subsequently, McHenry angered President Adams by supporting Washington's choice of Hamilton to be second in command of the standing army.

McHenry continued to hold his post during the Adams presidency but affairs did not go smoothly with President Adams. During the presidential election, Jefferson won in New York. Adams thought that McHenry conspired with Hamilton against him in the election. In an stormy conversation with McHenry on May 5, 1800, an incensed Adams was confrontational: "Through all parts of the Country, Sir, Your conduct in the Department is complained of. Every member of Congress I have spoken with ... tells me that you want capacity to discharge its duties ... You cannot, Sir, remain longer in Office."

In reply to this combative outburst, McHenry helplessly endeavored to explain himself. Exasperated, he finished with: "I shall certainly resign." He did so in June 1800. His letter of resignation concluded: "Having discharged the duties of Secretary of War for upwards of four years with fidelity, unremitting assiduity, and to the best of my abilities, I leave behind me all the records of the department, exhibiting the principles and manner of my official conduct, together with not a few difficulties I have had to encounter. To these written documents I cheerfully refer my reputation as an officer and a man."

Even after his resignation, McHenry encountered the wrath of the anti-Federalists. In December 1801, a Congressional committee investigated his management of the War Department and its alleged mishandling of $3 million in War Department funds. On April 29, 1802, the committee presented an unfavorable report and Congress adjourned four days later. Feeling himself disparaged, McHenry prepared an elaborate defense in *A Letter to the Honorable the Speaker of the House of Representatives*. In the next session on December 28, 1802, Speaker Nathaniel Macon read McHenry's reply to the Representatives. McHenry responded that the first charge, at most, was an error in judgment regarding excessive expenditures on a military arsenal to make and store arms and munitions of war. Another charge claimed that large amounts were due from the Secretary's accounts which were not properly settled. In responding to this accusation, McHenry produced a long array of figures and accounts to vindicate himself. Still another charge stated that $1,320 was spent in some secret service even though President Adams had vouched for the expenditure. In response, McHenry asked if private and confidential transactions are "to be exposed to the examination of a series of clerks, to be recorded in a public office, and the agents betrayed? ... How little, how very little in this way has been expended." Friends of McHenry arranged to have his 91 page document printed for private circulation. McHenry noted that he "distributed only a few of them ... This is the only notice I ever took of these calumnies, public or private."

Critics of McHenry's tenure as Secretary of War are plentiful. There appears to be no doubt that McHenry lacked the administrative experience to head a large War Department. He simply did not have the ability to organize its affairs. Four possible reasons for his administrative weakness existed: (1) There was just too much work for a single cabinet Department. When the Navy Department was created in 1798, the burden decreased. (2) There was an unclear definition of responsibility for specific tasks. This was clarified in the 1798 legislation. (3) McHenry was not decisive enough to command respect. He was not an original thinker nor a leader. (4) Differing views between the President and the Secretary confounded the administration of the War Department.

Not only was McHenry loaded down with the heavy burden of

being Secretary, but he was frequently unavailable because he was ill. Aware of his shortcomings, McHenry built up a deepening dependability on Hamilton for advice and actual actions. This publicly known political affiliation created a chasm of mistrust between McHenry and President Adams. Notwithstanding the criticism, McHenry achieved much in increasing the size of the standing professional Army, in augmenting the meager naval forces and in pacifying the Indians and the frontiersmen. Despite these accomplishments, there was no question that McHenry was ineffective as Secretary. Historians rate McHenry as a third-rate incompetent who stumbled through his term in office.

McHenry's tenure as Secretary of War materializes as "a classic example of too small a man in too large a job under too many pressures." Yet, he was "a pleasant man of moderate abilities in a position of greater responsibility than he could effectively handle."

In March 1776, the British sloop *Otter* approached Baltimore with captured American ships in tow. Fearing an attack, the Maryland ship *Defence* made a surprise assault and succeeded in chasing the British and recapturing the American ships. This incident stimulated the completion of the defenses of the city. About 250 men erected a line of connecting timbers across the water between Whetstone Point and the Lazaretto. They built batteries and mounted eighteen guns to guard the harbor entrance. In addition, they constructed beacons and signal stations along the Patapsco River and Chesapeake Bay. When completed, Colonel Mordecai Gist assumed command of the earthen Fort Whetstone. Even though there were recurring threats, the fortification never saw any battle action in the Revolutionary War. Although he need for a stronger fort was recognized, the federal government initially did not allocate enough funding. Between 1798-1800 significant changes occurred at the fort. Despite increased funding, a shortfall was expected. As Secretary of War, McHenry supported and increased the appropriations. In 1798, a French engineer, Jean Foncin, was selected to plan a new fort on Whetstone Point. Almost $94,000 was spent to complete the fort with walls 35 feet thick. In as McHenry was instrumental in promoting improvements and new construction for the garrison in his home town, the star-shaped fortification was renamed Fort McHenry in his honor. Fort McHenry gained its place in history during the War of 1812.

In 1932, at the 118th anniversary and reenactment of the Battle of

North Point, bronze tablets were unveiled at the fort honoring McHenry and others.

McHenry married Margaret Allison Caldwell on January 8, 1784. On almost every anniversary of his wedding, he wrote a poem to his wife. In a review of more than 100 pages of his poetry in a manuscript collection, McHenry garnered faint praise. He could express an idea neatly using turns of phrase that were frequently attractive and even charming. McHenry was labeled a very pleasant minor poet. On the negative side, he had no major poetic gifts, no penetrating insight and no power of distinction.

McHenry's last years were spent in retirement at his Maryland estate *Fayetteville*, named after the Marquis de Lafayette. He published a *Directory of Baltimore City* in 1807 and followed it in 1811 with a political pamphlet about Thomas Jefferson, James Madison and James Monroe, entitled *The Three Patriots*. Two years later, he served as president of the first Bible Society in Baltimore. Being a dedicated Federalist, McHenry opposed the War of 1812. Ironically, his son John participated as an Ensign in the Battle of North Point during the 1814 defense of Fort McHenry. In his private life, McHenry remained active in community affairs. On May 3, 1816 at the age of 62, McHenry died at his estate.

Toward the end of 1889, McHenry's executors donated his 700 papers, including 100 original letters, to the Maryland Historical Society. At an auction in 1944, McHenry's Constitutional Convention diary was sold for $3,600. His journal of the march from Valley Forge to the Battle of White Plains brought in $500. A total of $34,901 was collected for McHenry's papers by the end of the auction.

There seems to be no argument that McHenry was a man of integrity and honesty with a enjoyable and pleasing personality. He was a friendly and likeable man who spoke with a trace of an Irish accent but evidenced no outstanding ability. He had no marked proficiency as legislator, orator, soldier or surgeon. Yet, he was a high-minded gentleman, a conservative politician and an associate of great men in stirring days. "Here we come to the end of the life of a courteous, high-minded, keen-spirited Christian gentleman. He was not a great man but ... great men loved him, while all men appreciated his goodness and the purity of his soul."

## A RED DEVIL AND THE NATIONAL ANTHEM

Not all of the British military personnel were called Redcoats. One particular officer earned a more ominous appellation. If the "Red Devil of Chesapeake Bay," British Rear Admiral George Cockburn, had not sent a detachment of royal marines to seize and imprison a Maryland physician, *The Star Spangled Banner* may never have been written. If our national anthem was not *The Star Spangled Banner*, we might be singing *America, the Beautiful* at public gatherings today. This star spangled medical connection occurred during the War of 1812 as the United States struggled to protect its territory and its people from the invading British naval vessels and foot soldiers.

Landing troops at Benedict on the Patuxent River in Maryland, the British marched to attack Washington, D.C. On their route, Major General Robert Ross camped in Upper Malborough, Maryland on Monday afternoon, August 22, 1814. Most of the local residents fled before the British arrived. However, Dr. William Beanes remained in town. He was a member of the Federalist party and opposed the War. Graciously, he offered his house to General Ross and Admiral Cockburn to use as their headquarters. These British officers were treated with convivial hospitality by Beanes who shared his choice tobacco and wine with them. In turn, the doctor's courtesy was reciprocated and British soldiers protected his property.

On the way toward Washington, the British decisively routed disorganized American troops at Bladensburg, Maryland. At this point Ross was uncertain about marching on to destroy Washington. After a council of war in Beanes' house, Cockburn persuaded him to continue on to attack the American Capitol. Their smashing victory at Bladensburg reinforced Ross' determination.

At age 65, Dr. Beanes was the most prominent citizen in Upper Malborough: a physician, a major landowner, proprietor of the local grist mill, an accomplished scholar, and a popular gentleman. Beanes owned an 114 acre estate including Academy Hill, the finest house in town.

As was common, Beanes secured his medical education through apprenticeship to a local experienced physician. There was no medical college in the colonies at that time. After the battle of Lexington during the Revolutionary War, the Congress established the first General

Hospital in Philadelphia. For two years, Beanes was a staff surgeon at the hospital although he never formally joined the army. He treated wounded soldiers brought in from combat on Long Island, at Brandywine and from the dismal winter encampment at Valley Forge. In 1799, he was a founding member of the Medical and Chirurgical Faculty of the State of Maryland. Dr. Upton Scott, Francis Scott Key's uncle and a British surgeon in the Revolutionary War, became the first President of the Faculty. Beanes was elected to the Board of Examiners for the Western Shore. Young practitioners underwent examination by the Board before being permitted to practice. Their medical license cost $10.

Terrible destruction occurred as the British incinerated and looted the Capitol. At the White House, Dolley Madison scurried to remove Gilbert Stuart's painting of George Washington from its frame to prevent its destruction by the pillagers. Cockburn took particular delight in demolishing the Washington newspaper office of the *Daily National Intelligencer*. As his troops crushed the printing equipment and type, Cockburn commanded: "Be sure that all the C's are destroyed so that the rascals can have no further means of abusing my name as they have done." Both Ross and Cockburn pocketed souvenirs of their pillaging. Washington's *Daily National Intelligencer* remarked: "Cockburn was quite a mountebank in the city, exhibiting on the streets a gross levity of manner, displaying sundry articles of trifling value of which he had robbed the President's house."

A mocking *London Journal* article commented: "Our fleet ... appears to have created great alarm and done considerable mischief by a warfare of a somewhat ambiguous character." In France, the *Journal de Paris* delivered a candid and caustic observation: "How could a nation eminently civilized, conduct itself at Washington with as much barbarity as the old banditti of Attila and Genseric? Is not this act of atrocious vengeance a crime against all humanity?"

British soldiers and marines liberally applied torches. Ross reported: "... the following buildings were set fire to and consumed; the Capitol, including the Senate-House and House of Representatives, the arsenal, the dock-yard [navy yard], treasury, war office, President's palace, rope-walk and the great bridge across the Potomac." Damaged property was worth more than $2 million.

As they retreated on August 26, the British passed through Upper

Malborough again. Some of the marauding British soldiers were boisterous, drunk, and disorderly as they looted and plundered the countryside. Beanes incited several neighbors to assist him in imprisoning six or seven obstreperous soldiers in the local jail. A British officer, Lieutenant George Robert Gleig, described and embellished the incident in his diary: "... the inhabitants of that village, at the instigation of a medical practitioner called Baines [sic], had risen in arms as soon as we were defeated, and falling upon such individuals as strayed from the column, put some of them to death, and made others prisoners. A soldier whom they had taken, and who had escaped, gave this information to troopers just as they were about to return to headquarters; upon which they immediately wheeled about, and galloping into the village, pulled the doctor out of his bed, [for it was early in the morning]. and compelled him, by a threat of instant death, to liberate his prisoners, and mounting him before one of the party, brought him in triumph to the camp ... To our no small surprise, we saw our friend Dr. Baines brought in as a prisoner."

Washington's Sunday *Morning Chronicle* printed a different version. Beanes was said to be celebrating a rumored defeat of the British at Washington with copious libations. Suddenly, "three foot-sore, dusty and weary British soldiers made their appearance on the scene in quest of water." Under the influence, Beanes and his friends made them prisoners.

Regardless of how they became imprisoned, one soldier escaped and encountered a passing group of British troopers. In the early hours of August 28th, a party of British horsemen dispatched by Cockburn rode up to Beanes' door. They crashed into the house and pulled Beanes out of bed barely giving him time to dress. Beanes was forced to ride a barebacked mule the 35 miles back to the fleet anchored in Chesapeake Bay. On arrival, he was chained and imprisoned in solitary confinement in the brig on the British flagship, *Tonnant*. Treated as a culprit and not as a prisoner-of-war, Beanes suffered exceptionally harsh treatment, indignity and humiliation.

Upon hearing of Beanes' imprisonment, his well connected friends and neighbors sprang to his defense. A fellow Scottish trained physician, Dr. William Thornton, head of the Patent Office and architect of the Capitol, pleaded his case with Secretary of State James Monroe. Maryland Governor Levin Winder had a strongly worded letter delivered to General Ross urging Beanes release. American General John Mason's letter to Ross declared that the prisoner was "unarmed and [of] entirely noncombatant character" and his arrest was a "departure from the known usages of civilized warfare." Beanes' neighbor and patient, Richard West, went to see his wife's brother-in-law, Francis Scott Key, in Washington.

Key, a practicing lawyer in D.C., was an aide to Major General Samuel Smith, commander of the 3d Division of the Maryland Militia. Like Beanes, he was a Federalist and opposed the War. However, Key did fight the British at Blandensburg and in the battles defending Washington. At West's urging, Key went to see President James Madison seeking approval to negotiate with the British for the doctor's release. President Madison approved. Shortly afterward, John S. Skinner, the American prisoner-of-war exchange agent, was designated to accompany Key on his mission. As Key began the mission on September 2, 1814, he wrote to his mother: "I am going in the morning to Baltimore to proceed in a flag-vessel to Gen. Ross. Old Dr. Beanes of Marlboro is taken prisoner by the Enemy, who threaten to carry him off - Some of his friends have urged me to apply for a flag & go & try to procure his release ... I hope to return in about 8 or 10 days, though [it] is uncertain, as I do not know where to find the fleet."

On the same day, Key also wrote to his father about his trip to try to free Beanes. However, Key revealed his apprehension to his father: "I hope I may succeed but think it very doubtful."

In Baltimore, Key and Skinner took a small boat out to the British fleet under protection of a flag of truce. They arrived at dinner time. In keeping with the prevailing gentlemanly conduct of war, Vice Admiral Sir Alexander F. I. Cochrane, the British commander of the North American Station, invited Key and Skinner to dine with his officers on the Admiral's flagship. Cochrane did so even though he hated Americans.

During the dinner, conversation flowed easily without regard for the enemy ears of Key and Skinner. Being a lawyer, Key argued for the release of Beanes emphasizing that he was an elderly non-combatant civilian. Ross had only contempt for the doctor because he believed Beanes violated his tacit pledge to refrain from hostile acts against the British. Both Cockburn and Ross had mistakenly interpreted Beanes' Federalist leanings and hospitality as sympathy for the British cause.

Rebutting Key's arguments, Ross and Cockburn asserted that Beanes betrayed their trust by being the ringleader in rounding up the stray soldiers and putting them in jail. Ross felt that Beanes deserved much more punishment than he had received.

Cockburn bitterly denounced Beanes and was relentlessly opposed to releasing him. On the contrary, the Admiral suspected that Beanes was born in Scotland and wanted to send him to Halifax, Nova Scotia in chains to stand trial for treason. In reality, Beanes was descended of a Scotsman who settled in Maryland in 1672. Beanes himself was born in Maryland on January 24, 1749.

Key's prison interview with Beanes was remembered by his brother-in-law, Supreme Court Chief Justice Roger B. Taney: "He found him in the forward part of the ship, among the sailors; he had not had a change of clothes from the time he was seized; was constantly treated with indignity by those around him, and no officer would speak to him. He was treated as a culprit, and not as a prisoner of war. And the harsh and humiliating treatment continued until he was placed on board of the cartel."

Anticipating that the British might need persuading, Skinner carried with him hastily scribbled letters from British soldiers who were wounded and captured during the siege of the Capitol. These letters told of their medical care from Dr. James Ewell and other American doctors and the kindness shown to the wounded British officers. These notes persuaded the Admiral and the General. Skinner's rough, easy-going deportment beguiled a similarly affected Cockburn. Ross told Key and Skinner: "Beanes deserves more punishment than he has received ... it gives me great pleasure to acknowledge the kindness with which our officers have been treated ... confirmed by their own letters ... say to him [General Mason] and to the friends of Dr. Beanes that, on that account, and not from any opinion of his own merit, he shall be released, to return with you."

Key and Skinner prepared to escort Beanes back to their small boat. Smilingly, Admiral Cochrane abruptly intervened. "Ah, Mr. Skinner, after discussing so freely our preparation and plans, you could hardly expect us to let you go on shore in advance of us." During the free-flowing dinner conversation, the plans for an attack on Baltimore and the bombardment of Fort McHenry were revealed. Key was told that they would be detained until after the battle.

Skinner objected strenuously to the British forcefully requiring American citizens to remain on a enemy man-of-war while their own country was attacked. Cochrane courteously agreed and ordered that Key, Skinner and Beanes be returned to their own vessel. There was an entry in the Admiral's flagship log: "Sent a Mate and 4 Marines to take charge of a Sloop with a Flag of Truce."

While held captive on their own boat, Key, Skinner and Beanes apprehensively watched as Ross and Cockburn disembarked. Along with 9,000 soldiers and marines, they went ashore 12 miles from Baltimore at North Point on the Patapsco River. As the troops marched to attack Baltimore, the "Yankee-Doodles" resisted in paltry skirmishes until the British were about half-way to the city. As was his habit, Ross was leading his men on horseback and Cockburn was nearby. Sharpshooters, Privates Daniel Wells and Harry McComas of Captain Asquith's Rifles, fired from the tree tops and picked off the General. A sniper's rifle bullet pierced Ross' right arm and went into his chest. Ross toppled off his horse and died later in the day. Ross' replacement, Colonel Arthur Brooke, made little headway toward Baltimore, and the British retreated to board the troop ships still waiting in Chesapeake Bay.

Pacing their own vessel In painful suspense, Key, Skinner and Beanes watched the bombardment of Fort McHenry. All night long they saw the rockets' red glare and heard the bombs bursting in air. Inspired, Key scribbled an eloquent poem on the back of an old letter. As dawn's early light arrived, the tired and weary Beanes asked the keener-sighted Key: "Is the flag still there?"

After the unsuccessful bombardment ended on September 14th, the British allowed Key, Skinner and Beanes to sail back to Baltimore. They debarked at Hughes' Wharf about 9:00 P.M. on September 16th. Key finished his poem at the Indian Queen Hotel at the intersection of Market and Hanover Streets and titled it *The Defence of Fort M'Henry*. A few days later Key's poem was published anonymously in the *Baltimore Patriot* and the *Baltimore American*. Both papers suggested that the words be sung to the tune of *To Anacreon in Heaven*. Paradoxically, that was a British drinking song by John Stafford Smith and also the tune of Robert Treat Paine's revolutionary political ditty, *Adams and Liberty*. Almost immediately, the song was retitled and Carr's Music Store in Baltimore listed *The Star Spangled Banner* in its 1814 catalogue. Actor Fredinand Durang first sang the song in public at

Captain McCauley's tavern next to the Holiday Street Theater in Baltimore.

John Stafford Smith was the composer of the Anacreontic tune and, hence, of *The Star-Spangled Banner*.. This Anacreontic song was not intended for group singing or for amateur singing at all. It was not a barroom ballad, a drinking ditty to be chorused with glasses swung in rhythm. Anacreontic Society meetings were convivial, but "of the strictest propriety and decorum," devoted to music, both instrumental and vocal, and to suitable food and drink as well.

From 1793 through 1813, there were 66 different American parodies, new sets of words written to the tune published in 63 songsters that used this melody. Relevantly, Key knew the music and may have seen the 1804-05 publication of *The Baltimore Musical Miscellany* which contained both the words and music of *To Anacreon in Heaven*. This music book also included the first American publication of a 1792 song, *The Social Club*, which contained the line, *Which with star-spangl'd lustre celestially shone*.

Coincidentally, In 1805, Key attended a banquet in Georgetown honoring naval heroes Stephen Decatur and Charles Stewart for defeating the Barbary pirates off the North African coast. In a tribute to them, Key composed the song *When the Warrior Returns From the Battle Afar*. Furthermore, Key may have sung the song at the banquet vocalizing the following memorable phrases: *"By the Light of the Star Spangled flag of our nation / Where each radiant star / Gleamed a meteor of War /* [reprise after each of the five stanzas] *Where, mixed with the olive, the laurel shall wave, / And form a bright wreath for the brows of the brave.*

*When the Warrior Returns From the Battle Afar* was published in the Boston *Independent Chronicle* on December 30, 1805 but there was no mention of Key as the author. A second newspaper printing prefaced the text with "Song - Tune Anacreon. Prepared for, and sung by, a gentleman of George-Town, at an entertainment given in honor of Capts. Stephen Decatur, jun. and Charles Stewart." Gentleman from George-Town refers to Key.

On October 5, 1814, Key wrote to his friend, John Randolph: "I went with a [truce] flag to endeavor to save poor old Dr. Beans [sic] a voyage to Halifax, in which we fortunately succeeded." Key passed on his observations about the British officers: "... they appear to be illiberal, ignorant and vulgar and seem to be filled with a spirit of malignity against everything American."

Beanes returned home to live out his days peacefully in Upper Marlborough. Although his tombstone declares that he died on October 12, 1828, there is some confusion about the year being 1823, 1828 or 1829. In any event, Beanes and his wife, Sarah Hawkins Hanson, had no children. Beanes bequeathed his medicine, medical books and instruments to his brother, Dr. Colmore Beanes and his nephew, William Beanes Magruder, who later became a physician. Eventually, Beanes' property was acquired by the county and became the site of the Marlborough High School.

Almost 120 years later, *The Star Spangled Banner* was legally adopted as the official national anthem when Public Law 823 was signed by President Herbert Hoover on March 3, 1931.

Incidentally, the star spangled banner flying over Fort McHenry had 15 stars and 15 stripes - one star and one stripe for each state. That Fort McHenry flag should not be confused with "Old Glory" or the "Stars and Stripes," flags which had 13 stripes and the number of stars representing the number of states. Mrs. Mary Young Pikersgill and her daughter, Caroline, sewed the huge 30 by 42 foot flag together on the floor of Baltimore's Claggett's Brewery and received $405.90 for the flag.

Francis Scott Key never wrote another extraordinary line. If the British had not imprisoned physician William Beanes, Key might be unknown today or at best remembered as a sometime poet, the author of the hymns *Before the Lord We Bow* and *Lord With Glowing Heart I'd Praise Thee*, the three times United States Attorney for the District of Columbia and/or as the father of 11 children - six sons and five daughters.

In retrospect, there may have been something mystical in the interactions between the British Red Devil, the elderly physician, and the reluctant American soldier. That ethereal mix produced the U.S. national anthem, *The Star Spangled Banner*.

## A FIGHTING DOCTOR WINS THE MEDAL OF HONOR

With the blood of his forebearers surging in his veins, it may have been genetically ordained that physician, Bernard John Dowling Irwin, would become a career Army officer, a ruthless Indian fighter, and a hero. Irwin's lineage traced back to Sir William de Irrwyn, armour bearer to Scotland's King Robert Bruce. Reminiscences of Irwin by his army colleagues characterized his personality: "Many people accept danger when it is presented; the Irish seek danger for the love of it." On 28 November 1858, Captain Richard S. Ewell wrote to his niece, Betty, suggesting she come to Fort Buchanan [NM] and meet two bachelors: (referring to Irwin, the new post surgeon) "one an Irishman, doctor U.S.A., red head and hot-tempered." Afterwards, Ewell became a Confederate Lieutenant-General. With those characteristics, it is not surprising that Irwin displayed courageous actions with New York's Seventh Infantry Regiment battling hostile Apache Indians. A *Southwestern Medicine* article labeled Irwin "a brilliant surgeon who helped make Arizona safe for the white man."

Irwin was born on June 24, 1830 at Fort Round House, County Roscommon, Ireland, to James and Sabina Maria (Dowling) Irwin. He and his family emigrated from Ireland in 1845 and settled in New York City. Fifteen-year-old Irwin was educated by his father and private tutors as he studied classical and modern languages along with the usual subjects. In adulthood, he became proficient in five languages. He also attended the University of New York from 1848 to 1849. At eighteen, he enlisted in the New York State National Guard as a private.

Irwin began his medical education at Castleton Medical College [VT] and then enrolled in the first class of a new medical school. He attended the New York Medical College which was chartered on April 8, 1850 and opened for its first course of lectures on October 16, 1850. He paid a matriculation fee of $5, a fee of $105 for the full course of lectures and a demonstrator's fee of $5. Students needing room and board in the area paid $3 to $4 a week. There was also a fee of $30 for the final examination. The first commencement took place in early 1851 and the college closed in 1864. A history of medicine in New York said that the New York Medical College "represents a veritable oasis in the desert of low grade medical education in America at this time."

At Irwin's graduation on February 28, 1851, George Wood, a

prominent lawyer and President of the Trustees, bestowed the degree of Doctor of Medicine on the thirteen graduates. Professor Horace Green delivered the valedictory address on *The Prospective Progress of Medicine in America*. Comparing American and European medicine, Green remarked: "The healing art will make progress among us, because we are characterized by a fondness for novelty and experiments ... But let us never forget, that the most glorious, though least gainful triumphs of our art, should be to prevent, not to cure disease." There was sustained and rousing applause after Green welcomed the graduates into a noble profession. After listening to Green's speech, a *New York Daily Tribune* reporter commented: "It was well received and exhibited a perfect knowledge of the subject." To celebrate their graduation, Irwin and his friends paid $5 for a private box at Niblo's Gardens. They saw a new vaudeville *La Maitresse Des Langues* and the grand ballet of *Catarina Ou La Reine Des Bandits*. At a meeting of the graduates and students on March 11, 1851, Irwin was selected to chair a committee and wrote to Dr. Green "for the purpose of soliciting for publication a copy of your eloquent and patriotic Address delivered at the Annual Commencement."

At the time of Irwin's graduation, the "Medical" column of the newspapers advertised Dr. Delany's cures for private diseases in the first stage; a no cure - no pay offer by Dr. Corbitt; Dr. Glover offered to cure all those difficult and protracted cases that escaped from medical pretenders; Dr. T. L. Nichols and Mrs. Gove Nichols, Water Cure Physicians, offered consultations from 12 to 4 P.M.; Dr. J. S. Fancher described his Grecian Fancheronian Drops to positively cure dyspepsia, chills and fever, jaundice, diarrhea and cholera; and Horeshound Cough Syrup, Bryan's Pulmonic Wafers, Vegetable Pain Killer and Mrs. Burns Antique Ointment all proclaimed their unique benefits.

Perhaps, Irwin's familial military heritage subliminally guided him into medical service in the U.S. Army. There is no clear indication of why he chose the Army rather than private practice. After a few interim medical experiences, he became a career army medical officer who served in the U.S. Army for more than forty years.

In a April 10, 1849 letter to the American Medical Association Committee on Medical Education, Acting Surgeon General H. L. Heiskell detailed the duties and examinations for admission into the Army's medical staff. Regulations stated that the medical officer is required to investigate the physical agents that affect the health of the troops, to make reports upon the medical topography of his station, and to aid in the selection of military positions. Regarding military hygiene, he is to express his views in respect to the diet, clothing, watering, and exercise of the troops. "From necessity, the Army medical officer is a *general practitioner* in the most extended sense of the term (author's emphasis) ... From location, he often must rely entirely upon his own resources. Thus, he is deprived of the advantage of seeking aid and friendly counsel from professional brethren."

To be appointed to the Army medical corps, Irwin had to pass an examination by its Medical Board of Examiners. Prior to the exam, he had to prepare, in writing, a brief extemporaneous description of the causes, symptoms, pathology, and treatment of a disease assigned by the Board. In addition, the applicant had to prepare one or more prescriptions appropriate to the case, written out in the required form for the apothecary. Examiners raised questions on subjects usually taught in medical schools, on literary and scientific achievements, looked for grammatical knowledge of the English language, knowledge of Latin, and natural philosophy (or physics) since those were deemed important to those entering on the study of a liberal profession. Furthermore, the examiners evaluated the applicant's natural endowments, his general professional intelligence, his exact knowledge, his practical ability, and his strength of judgment.

In the 1850s, a medical career in the army seemed to be a highly competitive position. A report from the U.S. Surgeon General noted that only five of twenty-two applicants qualified for the Army medical corps. Reiterating criticisms of medical education at the time, the Army disclosed the most striking causes of failure: insufficient preparatory education, a hurried course of professional pupilage, and a want of proficiency in practical anatomy, pathology and clinical medicine.

Apparently, Irwin had no trouble meeting the comparatively stringent U.S. Army requirements. He passed the entrance examination on November 4, 1853 and was number fifteen on the list. While waiting for a vacancy, he was a resident physician and house surgeon at the Emigrant's Hospital [NY] from 1853 to 1855. In 1855, Irwin was respectively an Acting (contract) Assistant Surgeon at Fort Columbus [NY] and then accompanied troops to Corpus Christi [TX] and then to Santa Fé [NM]. Accepting a regular Army commission as an Assistant

Surgeon in 1856, Irwin served with expeditions against hostile Navajo and Apache Indians. He successively became the Post Surgeon at Fort Union [NM] and Fort Defiance [NM]. After these brief assignments in New Mexico, First Lieutenant Irwin was assigned as Post Surgeon to Fort Buchanan [AZ] in December 1857. Fort Buchanan was about ten miles from the Mexican town of Santa Cruz at Hot or Monkey Springs near the headwaters of the Senorita Creek, a branch of the Santa Cruz river.

During the latter part of 1860, hostile Indians raided a Senorita Creek frontier ranch where John Ward, a government beef contractor, lived with his mistress, Jesusa Martinez, and her son, Felix. Jesusa, a Mexican woman, was abducted by Indians and her son was sired by an Apache warrior during her captivity. These raiding Indians stole cattle and kidnaped the young boy. Ward traveled the eleven miles to Fort Buchanan to ask for help in recovering the cattle and his foster son. He told the officers that he believed the Chiricahua Apaches under Chief Cochise were responsible. Colonel Pitcairn Morrison pledged to help but bad weather and pressing business prevented direct action until February 1861. With Second Lt. George N. Bascom in command, about sixty men from the Seventh Infantry Regiment were sent to rescue the boy and to recover the cattle. Bascom found Cochise and invited him to parley and dine in his Army tent. Cochise was accompanied by his brother, two nephews, a woman, and a boy. A great-granddaughter of Cochise on the Mescalero Rez identified the woman as a wife and the boy as Cochise's youngest son, Naiche. Acting on his orders, Bascom demanded the return of the Ward boy and the cattle. Cochise explained that he knew nothing of the raid and offered to help get the boy and the cattle back.

Unyielding, Bascom called Cochise a liar and attempted to hold Cochise and his party as hostages. Acting with lighting speed, Cochise slit the tent with his knife and boldly made a dash for freedom. Although about fifty bullets were fired at him, Cochise escaped and several soldiers were wounded in the mêlée. However, Bascom did hold Cochise's five family members captive. Shortly, Bascom was surrounded by hundreds of Apaches. Cut off from Fort Buchanan, Bascom sent a messenger to the Fort under cover of darkness.

On hearing from the messenger, Colonel Morrison had few soldiers available and asked Fort Breckenridge to send support troops.

Knowing that Bascom had wounded men, Irwin volunteered to command the relief party. Irwin led fourteen picked infantrymen, mounted on mules, out into a blinding snowstorm on February 13, 1861. At Sulphur Springs Valley, Irwin encountered a band of Coyotero Indians returning from a cattle raid. Irwin led the hard chase of six or seven miles, retrieved thirty ponies and forty cattle, and captured a Coyotero Chief and two warriors.

Finally, after one hundred miles, Irwin entered the long winding canyon leading to Apache Pass on February 14. Apache Pass is a narrow defile lying between the Dos Cabezas and Chiricahua mountains approximately fourteen miles southeast of Bowie [AZ]. At the entrance to the canyon, Irwin's troops found the remains of a wagon train; five wagons burned and plundered. Lashed to the wagon wheels were the naked remains of eight people. Experienced troopers explained that the victims had been stripped, tied, tortured slowly, and burned alive. Troopers knew that Apaches often bound their victims to wagon wheels with their heads pointed down about eighteen inches from the ground. Then the Apaches built fires under them and roasted their brains until their heads burst open. Realizing his men were in imminent danger, Irwin began making plans to reach Bascom's men. Fortunately for Irwin's outnumbered troops, Apache scouts sighted the relief column from Fort Breckenridge under Lt. Isaiah N. Moore. Fearing an attack from the eastern side of the pass, the Apaches retreated, allowing Irwin to unite with Bascom's troops from the unguarded western side. Immediately, Irwin tended to the wounded as troops spent several days finding Cochise's abandoned village and destroying it.

On the march back to Forts Buchanan and Breckenridge, the movement of the troops disturbed a flock of buzzards. Upon investigation, Bascom and Irwin found vultures feasting upon the ghastly remains of six unrecognizable bodies, men who had been tortured, littered with lance holes, and killed by Apaches. Irwin reflected the culture of his times in his characterization of the Apaches: "One and all were then alike; treacherous, bloodthirsty, and cowardly, and ever on the alert to ambush small parties or incautious travelers ... Apaches were open or covert enemies of the white races ... insatiable thirst of the Apache for cruel and cowardly assassination."

James H. Tevis, a frequent correspondent to the *Weekly Arizonian*, knew Cochise well and assessed the chief's character in the

July 14, 1869 issue: "Ca-chees is a very deceptive Indian. At first appearance a man would think he was inclined to be peaceful to Americans, but he is far from it. ... have come to the conclusion that he is the biggest liar in the Territory! ... would kill an American for any trifle provided he wouldn't be found out."

While a historian branded Irwin and Lt. Moore as "blood thirsty," Irwin's own words reflect contemporary societal attitudes as well as his own personality: "I suggested their (the captured Indians) summary execution, man for man. On Bascom expressing reluctance to resort to the extreme measure, I urged my right to dispose of the lives of the prisoners captured by me. After which, he acceded to the retaliatory proposition, and agreed that those prisoners and three of the hostages taken by him, should be bought there and executed. After full and deliberate consideration, it was accordingly done the next day as the troops marched by that point on their return to their Forts. The punishment was an extreme mode of reprisal, but was demanded and justified by the persistent acts of treachery and the atrocious cruelties perpetrated by the most cowardly and intractable tribe of savages infesting the territory."

Ten days later, the six Indians were marched about a mile to be hung to the boughs of two sturdy oaks that stood over the graves of their six white victims. After watching the hanging bodies swaying in the wind, the Apache woman and boy were released when the troopers returned to the Fort. Six months later, Irwin traversed the pass and observed that "the bodies of the Indians executed still dangled on the oak trees over the graves of our murdered people."

In a March 17, 1861 message from Departmental Headquarters at Santa Fe to Fort Buchanan, the commanding officer was instructed to commend Irwin and Bascom: "The Department Commander directs that you will publicly express to Dr. Irwin, U.S. Army, and to Lieutenant Bascom, 7th U.S. Infantry, his approbation of the excellent conduct of those officers, and the troops under their command in the operations against Apache Indians during the last month. He emphatically approves of Lieutenant Bascom's decided action in executing the Indian warriors, after the atrocious murders which had been committed by the tribe."

Enraged by the retaliatory hangings, Cochise initiated a bloody twelve year Indian war threatening to kill ten for every one of his people killed. Within sixty days, 150 white men traveling the Overland Trail were killed. This brutal Indian war may have begun with or without the Apache Pass incident; there were multiple factors. However, a commentator is caustic and direct about the responsibility for the war being "the stupidity, pigheadedness and uncontrollable temper of a young shavetail (Bascom), fresh out of West Point." A historical consensus agrees that Cochise almost certainly did not steal the cattle and kidnap the boy and that Coyoteros most likely were the raiders. Nevertheless, a review of new evidence concluded: "The prevailing view that Bascom is entirely to blame should be strongly challenged."

About one year later, on February 21, 1862, Captain Bascom, serving with the Union's 16th Infantry, was killed by a Confederate cannonball in a battle at Valverde, New Mexico. In 1988, 126 years later, there was an announcement about Bascom's death at an Apache Girls Puberty Ceremony at Mescalero. Immediately, after the information was announced over the PA system, the historical information evoked enthusiastic cheering because the deaths of Cochise's brother and nephews had been avenged by the Rebels.

Ward's foster son was never returned. As an adult, he changed his name from Felix to Mickey Free and became a noted scout for General George Crook in the 1870s and 1880s. Free was infamous for his mean disposition. In his later years, he was "a wandering, aged, unkept, dependent of the government, an Apache in nature and cunning, in mind and action." Apaches labeled him "the coyote whose kidnaping brought war to the Chiricahuas."

Thirty-three years later, on January 24, 1894, Irwin was belatedly awarded the Congressional Medal of Honor with the following citation: "Voluntarily took command of troops and attacked and defeated hostile Indians he met on the way. Surgeon Irwin volunteered to go to the rescue of 2d Lt. George N. Bascom, 7th Infantry, who with 60 men was trapped by Chiricahua Apaches under Cochise. Irwin and 14 men, not having horses, began the 100-mile march riding mules. After fighting and capturing Indians, recovering stolen horses and cattle, he reached Bascom's column and helped break his siege."

Chronologically, Irwin was the first recipient of the Medal of Honor for his heroic deeds in February 1861. Paradoxically, Irwin earned the Medal of Honor for his heroism. However, this recipient of the U.S. Army's first Medal of Honor may have been a party to the unjustified hanging of Apache prisoners. His intransigence about summarily hanging the captured Indians possibly precipitated Cochise's bloody twelve year war with the Americans.

Irwin's heroism occurred before the Civil War began and even before the Congressional Medal of Honor was created. On December 21, 1861, President Abraham Lincoln signed legislation authorizing a Navy medal of honor. A similar bill, on July 12, 1862, created the Army medal of honor for non-commissioned officers and privates. On March 3, 1863, a bill passed making officers eligible. Actual medals were first awarded on March 25, 1863 by Secretary of War Edwin M. Stanton to six men who participated in the brazen Andrews locomotive raid in enemy territory in April 1862. Jacob Parrott was the first to receive his medal followed by the rest of the raiding party: William Bensinger, Robert Buffum, Elihu H. Mason, William Pittinger and William H. Reddick.

On June 11, 1861, Irwin was transferred from Fort Buchanan to Fort Fillmore [NM] and accompanied troops evacuating Arizona. He turned over his baggage and personal effects to the transportation officer for forwarding. En route on August 3, 1861, the commanding officer, Captain Isaiah N. Moore, received a message from Fort Craig [NM] that the troops at Fort Fillmore had surrendered the post to Texan insurgents. Captain Moore was warned of an impending ambush by the Texan insurgents who were only one day's march away from his position. In preparation for a five or six days march over rugged mountain trails to Fort Craig, Captain Moore did not want to be encumbered by baggage and didn't want the material to fall into enemy hands. Soldiers were ordered to put the torch to all public and private property, including Irwin's baggage and household effects.

If a man can be known by the books he reads, can the same be said for the belongings he accumulates? In his claim Irwin listed $2,286.00 worth of personal items. What can be learned from the listing of Irwin's belongings? Army medical officers were usually the best educated men in the service. Furthermore, Irwin was well traveled, having made three trips to Europe in five years; 1851, 1854, 1855. While Irwin's life was busy and exciting, there were occasional lulls. In addition to his medical pursuits, he became a naturalist and collector in the Western United States with far ranging interests including anthropology, ethnology, entomology, herpetology, metallurgy and ornithology. His property included valuable cabinet collections of varied Indian tribal artifacts, mineral specimens from the Southwest, and a collection of animals, birds, reptiles, insects and Indian crania from Arizona and New Mexico. In 1857, Irwin discovered the remains of a meteorite in an alley in Tucson, Arizona. He presented the "Irwin Meteorite" to the Smithsonian Institution and published a seven page booklet on the history of the great "Tuczon (sic) Meteorite."

In the 1890s, Irwin instituted a law suit to recover for his losses saying he collected the specimens "at much labor during nearly seven years' service" in the Southwest. His demand was heard by the U.S. Court of Claims. However, the Court declared that the claim was not within their jurisdiction because the events occurred in the war for the suppression of the rebellion.

Army medical officers cooperated with scientists and institutions absorbed in obtaining specimens of animals, plants, and minerals. Naturalists requested data on the varied Indian tribal folkways and artifacts such as clothing, hunting equipment, warring weapons, and household implements. Irwin recalled his "frequent correspondence with Professor Spencer F. Baird" of the Smithsonian. Trained and encouraged by Baird, the Smithsonian Institution's Assistant Secretary, Irwin made natural history more than just a hobby. Baird supplied Army surgeons with containers for their animal, plant and mineral specimens, materials and instructions for preserving them, books relating to natural history, and one-to-one training. Irwin was among the many medical officers who kept forwarding a constant stream of specimens. Many of Irwin's letters are still in the Smithsonian's archives. In a letter to another Army medical officer naturalist, Irwin remembered "a collection of reptiles ... made by me for the Smithsonian Institute at Fort Buchanan and vicinity in 1858-60." There are still specimens credited to Irwin in the Smithsonian's anthropology and ornithology collections.

In addition, Irwin directed other Army personnel to collect specimens. Writing about Major Charles E. Bendire, Irwin reminisced that "it was I who initiated in him the taste for natural history which he cultivated with so much zeal and advantage as a naturalist." In turn, Bendire wrote about Irwin: "... Dr. Irwine (*sic*) is also an excellent man in every way, and in the early days of Arizona in 1857 and 1858 he used to be quite interested in making natural history collections and the Smithsonian is indebted to him for a great many nice things from the

Northern portion of the Territory. I am indebted to the doctor for my life and never would have pulled through if it had not been for his unremitting attention to me while at Fort Buchanan."

Interestingly, the U.S. Weather Bureau owes its origin to the Army Medical Department. Beginning in 1814, the Surgeon General directed Army medical officers "to keep a diary of the weather, together with an account of the medical topography ... as the influence of weather and climate upon diseases, especially epidemics, is perfectly well known."

By 1862, Captain Irwin was Medical Inspector, Army of the Ohio, for Major-General W. Nelson's 4th Division. Up to this time, there was no ambulance service to speak of and no efficient methods for transporting the wounded. Barely adequate medical personnel administered first aid at the front lines and base hospitals were far in the rear. There was nothing between these two.

Immediately before the battle of Shiloh, Tennessee on April 6-7, 1862, Irwin organized a three hundred bed army field tent hospital, the first of its kind for the treatment of the wounded during a war. However, the Prussians in Europe and the British in India used tent hospitals in 1848. Still, Irwin's was possibly the largest. Actually, his creation was a precursor to contemporary wartime MASH (Mobile Army Surgical Hospital) frontline units. Prior to Irwin's innovative idea, the wounded were treated in the barns, stables, churches, and any accommodations that might be found in the immediate area of a battle.

Displaying unusual resourcefulness, Irwin described how the tent field hospital evolved: " ... one of the operating stations moved forward to a deserted farmhouse, situated on an open piece of level, unbroken ground ... a spring of cool, potable water and the nearness of the building to a small branch of a creek were advantages ... A large number of wounded ... suggested utilization of the abandoned tents ... regimental hospital tents, commissary tents, and the wall tents were accordingly taken procession of ... removed to and pitched in regular camp order ... building afforded an operating room, dispensary, office, kitchen, and dining-room for the officers ... supplied [wounded] with an abundance of warm food, good bedding and shelter against the inclement weather ... camp enlarged to conveniently accommodate some three hundred patients ... All bedsteads, cots, bedsprings, cooking and necessary utensils, hay and straw appropriated for the use of the hospital ... A suitable number of attendants of each class were detailed for duty ... A fair supply of extra diet and delicacies were served to the inmates who needed special attention ... It soon became manifest that the wounded accommodated in that improvised field hospital were better provided for and more comfortable in every particular than those who were hurried aboard the crowded transports. One of the most valuable lessons ... was the demonstration of the inestimable value of the tent as a hospital, and as a reliable substitute for the pick-up structures, obtained by chance, into which the sick and wounded of armies in the field were up to that time huddled."

Union forces suffered more than 13,000 casualties during the battle of Shiloh. Assistant Medical Director Robert Murray issued a commendation: "Assistant Surgeon Irwin deserves great credit for his admirable management on the field as well as for his promptness and professional skill in the care of the wounded ... he succeeded in organizing and putting in good working order a hospital for three hundred patients ... These were so well taken care of in every way that I designated them as the last to send on board of the boats."

Rapidly, the importance of Irwin's field tent hospital was recognized. Armies of many nations soon adopted this type of modern field hospital. In recognition of his service, Irwin was made a Companion of the Military Order Loyal Legion, U.S., New York Commandery in December 1867. A memorial tablet on the Battlefield of Shiloh, with a bold red cross in each corner, honors Irwin.

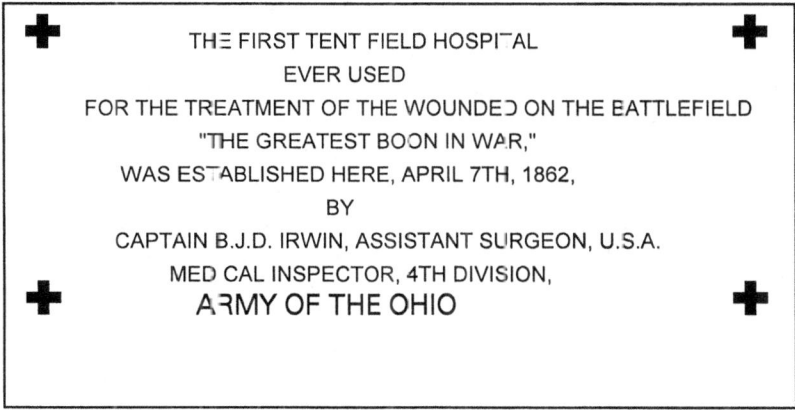

> ✚ THE FIRST TENT FIELD HOSPITAL ✚
> EVER USED
> FOR THE TREATMENT OF THE WOUNDED ON THE BATTLEFIELD
> "THE GREATEST BOON IN WAR,"
> WAS ESTABLISHED HERE, APRIL 7TH, 1862,
> BY
> CAPTAIN B.J.D. IRWIN, ASSISTANT SURGEON, U.S.A.
> MEDICAL INSPECTOR, 4TH DIVISION,
> ✚ ARMY OF THE OHIO ✚

On August 26, 1862, Irwin set out from Lexington [KY] to

Richmond [KY] to procure ambulances and medical supplies. Three days later, he secured twelve ambulances in Lancaster, about twenty-five miles from Richmond. Next day, Irwin was with General Nelson in a skirmish. After the General was wounded in the left groin, Irwin attended to the wound. However, the Rebels were still there and Irwin described his actions: "I was obliged to throw myself into the hands of a party of the enemy's calvary, thereby securing his [Nelson's] escape."

At the prison camp, Irwin discovered about 700 wounded Union soldiers and asked the Confederate commander to allow him to attend to the troops. While the ladies of Richmond nursed the men and Union loyalists brought foodstuffs, Irwin purchased $400 worth of medicines from a local druggist and borrowed instruments from civilian physicians. He secured permission to send to Lexington for clothing and medical supplies, under a flag of truce. In addition, Irwin got a pass through the lines to go to Ohio to arrange for transport for the wounded and two hundred prisoners were paroled on their own and sent forward to the Union lines. All-in-all, Irwin remained with the Union wounded for about three weeks. Shortly thereafter, he was exchanged and returned to the Union army.

With the end of the war, he successively served in various posts in the Western states. Between 1863 and 1873, Irwin served in St. Louis [MO], at Fort Riley [KS], at Fort Leavenworth [KS], and at Fort Wayne [MI].

In October 1873, Irwin became the Chief Medical Officer at the U.S. Military Academy at West Point. He conducted physical examinations of the candidates for admission handled sick call among both civilians and the military, and paid particular attention to public health, sanitation and the environment.

During Irwin's tenure, a very complete medical evaluation of West Point took place. Irwin was deeply involved in the research for and submission of a Special Sanitary Report in 1874. Recommendations advised: construction of new water closets and urinals, screened from view and connected to new sewers; removal of families from quarters in the guard house, discontinuation of the use of dark cells in the basement and abandonment of a ball and chain for prisoners; improvement of the heating system in the cadet barracks; substitution of Java coffee for the type used in the cadet mess; use of boiled instead of cold milk for coffee; addition of much more fresh milk to cadet menus; an appropriation of

$10,000 to complete a drainage and sewage system for the officers' quarters; and the rapid construction of a new cadet hospital. Irwin and the Academy's Board of Visitors continued to strongly urge the completion of the cadet hospital. Each cadet was regularly charged a monthly average of 61 cents to augment the hospital fund.

At the same time that Irwin reported a diphtheria epidemic in New York City in January 1875, he also observed a severe form of rampant tonsillitis at West Point. Assistant Surgeon A. C. Gerard, a staff physician, thought the tonsillitis might be linked to the low temperatures and the snow on the ground. Gerard had another theory: "... it (tonsillitis) is a modified form of the epidemic of diphtheria that has been ravaging the inhabitants of New York City wafted to us by the atmosphere and modified by our pure country air and superior hygienic conditions.' A large number of cadets were treated without interference with their classes.

In a space of 48 hours in August of 1875, 65 out of the 205 cadets were afflicted with nausea, fainting, vomiting, griping pain in the bowels and violent purging. Irwin and his medical staff diagnosed the illness as "cholera morbus," a term used for any acute gastroenteritis. An investigation attributed the outbreak to a breakfast serving of fish hash prepared with dried cod that was probably contaminated. Following Irwin's advice, the Superintendent prohibited the serving of fish, except for salt mackerel, at cadet meals between June 15 and September 15. Irwin also stopped the commissary from issuing, at one time, a ten day supply of meat to married soldiers.

In 1876, a scarlet fever scare developed with six cadets falling ill. A specialist, Assistant Surgeon S.Q. Robinson, was called to West Point to take charge of the outbreak. Later that year, Irwin tended to a measles epidemic among civilians with a total of 125 cases, 95 occurring during November and December.

After an analysis of the statistics from 1864 to 1873, Irwin found that 20 percent (3,538) of the 17,442 cases of disease originated "in miasmatic poison, most of which could have been prevented by a proper system of hygienic police. Faulty drainage on the post has been the most potent and constant factor in producing disease, especially those of miasmatic and malarial type." Irwin recommended the early completion of a thorough and perfect system of drainage.

On August 28, 1878, Irwin was relieved from duty at the Military

Academy and ordered to report to the Surgeon General. He took a year's leave and toured military hospitals in Austria, Belgium, Great Britain, France, Germany, Hungary, Italy, and Switzerland. Returning to service, between late 1879 and 1885, Irwin served as Post Surgeon at Fort Meade [Dakota] and Fort Snelling [MN] before becoming the Medical Director for the Department of Arizona,

While tending to his medical duties, Irwin contributed articles to the professional literature, mainly about his medical experiences in the West. Eight of Irwin's articles appeared in the *American Journal of the Medical Sciences*. Traveling 100 miles from Fort Buchanan to treat a patient, Irwin described an amputation of the shoulder joint on April 10, 1859. In graphic detail, he explained his procedure for this serious surgical intervention. He concluded: "On the 24th day after the operation he (the patient) was walking about, and in less than six weeks he started for the Eastern States, restored to perfect health."

Still at Fort Buchanan in September 1860, Irwin made a "proper investigation" of a herb, *Euphorbia prostrata*. This herb was labeled "Gollindrinera" by the Mexican population and used as an antidote to rattlesnake venom. For several months, Irwin experimented on many dogs with satisfactory results. After minutely detailing the herb, the source of its medicinal properties, its physiological effects and his inability to explain the *modus operandi*, he described two experiments in detail. In summary, Irwin stated that the herb "never fails to produce a sure and speedy cure." Furthermore, he recommended the herb as being more advantageous than the standard "Bibron's Antidote" then in use.

During the incident at Apache Pass, one of the Indian hostages was bayoneted and transfixed to the ground. When Irwin arrived, he took care of the Indian. His treatment of the puncture wound and recovery of the patient was related in *American Medical Times* the next year.

At Fort Buchanan in May 1861, Irwin treated a soldier who had a gunshot wound of the arm. Since the humerus was splintered, he amputated at the shoulder joint. About two months after being shot, the patient died. However, during the surgery Irwin pricked the end of his left index finger and apparently was poisoned by absorption of some putrid matter. Suffering pain and throbbing, he administered medications, constant irrigation, and sought consultation with a physician friend who had arrived from Tuczon (*sic*), Arizona. After going through six days of intense pain, intermittent fever, and wild delirium, his finger was incised to relieve the pain. Noting the destruction of muscular tissue at the first metacarpal, Irwin commented that "the condition of the first phalanx is irremediable by any other than surgical means."

Irwin recounted an 1863 case dealing with the immobility of the temporo-maxillary articulation following a gunshot wound. This patient was unable to separate his jaws for more than a year. Using a "unique and entirely original" approach combining wooden wedges and leather straps, Irwin relieved the problem by novel mechanical means. He was able to pry open the man's jaws without harming him.

In 1874, Irwin described a case of osteophytic inflammation of the right radius of a young woman. She was going East to have her arm amputated, but Irwin's examination convinced him that such an extreme measure was unnecessary. With impressive surgical skill, he did a resection and was able to preserve a useful hand. Citing a few prior examples, he remarked that "the exsection of any extensive part of the lower extremity of the radius does not appear to have been performed except in the instances already mentioned."

Additional professional articles dealt with extensive laceration of the hand from an explosion, three cases of penetrating gunshot wounds of the thorax with perforation of the lungs, concussion of the brain, fracture of the sternum with dislocation of the fragments, and his introduction of tent field hospitals in war.

In 1877, at West Point, Irwin published a seven page pamphlet: *Catalogue of the Library Pertaining to the Cadet's Hospital*. A total of 524 volumes were listed alphabetically by author including 179 books, 259 volumes of periodicals, and 86 miscellaneous volumes.

Irwin was promoted to Lt. Colonel in 1885 and put in charge of the Army medical purveying depot in New York City until 1886 when he was transferred to the same position in San Francisco. In a political remonstration in 1890, Irwin sent a seven page letter to the Military Committee of the U.S. Senate and to the Adjutant General of the Army. He protested the appointment of Colonel Edward P. Vollum as Chief Medical Purveyor for the Army. He contended that Lieutenant-Colonel and Assistant Medical Purveyor B.J.D. Irwin was Vollum's senior and the appointment, by law, should have gone by seniority and not by selection. However, Vollum was appointed despite Irwin's efforts.

In 1886, a newspaper's bold headlines proclaimed: *Why Apaches Made War: Officer Oberly of Brooklyn Tells What He Knows About It* Officer Oberly served in Arizona and was a color sergeant of the Seventh Infantry during the Apache wars. He downplayed the savagery and ruthlessness of the Apaches. Upset by the tone of the article, Irwin felt compelled to prepare a written response and did so in 1887. However, this article was not published until 1928 as Irwin recalled his heroic encounter with Cochise and the Chiricahua Apaches in *The Infantry Journal*. Irwin set the record straight contending that the newspaper article did not do justice to the severity of the Apache atrocities. and "distorts a conspicuous incident in the early history of that territory, and, at the same time, does gross injustice to the reputation and memory of a brave and efficient officer of the Army, Captain George N. Bascom."

Two years after joining the newly organized Association of Military Surgeons in 1891, Irwin was elected First Vice President. He was a member of the Public Health Congress, Auxiliary to the World's Columbian Exposition, 1893; Vice-President of the Pan American Medical Congress, representing the Medical Department of the U.S. Army, 1893; Delegate of the U.S. to the Eleventh International Medical Congress in Rome, 1894; Commander, of the Order of Indian Wars, 1903-1905; and Vice-President of the American White Cross First Aid Society, 1904.

Irwin retired in 1894 and was promoted to Brigadier General in 1904 by an Act of Congress. Although Irwin died at his summer home in Coburg, Canada on December 15, 1917, his final resting place is at the West Point military academy in New York. Irwin General Hospital in Fort Riley, Kansas is a memorial to Bernard J. D. Irwin, "the fighting doctor" and displays a large portrait of him in the lobby.

Although constantly on the move, Irwin managed to have a family life as well. He married Antoinette E. Stahl in 1864 and they had two daughters and a son. Margaret Irwin married a physician, Dr. Arthur A. Small, who became the long time medical director of the Chicago Surface Lines. She died some time after her husband's death in 1952. Aime [sometimes Amy] Irwin married Robert R. McCormick, publisher of the *Chicago Tribune*. She was an accomplished artist and painted an oil portrait of her father that hung in the National Library of Medicine. She died in 1939 and was buried with full military honors. George

LeRoy Irwin became a career Army officer and graduated from West Point in 1899. As a Brigadier-General, he commanded an artillery unit in World War 1. By 1928, he was a Major-General in command of the Panama Canal fortifications. He died in 1931 and was buried with full military honors in West Point beside the grave of his father. Irwin's grandson, Stafford Leroy Irwin also became a career Army officer who died in 1955.

Bernard John Dowling Irwin combined the adventure and travel of a military life while making profound contributions as a scientist. As a well educated physician, he applied his intellectual abilities in the variegated locations where he served with undiluted gusto. His special achievements included his winning the Congressional Medal of Honor, his creation of the first army tent field hospital during the Civil War, his numerous contributions as a naturalist, and as a medical practitioner. In Surgeon General Ireland's Presidential Address to the Association of Military Surgeons in 1927, he referred to General Irwin: "Irwin was a very distinguished man ... a man of great energy and character, and he saw to it that the Medical Department received whatever was coming to it in his department." He (Irwin) used to say: "The doctor first and last is a medical officer."

## CLARA BARTON: FOUNDER OF THE AMERICAN RED CROSS

Clara Barton lived in an age of conformity, the antebellum/Victorian era in the United States. Societal expectations of women demanded "piety, purity, domesticity, and submissiveness" and resulted in women being totally dependent upon men for their survival. Furthermore, before the Civil War, women were considered generally unhealthy: "... the fact is certain that the American girl is a very delicate plant ... not generally strong in nerve and muscle, and too ready to fade before her true mid-summer has come." Contrary to these dire Victorian expectations, Barton confided: "I must have been born believing in the full right of woman to all the privileges and positions which nature and justice accord her in common with other human beings. Perfectly equal rights -- human rights. There was never any question in my mind in regard to this."

Phrenology taught Barton a lifelong philosophy. Her bouts with gender discrimination made her a pioneer in competing with men on an equal footing and at equal pay while fortifying her for future battles with reluctant men. Barton's non-conventional therapy for nervous prostration prepared her physically and mentally for the monumental task of moving governments and politicians toward the formation of an American Red Cross organization.

On Christmas day in 1821, Clarissa Harlowe Barton was born in North Oxford, Massachusetts. She was the youngest of five children with the next child 10 years older. Her father, Stephen Barton, commented that Clara was a tomboy as a child. In contrast, Barton reminscienced: "In the early years of my life, I remember nothing but fear." Changing her name upon maturity to Clara Barton, she gained fame for ministering to the soldiers during the Civil War and other wars and as the founder of the American Red Cross. In addition to all the adulation for her well known feats, she was more ambitious than selfless, more middle-class than wealthy, and more of a politician than a nurse. Although usually associated with being a nurse, Barton gave her own assessment "I never claimed to be a nurse. There were hundreds of women who could nurse as well or better than I could." In fact, Barton was an idealistic leader in humanitarian activities.

Phrenologist Lorenzo Niles Fowler was a guest of the Bartons when he delivered several lectures in their Massachusetts area in 1836.

Phrenologists studied the grooves and bumps of the human skull, searching for signs of intelligence, character and other faculties of the mind. Practitioners claimed that the brain was divided into 37 separate physical "organs." Each organ corresponded to a different "mental faculty" or "propensity" such as "firmness," "secretiveness," or "destructiveness." Individual faculties could be modified in size and shape through proper exercise and control. A Viennese physician, Joseph Spurzheim, coined the term "phrenology," calling it "the science of the mind." Phrenological examinations became popular in the U.S. in the 1830s. As late as 1925, "Jessie Fowler, Phrenologist," was still listed in the New York City Directory.

Barton was phrenologized by Fowler at her agonized mother's request because her most difficult child was "sunk in timidity and self-abnegation." Responding to her anguish, Fowler told Barton's mother: "She will never assert herself for herself ... but for others she will be perfectly fearless. Throw responsibility upon her. She has all the qualities of a teacher. As soon as her age will permit, give her a school to teach." Barton described her reaction to this chance meeting: "Mr. Fowler placed in my hands their well written book and brochures on Phrenology, 'The Science of the Mind ... Know thyself' became my text and my study ... 'Know thyself' has taught me in any great crisis to put myself under my own feet; bury enmity, cast ambition to the winds, ignore complaint, despise retaliation, and stand erect in the consciousness of those higher qualities that made for the good of human kind, even though we may not clearly see the way."

"Know thyself" was not original with phrenologists. Socrates' most famous aphorism "nosce te ipsum" dictated the same philosophy. Barton had "great faith" in phrenology according to Frances (Fanny) Childs Vassall, a fellow teacher and niece by marriage. Barton considered Fowler one of the significant forces in her destiny who changed her way of thinking and her way of life. She corresponded with Fowler and about 40 years later was happy to meet him and his wife in London. Interestingly, his wife, Lydia Folger Fowler, was the second woman to earn the degree of Doctor of Medicine in the United States. She graduated Central Medical College [Syracuse, NY] in February 1850, about one year after Elizabeth Blackwell became the first woman physician.

Although Barton may have taught school earlier, she obtained her first teacher's certificate on May 5, 1839, when she was 17. Her assignment was at District School Number 9 near her Massachusetts home. In a prophetic comment, considering her future 1852 teaching job, Barton stated: "I may sometimes be willing to teach for nothing, but if paid at all, I shall never do a man's work for less than a man's pay."

For about 10 years Barton taught school in Massachusetts. In 1850, she enrolled in the Clinton [NY] Liberal Institute and took as many classes as possible. Her broad based education fit easily into her family's progressive traditions and her own political and religious feelings. Moreover, she was aware of the intellectual and moral liberalism occurring in New England and New York during the 1830s and 1840s. Horace Mann initiated educational reforms in Massachusetts and Ralph Waldo Emerson wrote about the philosophic basis of human liberty. William Lloyd Garrison expounded on the plight of the enslaved black and Elizabeth Cady Stanton protested that women were little better than slaves. Religion lost its evangelistic approach in the liberal atmosphere. By the time Barton finished her educational endeavors, she was ready to step out on her own. When she did so, she encountered calloused gender discrimination in her first two work experiences.

After her study at the Liberal Institute, Barton spent a few weeks with a classmate, Mary Norton, who lived in New Jersey. During her stay, Barton noticed young boys wandering on the streets. "Every street corner had little knots of them, idle, listless " She spoke with them. "Lady, there is no school for us. We would be glad to go if there was one." Barton secured an interview with Peter Suydam, chairman of the Bordentown School Committee. Suydam told her that these boys were renegades, more fit for the penitentiary than for school, and their parents would never send them to a "pauper school." Forthrightly and politically, Barton attacked the issue telling Suydam: "I would open and teach such a school without remuneration, but my effort must have the majesty of the law, and the power vested in its offices behind it or it would not stand ... that the School Board, as officers of the law, with accepted rights and duties must so far connect themselves with the effort as to provide quarters, the necessary furnishings, and to give due and respectable notice of the same among the people. In fact, it must stand as by their order, leaving the work and results to me ... I had no ambitions to serve, but as an observer of unwelcome conditions, and, as I thought, harmful as well, to try, so far as possible, the power of a good, wise, beneficent, and established state law, as against the force of ignorance, blind prejudice, and the tyranny of an obsolete, outlived, public opinion."

On July 1, 1852, Barton was granted a teacher's certificate and signed a contract to teach or keep a free school in Bordentown. She was to receive no pay until she was successful. Barton marked the beginning of the Crosswicks Street school by saying: "One bright morning I found myself there with six bright renegade boys (not a girl could be trusted with me) and the public school was commenced." In two weeks there were 55 pupils. One year later Barton had 600 pupils, had hired a North Oxford (MA) woman, Fanny Childs as another teacher and both were earning $250 year. Jenny Suydam became a student assistant. Barton's successful efforts prompted the town to raise $4,000 for a new school building. However, when the new building opened, the school board selected a man, J. Kirby Burnham, to be the principal at $650 per year. In 1853, it was almost impossible for the people to think that such a large institution could be headed by a woman. Bordentown citizens objected to her sex; not to Barton's skills. She was demoted to a "female assistant" and suffered from the harassment, the rivalry, the unhappiness taking orders from Burnham and the bitter collapse of her hopes. She and Childs called Burnham "the critter" and Barton summed up her bitterness by saying: "I could bear the ingratitude, but not the pettiness and jealousy of this principal, under whom I am set to work." Barton's health suffered; she had a nervous breakdown, her eyes bothered her, and she lost her voice for a while. In February 1854, she and Fanny Childs resigned and the *Bordentown Register* bitterly admonished them for "forsaking their posts without leave or warning." School board members were disturbed by all the squabbling and at the end of the term, three months later, Burnham was fired.

In this first independent work experience, Barton displayed the traits that characterized her whole career: a quick and practical response to an immediate need; an aggressive independence; persistence; courage; delight in directing a difficult enterprise; and an intense nervous energy. This sequence of events -- depression, loss of health, and flight -- established a pattern that Barton fell into when she encountered great personal frustration.

Barton arrived in Washington, DC in the Fall of 1854 at the age of 32. President Franklin Pierce presided over an untidy city of about

50,000 people. Most of the capital's streets and sidewalks were unpaved and swirled in dust in the summer and were full of mud puddles in the winter. There were few street lights, parks were overgrown with weeds, and a water system was yet to come. Many government buildings were not finished; wooden scaffolding encased the top of the Washington Monument; and the Capitol had two unroofed wings.

Almost immediately, Barton requested help from her Massachusetts congressman, Colonel Alexander De Witt. In the interim, she was considering a job as governess in Burlington, Iowa for Mary, the 12 year old daughter of Judge Charles Mason, Commissioner of the Patent Office. De Witt recommended Barton to Mason for employment in the Patent Office. Impressed by Barton's neat, precise, beautiful round "copperplate" handwriting, Mason hired her as a temporary clerk to copy patent applications, regulations and caveats at 10 cents per hundred words; the same rate as male copyists. During the months of April, May, and June 1855, Barton respectively earned $71.35, $93.39 and $83.35. It was rare for copyists to earn more than $900 per year.

Commissioner Mason was the first head of a government department in Washington to give regular employment to a woman, contending that if a woman's work equalled that of a man, she should have a man's pay. By this time, Mason broke with tradition by allowing female copyists to work in the basement of the east wing of the Patent Office and he was the first to do so. Barton described Judge Charles Mason as "a man of stern moral fiber." Mason graduated first in his class from West Point in 1829; Robert E. Lee graduated second. He taught engineering at West Point, practiced law, was a journalist at the *Evening Post* (NY), a public prosecutor in Iowa, the chief justice of the Iowa supreme court and president of two railroads. In rewriting the Iowa 1851 code, Mason kept in step with the most advanced legislation of his time as to the property and personal rights of women. Mason believed that women possessed the same inherent rights as men, an uncommon concept among men of that period. President Franklin Pierce appointed Mason U.S. Commissioner of Patients on March 24, 1853.

Three months after Barton began working, on July 4, 1855, Mason resigned to take care of real estate transactions as President of the Des Moines River Improvement Company. Under a prearranged scheme, Mason's chief clerk, Samuel T. Shugert, became acting commissioner until Mason's scheduled return in four months. During

July, August and September, Barton received no pay indicating that she was kept on the rolls but not given any work to do. Although Shugert was friendly toward Barton, he yielded to pressure from Interior Secretary Robert McClelland and scribbled a note to the Chief Clerk of the Interior Department on August 30, 1855: "I have communicated to the Ladies employed in the Patent Office that they must vacate their room within the present month, and also, that the Hon. Secretary promises to give them work from the Land Office, when practicable –."

Barton and the other ladies appealed to their congressmen. On September 22, 1855, De Witt wrote to Secretary McClelland: "Having understood the Department had decided to remove the ladies in the Patent Office on the first of October, I have taken the liberty to address a line on behalf of Miss Clara Barton, a native of my own town and district, who has been employed in the past year in the Patent Office, and I trust to the entire satisfaction of the Commissioner."

Interior Secretary McClelland forcefully expressed his views about this situation: "... I have no objection to the employment of the females in the Patent Office, or any other Bureaus of the Department, in the performance of such duties as they are competent to discharge, but there is such *obvious impropriety in the mixing of the sexes* [emphasis added] within the walls of a public office, that I determined to arrest the practice, though not until after full consideration, on account of the probable effect on some, now enjoying the emoluments of such labor ... There is every disposition on my part, to do any thing for the lady in question, except to retain her, or any of the other females at work in the rooms of the Patent Office."

McClelland advised Acting Commissioner Shugert that he had no objection to finding work for Miss Barton "out of the office."

Mason reacted to the news in his diary on October 14: "I understand that the Secretary has dismissed the female clerks whom I had employed in the office and sent instead a detachment of male clerks from the Pension Office. To this I shall have some great objections if I understand the matter rightly. They were some of my best clerks and besides, charity dictated their appointment and retention."

Upon returning as Commissioner on November 1, 1855, Mason took drastic steps to stop dishonest clerks from fraudulently copying secret inventions to sell to unscrupulous business men. At this point, Mason appointed Barton to an administrative post. "After some rest I was requested by the commissioner of patents to take charge of a confidential desk with which he had found some difficulty. The secrecy of its papers had not been carefully guarded. I accepted and thus became as I believe the first woman who entered a public office in the Departments of Washington in her own name drawing the salary over her own signature. I was placed equal with the male clerks at $1,400 per year. This called for no little denunciation on the part of those who foresaw dangerous precedents."

Male employees subjected Barton to dreadful abusive behavior due to jealousy, suspicion and hatred. She said: "I found the frauds. It made a great commotion among the clerks; they knew what it meant and they tried to make the place too hard for me."

Each morning, the jeering men formed a human gauntlet along both walls of the corridor leading to her desk and taunted the "pest in petticoats." They stared at her with undisguised disgust. Barton walked rapidly with her head down, seeing only the floor and their boots. They whiffed cigar smoke in her face and spat tobacco juice on the floor before her as she walked. They tried to obliterate her with their insulting obnoxious remarks, whistles and catcalls that increased in volume, number and maliciousness as she reached the end of the gauntlet. In recounting this story to numerous people, Barton explained that "It wasn't a pleasant experience, in fact it was very trying, but I thought perhaps there was some question of principle involved and I lived it through."

Her infraction was quite straightforward. She was ambitious, competent, and a leader, and demonstrated an ability to equal or surpass men doing the same work. Even though teapots and hoop skirts equated with cigars and spittoons in the working environment, many bureaucrats and managers were irritated by the sight of female co-workers. Even President Pierce was known not to favor women in government offices.

Thoroughly beaten by Barton's efficiency, her detractors resorted to vilification and whispered slanders regarding promiscuity, drink, and debauchery. In the public's mind, female clerks were considered immoral. They accused Barton of lax sexual conduct, being a "slut" with illegitimate Negroid children and believing in free love. Upon hearing of this, Judge Mason said to the ringleader: "Show me proof and I will discharge the clerk. If you cannot, you *will* go." The defamer went.

Barton's salary reflected Mason's principle of paying equally for equal work. Her wages jumped from $73.56 in October to $135 in November and to $136.60 in December, equaling that of the male clerks. Considering that Mason was paid $3,000 per year as Commissioner, $1,400 was a magnificent salary for a clerk.

Being the first woman employed independently full-time in a government office at a salary equal to men was no small accomplishment. In the 1840s and 1850s, part-time clerks hand-copied documents working at home or outside of government offices. Of 26 temporary clerks listed in 1848, five were identified as "Female." Their compensation for the year ranged from $44.19 to $174.11. As late as 1863, *The Employments of Women; a Cyclopedia of Woman's Work* stressed the point that in ordinary employment women were paid about half of the salary of men doing the same work.

Friction continued without abatement in the Patent Office as President James Buchanan came into office. McClelland pressured Mason to remove government officials having differing political views than Buchanan. Distressed by the "spoils system," Mason protested saying that the law allowed the Commissioner exclusive rights to make all temporary appointments. McClelland ordered Mason to forward nominations to him and the Secretary would make the appointments. Reacting, Barton commented: "There is great talk about cutting off official heads, but no specimens of decapitation yet."

Barton received her last voucher for $88 in May 1857 after Buchanan's inauguration. She had supported John C. Frémont for president and was considered as harboring "black Republican" liberal anti-slavery sentiments. Mason resigned on August 4, 1857. A Washington *Daily National Intelligencer* article reported that Mason had discharged his duties with responsibility and delicateness hardly equalled by any one of his able predecessors.

During the next few years Barton was at her home in North Oxford, Massachusetts. Although pressured to return to teaching, she responded: "I have outgrown that, or that me." After Lincoln's election in 1860, she was recalled to a job in the Patent Office in December. This time, she was a humble copyist being paid at eight cents per 100 words for recording specifications and making office copies. Rates for copyists were reduced from 10 cents due to budget restrictions. Under an act of Congress, those people so affected did get compensation at a later date.

Barton received more than $1,000 in back pay to make up for the lowered war-time salary.

Congressman De Witt was defeated for re-election and Barton sought out Massachusetts Senator Henry Wilson to be her patron. Wilson did much to aid her later activities.

Although Barton stated that "I resigned and went into direct service to the sick and wounded troops," it appears that she was carried on the Patent Office payroll during the entire war until August 1865. However, after the summer of 1862, Barton may have hired Edward Shaw to perform her duties and shared her earnings with him. This practice was common under D.P. Holloway, the new Commissioner of Patents, who made exceptions for anyone helping the army.

Barton's first experience nursing occurred in 1832 when she was only 11 years old and lasted for two years. Her brother David fell from a ridgepole during a barn raising and was seriously injured and bedridden. She described her childhood nursing: "From the first days and nights of illness, I remained near his side. I could not be taken away from him, except by compulsion ... I learned to take all directions for his medicines from the physician, and to administer them ... I was the accepted and acknowledged nurse of a man almost too ill to recover. "

David survived the heroic medical measures of the times: the bloodletting, the leeches and the plasters that Barton applied. Eventually, he recovered after being treated with "steam baths" by unorthodox botanic practitioners. It's possible that this childhood encounter with regular physicians may have engendered Barton's distrust of medical practitioners.

As the Civil War began in April 1861, a 39 year old Barton wrote in her diary: "I'm well and strong and young -- young enough to go to the front. If I can't be a soldier, I'll help soldiers." Her ambitions did not receive enthusiastic support from male administrators at all levels of the army. After intense lobbying, Barton secured a historic directive from the U.S. Army Surgeon General, William A. Hammond in July 1862: "Miss C.H. Barton has permission to go on the sick transports in any direction -- for the purpose of distributing comforts for the sick and wounded and nursing them -- always subject to the direction of the surgeon in charge."

Immediately after the Battle of Cedar Mountain in August 1862, Barton rushed to the front to render aid to the several thousand Northern casualties. Army surgeon Dr. James I. Dunn described the scene in a letter to his wife: "She appeared in front of the hospital at twelve o'clock at night with a four-mule team loaded with everything needed: and at a time when we were entirely out of dressings of every kind, she supplied us with everything, and while the shells were still bursting in every direction ... she staid (*sic*) dealing out shirts to the naked wounded ... and preparing soup and seeing it prepared in all the hospitals ... I thought that night if heaven ever sent out a homely angel, she must be one, her assistance was so timely."

Dunn's letter was unofficially published in newspapers throughout the country. However, the M and the E in homely were deleted and Baron became known as the "holy angel" and the "Angel of the Battlefield."

As early as December 12, 1862, a headline in the *New York Times* referred to "Clara Barton, the Florence Nightingale of America." Rev. D. Francis Vinton "told with thrilling effect the story of the labors of one devoted woman who had most assiduously attended the sick and wounded at various battles, and who came most opportunely with aid after the terrible contest of Antieiam ... After paying a passing compliment to Victoria, the mother Queen, and Florence Nightingale, Dr. Vinson said the trinity would be completed by the name of this noble woman already alluded to, whose name is Clara Barton, [applause]..."

Barton was present at 16 battlefields during the Civil War. An historian vividly detailed Barton's activities on the battlefields in a 527 page book, extolling her valor during the war.

In February 1865, Barton's friend, Senator Wilson, urged President Lincoln to establish an agency to locate missing Northern soldiers. At least 143,155 graves were unidentified and 44,000 deaths were not even recorded. On March 11, about a month before he was assassinated, he wrote to Barton approving her offer to locate missing prisoners: "To the Friends of Missing Persons: Miss Clara Barton has kindly offered to search for the missing prisoners of war. Please address her at Annapolis, giving her the name, regiment, and company of any missing prisoner."

More than 105,000 handwritten letters were prepared and sent by Barton and her few assistants in this four year project to locate the missing men. Barton accomplished her most striking work at the infamous Confederate prison camp in Andersonville, Georgia. Almost

13,000 soldiers were identified and given proper memorials as Barton wrote: "I saw their little graves marked ... raised over them the flag they loved, and died for, and left them to their rest ..." Congress was so impressed with Barton's work that an appropriation of $15,000 was voted to repay her for her expenses.

Beginning in October 1866, Barton took to the lecture circuit to stimulate public support and to raise money for her missing soldiers project. Despite chronic stage fright and recurrent earaches, bronchial distress and sore throats, she maintained a formidable speaking schedule. In one month in 1868, Barton made 14 appearances and a total of 300 in 1867 and 1868 alone. An agent booked her talks, but she also scheduled some herself. Barton was paid from $75 to $125 per lecture, the same rate as male lecturers. Her speeches included topics such as "How the Republic Was Saved," "Work and Incidents of Army Life," and "War Without the Tinsel." On announcements, Barton was billed as the "Heroine of Andersonville" and the "American Florence Nightingale." The admission price was 25 cents. Barton was extremely effective as a public speaker even though the task was always a strain for her. "All speech-making terrifies me. First, I have no taste for it, lastly I hate it." About one speech, the *Syracuse Times* reported: "Few eyes but were dim; few hearts but were saddened." Eventually, the exhausting schedule took its toll.

During a lecture in Portland, Maine on a winter's night in 1868, Barton's voice gave out. After she left the stage, a doctor told her: "Your throat is exhausted. Rest is the only cure. You ought to go to Europe. Get away from everything and everybody, and let your system build up again." During 1868, Barton's diary mentions taking prescriptions of "pickley ash bark, peach stoned meats, wild cherry bark, poplar bark, red peruvian bark, golden seed, sassafras," all steeped and sweetened with white sugar, and to mix "a pint of Bay rum" with "allspice." A year later she was still too ill to speak at the twentieth anniversary of the Seneca Falls feminist convention. Barton wrote: "Nervous prostration had declared itself ... ordered to Europe by my physician." Her doctor prescribed three years of complete rest. In August 1869, Barton recovered enough to take the trip abroad and sailed for Europe. She disembarked and toured in Scotland, then went sightseeing in London with a stopover in Paris on her way to Geneva, Switzerland where the climate was supposedly ideal for throat ailments.

In Geneva, Barton met Dr. Louis Appia and learned about the 1864 Treaty of Geneva and the International Committee of the Red Cross. When Barton learned of the Treaty, she was intrigued by the concept. It had already been ratified by 32 nations, but not the U.S. Under the Treaty, ambulances, hospitals and personnel rendering care to the wounded were to be treated as neutrals in any war. After a visit to Napoleon's birthplace in Corscia, Barton returned to Geneva. In July 1870, the Franco-Prussian war erupted and Barton went to the front under the auspices of the Red Cross to participate in their activities. A *New York Tribune* reporter cited her work in Strasbourg in April 1871: "Miss Clara Barton, scarcely removed from the fatigues and indispositions resulting from her arduous and useful duties during the War of the Rebellion, was found again formost (*sic*) bestowing her care upon the wounded ..." After several visits to France and Italy, Barton left to sail back home on September 30, 1873, still "worn out, sleepless, wretched, and despairing." Barton rushed home extremely distressed that her sister Sally was ill with stomach cancer. After Sally died in May 1874, Barton suffered a complete nervous breakdown within days and was subject to colds, severe headaches, digestive trouble, and attacks of diarrhea. In November 1874, Barton suffered another crushing blow when her friend and protector, Henry Wilson, died. Barton reflected on the effect of his death on her: "It was too much. Body and soul were stricken ... I could not tell you the suffering, physical and mental ... and I would not if I could ... Only a small portion of the time could I stand alone; averaged less than two hours' sleep in 24 for almost a year; could not write my name for over four months, and could not have a letter read to me or see my friends or scarcely my attendants."

For two years Barton remained a helpless invalid who would "lie miserably whimpering in her bed." Believing that physicians didn't know how to relieve her suffering, Barton declared: "I must confess that my previously small share of confidence in medical aid and wisdom has not increased by last year's experience."

There can be no doubt that Barton's collection of multiple and ambiguous symptoms paralleled a new diagnosis emerging as an epidemic in the nation. A sampling of symptoms included: tenderness of the scalp, the spine, the teeth and gums; itching; abnormal secretions; "flying neuralgias;" "fidgetiness;" palpitation of pulse; sensitiveness to weather changes; ticklishness; need for stimulants; forgetfulness;

seminal emissions; distaste for certain foods or medicines; depression; timidity; headaches; chills; muscle spasms; and "atonic voice." Barton's symptoms obviously fit into the diagnosis and she joined other famous woman patients including authors Charlotte Perkins Gilman and Edith Wharton; and social activists Jane Addams, Susan B. Anthony and Catherine Beecher.

In 1869, neurologist Dr. George M. Beard coined the term "neurasthenia" to identify a lack of nervous force, a state of nervous exhaustion afflicting the new urban "brain-workers" in America. This condition, also known as "Americanitis" or "the American disease" appeared to be unique to the U.S. with a proclivity for women since they had "a natural tendency toward nervousness." Neurologist Dr. S. Weir Mitchell attributed the rapid increase of women with this disease to their attempts to compete with men which caused "mischief" with their health. Mitchell boasted of treating more women with neurasthenia than any other physician. Although overwork or stress were commonly cited as causes, there were physicians who thought that the reason for neurasthenia in women was more related to idleness and remaining passive to the creative power, more than anything else. Based on his Civil War experiences, Mitchell devised the "rest cure" as the standard therapy for neurasthenia. However, an enticing spectrum of prescription medicines, commercial medications and patent medicines were readily available to treat the illness.

Today, neurasthenia is a popular diagnosis in China, Korea, and Japan, where nerve forces remain an integral part of medical diagnosis. In Western Europe, a transitional society in Yugoslavia considered neurasthenia as a model of social psychopathology. In the U.S., investigators found a striking resemblance between chronic fatigue syndrome and neurasthenia and implicated the role of culture in making a diagnosis. This exposition elicited a host of critical letters to the editor of the *American Journal of Psychiatry*. Intriguingly, an April 1994 perspective in the *Journal of the American Medical Association* asked: Was Neurasthenia a "Legitimate Morbid Entity"? Regardless of whether the disease was legitimate or not, numerous diagnosed patients sought out the water-cure treatment, just as Barton did in 1876.

Sectarian therapists borrowed and adapted remedies from each other during the ebbs and flows of each particular sect. Phrenologists, Grahamites, botanic practitioners, vegetarians, hydropaths, and eclectic physicians used whatever worked in their practices. People sought out sectarian physicians in a revolt against the overuse of bleeding, mercury, antimony, harsh purgatives and salts by orthodox doctors. At its height in the 1850s, hydropathy was regarded as a panacea in America; there were more than 200 establishments. Hydropaths could earn a medical degree in about three months and between 20 to 30 percent of hydropathic physicians were women. "Wash and Be Healed" was the slogan of *The Water-Cure Journal* and more than 100,000 people addicted to aqua-mania subscribed to the publication which was printed by Orson and Lorenzo Fowler, renowned phrenologist brothers.

In an 1876 letter to the editor of the *Dansville (NY) Advertiser*, Dr. James Caleb Jackson briefly and concisely explained the purpose of his "Our Home on the Hillside" sanitarium: "Our Home is not a water-cure, nor a diet cure; it is a great institution come to be widely known all over the land as a place where the sick can come, and having the right conditions of life created, get well." Dr. Jackson used ten natural remedies: fresh air; health food; internal and external water; sunlight; comfortable dress; outdoor exercise; sleep; rest; and social influence. Patients at Our Home followed a slightly modified Sylvester Graham regimen with a no-meat diet, no tea, no coffee, no alcohol, fresh air, exercise, cleanliness, cold bathing, and the avoidance of tightly laced corsets. Our Home served two meals daily, breakfast at eight and dinner at 2:30. Hard beds of sea grass and cotton mattresses on wooden slats induced healthful slumber.

Jackson felt invalids needed emotional support more than medicine and his regimens used no drugs. Patients were provided with psychological succor and encouraged to accept themselves as they were. In a pre-Freudian insight, Jackson realized the connection between mental attitude and good health. One cynical theory speculated that the lengthy water-cure treatment offered women a legitimate escape from the rigors of daily life.

In early 1876, Barton corresponded with Dr. Jackson and his adopted daughter, Dr. Harriet N. Austin. After they sent her a circular, Barton responded and copiously gave them "the facts in the case" in colorful detail: "Although I cannot at *present* lay claim to the *highest flow* of animal spirits, I hope I am not a confirmed hypochondriac. I am not hysterical nor epileptic [*sic*], nor cataleptic - nor 'given to drink,' nor bed-ridden at *present*; and I trust not wholly incurable, although I have no right to expect the health I once had, and I do not ... My troubles are, I *suppose*, of disturbed circulation, indigestion, the liver, bowels, nerve-centers, &c &c. ... I have been ill two or three years ... I am *mainly* about my house this winter, but cannot expose myself with safety, or endure much strain upon the nervous system in any way, which is sure to avenge every such injury by a prompt attack upon the liver and bowels. I have no cough, nor any trouble with the lungs ... My sleep has become *fair* again, not always reliable. I have less heat along the spine, especially between the shoulders [earlier Barton described this as 'a hot sore spot' in the spine, high up between the shoulders, leading up to the base of the brain, bursting into flame at every over-taxation of mental energy.' ... but I still have nervous feet, and tender soles."

Despite the litany of ailments that Barton described, she realized the vague nature of her complaints. In a letter to a visiting German scholar, Barton elucidated: "My illness ... is what is known as 'prostration of the nervous system,' and very complete at that, I suppose. I am not aware of any decided organic disease ... but ... the price of not only my liberty, but my life is 'eternal vigilance' ..."

Recovering enough to be able to travel, in May 1876, Barton arrived as a patient at Our Home. After a brief period, she wrote to a relative: "I have now been here seven weeks and find no occasion to regret coming ... The institution is flourishing ... with about three hundred patients, or persons *as* patients ... I think I never saw together any group of people that combines the degree of intellect, general intelligence, and culture as is collected here ... [faculty skillful and competent] ... general means for promoting health through proper food, water, bathing, dress, rest, sunshine, open air, and pleasant surroundings are mainly relied upon; little or no medicines are ever used ... We have several excellent lectures in the Hall during the week and services on the Sabbath ... The tables are *excellent* and most abundantly supplied. Meats plainly but well cooked, the freshest of vegetables from their own gardens, and such abundance of fruit as I never saw ... in large fruit dishes ... the greatest abundance of 'Shaker' dried fruits ... New milk from their own dairy ... freshest of oatmeals and grahams, sweet butter, tapioca, etc. The vegetables are largely cooked in milk, and harmless. ... No fevers, no colics, but all up and about in the sunshine and on the stretchers and hammocks under the trees. One has only to be lazy and jolly, and get well, if they can. ... There are something like fifty people employed as *help*, ... but not one *servant* ... There is an amusement society, and one of its features is a beautiful dance once a week from 5 till 8 PM. Piano and violin music - no round dances - but cotillions and all dances which are *not injurious*, and the prettiest and most elegant dancers in the hall are from among the help."

Referring to herself as "Byas," a name Barton's young nieces called her, she described the "American Costume" attire at Our Home: "Byas wears no flannel, neither under nor over, but cotton flannel, then one of her little thin white sheet underskirts, and her linen dress, but it is all made over, has no belt, high boots and short stockings, so as to have no trouble with elastics or supporters. She is dressed just as free and easy as a gentleman with lots of pockets and perambulates around to suit herself."

Following the water-cure regimen at Our Home was no problem for Barton: "I have done everything to surround myself with healthful and strength-giving influences ... My flesh is also returning and I am regaining some power of endurance." Barton concluded that Our Home gave her "the knowledge and humanity that will permit me to rest if I need it, to recognize my necessities without shame, and perhaps come back a little into life." In a long and affectionate correspondence with Dr. Jackon he became "Father" and Barton "Clara, Beloved." On March 3, 1890, she wrote Father: "It was, I think, worth all my illness to have known 'Dansville'." With emphasis, Barton declared that the cure was a "wonder" and she energetically returned to her idea of establishing an American Red Cross.

In 1877, at age 55, Barton turned her attention to her most ambitious task. With her physical and mental health in control, she began the political struggle to induce the U.S. to ratify the Treaty of Geneva and set the stage for founding an American Red Cross organization. Barton resumed corresponding with Dr. Appia and unequivocally suggested a leadership role for herself: "If you feel that I can serve your cause, and humanity through it ... let me know your desires *at once*. If you will write me immediately upon receipt of this, asking ... that I do all in my power to aid you in your work ... I will have your letter placed before our President and Government and ask their sanction...."

On August 19, 1877, Gustave Moynier, president of the International Red Cross Committee, sent Barton a letter to be delivered to U.S. president Rutherford Hayes. Political opposition to foreign "entangling alliances" put a damper on the idea. To meet this isolationist posture, Barton circulated a pamphlet, "What the Red Cross Is," proposing that the American Red Cross engage in humanitarian work in times of peace, as well as war, to render relief in extraordinary calamities. This expansive amendment was adopted by the International Red Cross in 1884.

Making no headway politically, Barton campaigned for James Garfield. When he was elected president in 1881, he supported the Red Cross concept. Unfortunately Garfield was shot in July and died in September without signing the Geneva Convention. Nevertheless, Barton arranged to incorporate the American Association of the Red Cross on October 1, 1881 under the laws of Washington, DC. Barton was elected President and remained so for 23 years. In keeping with the wishes of Garfield, President Chester Arthur signed the Geneva Convention on March 1, 1882. About 12 years after Barton initially learned about the Red Cross, the institution was officially sanctioned in the U.S.

Almost immediately, a host of disasters and calamities struck the nation. Barton was 60 years old in 1881 and 83 in 1904. Yet, she was on the scene at each one or directly involved in the following national and international disasters: 1881 - Michigan forest fires; 1882 - Mississippi River floods; 1883 - Mississippi and Ohio River floods; 1883 - Tornado in Louisiana and Alabama; 1884 - Ohio and Mississippi River floods; 1886 - Charlestown earthquake; 1887 - Texas famine; 1888 - Tornado at Mt. Vernon, Il; 1888 - Florida yellow-fever epidemic; 1889 - Johnstown, Pa. flood; 1892 - Russian famine; 1893 - Tornado at Pomeroy, Iowa; 1893-94 - Hurricane and tidal wave, South Carolina Islands; 1986 - Armenian massacres in Turkey; 1898-1900 - Spanish-American War; 1900 - Galveston, Texas storm and tidal wave; and 1904 - Typhoid-fever epidemic, Butler, Pa.

In the early 1900s, a controversy arose within the Red Cross leadership. Inflammatory accusations declared that Barton mismanaged the Red Cross, that her accounting was careless, that funds were misappropriated and there was a call for a reorganization. Critics argued that Barton embellished the truth, was dishonest in her accounting of contributed funds, demanded blind loyalty from her associates, and ruthlessly used her power and personal influence to achieve her objectives. At first, Barton fought the "remonstrants," but on May 15, 1904 she resigned after having been named "Red Cross president for life." Infuriated, Barton's supporters asserted that Washington society women wrested the Red Cross away from her and made it "the sport of the smart set." Her friends said that President Theodore Roosevelt, "the Imperial One," abetted the designing society women and denied Barton a "square deal." Baron was devastated and retired to live in her Glen Echo, Maryland home. At age 90, on April 12, 1912, Barton died of double pneumonia at her home. Appropriately, her tombstone in North Oxford, Massachusetts has a red cross on top of it. She was honored all over the world in memorials. An editorial in the *New York Sun* was typical: "Clara Baron was more than brave. She devoted her life to humanity. She was one of the most useful of women, self-sacrificing to a degree, generous to a fault. Health and fortune she devoted to her great cause ... Is it not the finest kind of glory that when the American Red Cross is seen or mentioned the name of Clara Barton comes to mind like a benediction?"

Clara Barton was a complex person whose character, ambitions and desires were tempered by experiences early in her life. Influences of phrenology, the bitterness of sex discrimination and the water-cure psychohygenic remedies for her persistent bouts of neurasthenia shaped her personality. A six word summary of her lengthy career exemplifies the key to her administrative capabilities: "Think straight, plan carefully, and act boldly."

## FIRST, AND ONLY, FEMALE EVER AWARDED THE CONGRESSIONAL MEDAL OF HONOR

Mary Edwards Walker lived in an era when society expected women to be totally subservient to men. Yet, a male speaker at the Fifth National Women's Rights Convention in Philadelphia on October 18, 1854 advocated women's rights: "Credit not the old-fashioned absurdity that woman's is a secondary lot, ministering to the necessities of her lord and master." Contrary to expectations, Walker digressed from the popular concept of a woman on a pedestal and established her own identity in a man's world not seeking to "act the man" but to become the "true woman." While doing so, Walker acted as an intelligent, independent, irrepressible and indefatigable proponent for the major social movements of her time. These movements included moral reform to curb man's sexual appetite, advocating temperance toward total abstinence from alcohol, anti-slavery activities aiming for emancipation and abolition and equal rights for women on all matters without regard for gender. Invariably, these causes were linked to Walker's parental upbringing, to her medical education and to her social experiences.

When Walker was sixteen years old, she eagerly read the newspaper reports on the first women's rights Convention held in Seneca Falls, New York, about forty miles from her home in Oswego. Patterned after the U.S. Declaration of Independence, on July 20, 1848, the Convention adopted a Declaration of Sentiments and Resolutions beginning with the self-evident truth that "all men and women are created equal." This document was soundly denounced in the press, from the pulpit and in parlor room conversations. In the face of the ridicule, many of the signers of the Declaration withdrew their names as supporters.

Within this Victorian environmental milieu, Walker became a physician, a journalist, an author of two sensational books, a professional and popular lecturer, a political lobbyist, and a women's rights advocate. In addition, Walker was a lifelong leader in the national dress reform movement. She was energetic in an organized crusade to promote revolutionary changes in "unhygienic" feminine attire. Both males and females argued that stylish female attire was harmful to the health of women. Ladies used restrictive steel ribbed or whalebone corsets with tight lacing along with the cumbersome hoop skirts. In total, the sheer weight of the voluminous garments added about fifteen burdensome pounds.

On top of all that, Walker was, and still is, the only female to ever be awarded the Congressional Medal of Honor for battlefield valor. On June 10, 1982, in her birthplace of Oswego, the United States Postal Service honored her with a commemorative twenty cent stamp featuring her portrait and the wording: "Dr. Mary Walker, Army Surgeon, Medal of Honor."

Considering Walker's accomplishments and the intense emotional and often derogatory reactions to her activities, a distant great grandniece concluded that "she was one hundred years ahead of her time and no one could stomach it."

Walker's unique career and significant achievements are directly linked to the guideposts established within her family. Additionally, contemporary medical theories, medical education and medical practices influenced her lifelong activities.

Mary Edwards Walker was born on November 26, 1832 to Alvah and Vesta [Whitcomb] Walker. Her parents traced their roots back to the early settlers of Massachusetts. Operating a farm on Bunker Hill Road outside of Oswego, New York, both parents were teachers, abolitionists, and liberal thinkers. In contrast to current thinking, Alvah Walker provided his five daughters, as well as his two sons, with an education. Often, he admonished his daughters about their health being impaired by vice-like "coffin" corsets and tight fitting clothes. Walker's father was learned in medicine and may have actually been a non-practicing physician. There were medical texts in her house that she thumbed through regularly. She probably acquired an inclination to study medicine from him. Both parents supported Walker's desire to become a physician despite obvious societal disapproval of women entering the profession.

Following her sisters, Walker attended the Falley Seminary in Fulton, New York. Leaving the Seminary in 1852, she taught school at Minetto, New York, for about two years. During this time, Walker saved her money and crystallized her plans to become a physician. She knew it was not going to be easy.

American society persisted in discrimination against women physicians into the twentieth century. In Cincinnati, Ohio, the *Lancet and Observer*, a professional medical journal, furiously denounced Starling Medical College for awarding a medical degree to a woman:

"Why not grant the degree to sucking babes? There never was a woman fitted to practice medicine, surgery and obstetrics, no matter how long she may have studied. The duties of the physician are contrary and opposed to her moral, intellectual and physical nature ... Is it then left for a respectable school to so far insult all gentlemen in the profession as to admit to the Temple of Aesculapius those who have no right in it?"

Women were not welcomed in the traditional medical schools. An 1848 obstetrics text declared: "She (woman) has a head almost too small for the intellect but just large enough for love."

Elizabeth Blackwell was the first woman accepted to an obscure regular medical school in Geneva, New York. Rumors persisted that a fluke vote of the student body in 1847 approved her acceptance. After 15 months of study, she graduated on January 23, 1849. Relevantly, in October 1849, the Central Medical College at Syracuse, New York was the first sectarian medical school to adopt an explicit policy of co-education. In February 1850, Central Medical College graduated the second woman physician in the United States, Dr. Lydia Folger Fowler.

Sectarian medical schools emphasized different medical therapies. A botanic medical school stressed natural remedies borrowed from the Indians combined with vapor baths/steaming, peppering and puking. A hydropathic school relied upon natural cures with an emphasis upon water cures. A homeopathic school taught students to use infinitesimal amounts of the illness to cure the ailment. Eclectic schools combined a variety of treatments borrowed from all the other sects. Furthermore, medical practitioners could incorporate mesmerism, phrenology, spiritualism or vegetarianism into their practice. Walker's medical education opportunities were much greater at the sectarian schools that sought to demystify and deprofessionalize traditional medicine.

Just after her twenty-first birthday, in December 1853, Walker was accepted by the eclectic Syracuse Medical College, which was unrelated to Syracuse University. Opening in 1851, Syracuse Medical College proposed that "nothing should be used as a remedy that will injure the human constitution, and that all means used should have a direct tendency to sustain and not depress the vital powers." There was a faculty of nine physicians including the founder of the college, Dr. S. H. Potter. In addition, Dr. Wooster Beach gave lectures on the theory and practice of medicine and Dr. S. O. Gleason on the water-cure.

Medical instruction consisted of three terms of thirteen weeks each. Between terms students apprenticed with practicing physicians. Walker took an assortment of imposing courses: anatomy; surgery; the practice of medicine and medical pathology; obstetrics; diseases of women and children; physiology; materia medica; therapeutics and pharmacy; chemistry; and medical jurisprudence. Tuition was $55 per term plus $5 for matriculation and $15 for graduation with about $1.50 a week for room and board. With an expenditure of about $253.50 and eighteen months of study, Walker became Dr. Walker in June 1855, the only woman in the graduating class. She joined woman physicians with similar training including Dr. Harriet Austin, Dr. Ellen Harman, and Dr. Lydia Stowbridge.

Following her medical school graduation, Walker married her classmate, Dr. Albert E. Miller, on November 16, 1855. Abiding by her beliefs, Walker was married in trousers and dress coat, and the promise to "obey" was omitted from the vows. Dr. Miller had an office at 60 Dominick Street in Rome, New York. Joining him, Walker supposedly concentrated her clinical efforts in obstetrics and pediatrics. However, Walker saw male patients, never gave up her maiden name, certainly was not subservient, and the marriage was short-lived. Her husband cultivated a nonclinical penchant for women and was unfaithful. They never lived together again after Walker ordered him out in 1859. In the summer of 1860, Walker moved to Delhi, Ohio to secure a divorce. However, she did not complete the requirements and her divorce did not become final until 1869.

As Walker started her own practice, a small ad appeared in the Rome, New York *Sentinel* on March 14, 1860:

---
**FEMALE PHYSICIAN**
DR. MARY WALKER HAS REMOVED TO NO. 48 DOMINICK STREET OPPOSITE THE "ARCADE," OVER MESSRS. H.S. & W.O. SHELLY'S CLOTHING STORE.
THE DOCTOR EXPRESSES HER GRATITUDE TO THE ROMANS FOR THEIR LIBERAL PATRONAGE, AND SOLICITS A CONTINUANCE OF THE SAME.
OFFICE FIRST DOOR AT THE RIGHT OF THE STAIRS.
OFFICE HOURS: 7 TO 8 A.M., AND 1 TO 3 AND 6 TO 8 P.M.

---

Referring to the ad, the newspaper editor added: "As there is generally alleged to be so much rivalry and jealousy between those of the medical profession, we hardly dare to venture to give one of them a 'puff.' Those who prefer the skill of a female physician to that of a male, have now an excellent opportunity to make their choice."

In 1862, Walker attended the Hygeio Therapeutic College in New York City, which was chartered in 1857 by Dr. Russell T. Trall. About fifty percent of the prior graduates of this water-cure medical school were women. Instruction included lectures and a few clinics at Bellevue Hospital. For Walker, this curriculum could only be considered a refresher or postgraduate training. This unconventional medical school did have a woman faculty member; Dr. Huldah Page, Professor of physiology, hygiene and obstetrics. Walker received another medical diploma on March 31, 1862.

Why did Walker attend this water-cure medical school? Water therapy captivated women with a reliance on natural cures as contrasted with the harsh, purgative, heroic and debilitating remedies of traditional medical care: blood-letting; leeches; wet cupping; cathartics; and emetics. In rebellion against those drastic remedies prescribed by regular medical practitioners, a non-physician zealot, Mary Gove Nichols, founded an unchartered school, the American Hydropathic Institute in 1851. Nichols explained her gender-specific rationale for women as physicians: "Women are particularly fitted to practice the art of healing ... [because of the] tenderer love, the sublimer devotion, the never to be wearied patience and kindness of woman."

Nichols detailed "the principles and results of water treatment in the cure of acute and chronic diseases" in her book, *Experience in Water-Cure*. Relative to child birth, Nichols stated that "gestation and parturition are as natural functions as those of digestion." She regularly wrote articles for the *Water-Cure Journal*, whose masthead slogan was "Wash and Be Healed." Walker and Nichols were kindred souls; "ideological radicals relative to sex stratification and gender roles."

During the Civil War, Walker's medical qualifications were questioned. Dr. Roberts Bartholow was appointed to a medical board to consider her employment as an Army medical officer:"She betrayed such utter ignorance of any subject in the whole range of medical science, that we found it a difficult matter to conduct an examination ... she had no more medical knowledge than any ordinary housewife ... She had never been, so far as we could learn, within the walls of a medical college or hospital, for the purpose of obtaining a medical education."

Despite the harsh criticism of Walker's medical education, her training was most likely average for the times. Her alleged "medical condemnation" may be attributed to the deep-seated prejudices against female physicians bolstered by the Victorian concepts of appropriate behavior for "genteel" women. Certainly, Walker's rebellion against gender constraints did not endear her and other female physicians to the male dominated medical profession. As late as December 1893, Dr. Ellen Curtis Gage bitterly complained to the American Medical Association that the all male Salt Lake Medical Society in Utah "turned a cold shoulder to me ... I was turned down for admission" because the society did not admit women. Dr. Gage was refused membership despite the fact that she was a member of the national association and the Chicago Medical Society for seven years before moving to Utah. In 1905, Dr. Carol N. Nadelson remembered attending a medical lecture and learning that "hard study killed desire in women, took away their beauty, brought on hysteria, neurasthenia, dyspepsia, astigmatism and dysmenorrhea."

In 1961, a physician reviewing Walker's life said "that her medical training was a diploma-mill, once-over-lightly affair cannot be doubted ... she took time out from her war-time service to garner another *phony M.D. degree...*"

There was considerable rivalry for patients and Walker's medical practice did not flourish. In 1861, after the first battle of Bull Run, Walker quickly gave up her meager practice in Rome, New York to go to Washington, D.C. She applied to Surgeon General Clement A. Finley for a commission as a medical officer. However, Union Army Examining Boards usually rejected all sectarian physicians as unfit for appointment and women were not even considered. As the need for physicians increased, competent doctors were appointed regardless of therapeutic training, but still no women. In contrast, the Confederate Army did accept botanic and eclectic trained male physicians.

Without waiting for an appointment, Walker volunteered to care for wounded and sick soldiers at the makeshift Indiana Hospital on the unfinished top floor of the U.S. Patent Office. At the hospital, she was "a whirling efficient combination of physician, nurse, orderly, mail clerk, Red Cross worker, and social service investigator." In a letter home, Walker wrote: "I am Assistant Physician and Surgeon in this hospital. We have about eighty patients now. We have five very nice lady nurses, and a number of gentlemen nurses ... Every soul in this hospital has to abide by my orders as much as though Dr. [J.N.] Green gave them."

Though she worked without pay, Walker acted "with the knowledge and consent of the Army authorities." She wore a modified Union officer's blue uniform: her jacket was cut like a blouse to fit loosely at the neck; her trousers were gold-striped, with the surgeon's green sash at her waist; and she topped off the uniform with a felt hat with encircling gold cord. She also served at the Forest Hall Prison in Georgetown, in tent hospitals at Chattanooga, Tennessee, and at Virginia battle sites in Warrenton and Fredericksburg.

Her activities inspired the imagination of a *New York Tribune* reporter in his colorful, most likely exaggerated, description of her wartime service: "Among the unmarshalled host of camp-followers of the army, not the least noteworthy personage is Miss Mary E. Walker, or "Dr. Walker" as she is usually styled ... She can amputate a limb with the skill of an old surgeon, and administer medicine equally as well. Strange to say that, although she has frequently applied for a permanent position in the medical corps, she has never been formally assigned to any particular duty ... We will add that the lady referred to is exceedingly popular among the soldiers in the hospitals, and is undoubtedly doing much good."

Walker wrote directly to President Abraham Lincoln asking to be assigned to the female ward of Douglas Hospital. On January 16, 1864, the President replied: "If they [Army Medical Department] are willing for Dr. Mary Walker to have charge of a female ward, if there be one, I also am willing." However, Lincoln would not "with strong hand, thrust among them anyone, male or female, against their consent."

Toward the end of January 1864, Walker was sent to the 52nd Ohio Volunteer Infantry Regiment in Chattanooga, Tennessee to replace the Company Surgeon who had died unexpectantly. Finally, on March 11, 1864, she received a contract as an Acting Assistant Surgeon at $80 per month. It was rumored that Walker's medical appointment was a cover-up for her activities as a spy. Supporting the spy rumor, an October 1865 Judge Advocate General's report stated that Walker "passed frequently beyond our lines far within those of the enemy, and at one time gained information that led General Sherman so to modify his strategic operations as to save himself from a serious reverse and obtain success where defeat before seemed to be inevitable."

During that tour of duty, she cared for starving and poverty-stricken civilians. In enemy territory on April 10, 1864, Walker was captured by confederate soldiers. She was transported to Castle Thunder, a political prison on Cary Street in Richmond, Virginia. Confederate Captain Benedict J. Semmes described the capture scene: "[we] were all amused and disgusted ... at the sight of a thing that nothing but the debased and depraved Yankee nation could produce ... She was dressed in the full uniform of a Federal Surgeon ... not good looking and of course had tongue enough for a regiment of men ... She would be more at home in a 'lunatic asylum.'"

During Walker's imprisonment, she caused quite a disturbance by refusing to wear clothes "more becoming to her sex." After four months in prison, in another possible first, Walker was exchanged "man-for-man" for a six foot confederate surgeon from Tennessee on August 12, 1864.

Following her release from prison, in September 1864 Walker received $432.36 for about five months of service as a contract surgeon; she was in prison for four of the five months. Awaiting assignment, Walker managed to confront Major-General William T. Sherman in Atlanta and demanded an army medical department commission.. Surprised, the General attacked Walker's wearing of "breeches:" "Why don't you wear proper clothing! That toggery is neither one thing or the other." Stridently, Sherman concluded the conversation: "Put on decent clothes ... enter the hospitals where our boys are dying of wounds and fever, and imitate the example of women in hoops and petticoats, who are devoting their time to the work of nursing."

By the 22nd of September, Walker was the medical officer at a Women's Prison Hospital in Louisville, Kentucky. Six months later, on March 22, 1865, she was placed in charge of an orphan asylum in Clarksville, Tennessee and was also responsible for refugee families in the area. Later, Walker was transferred to Washington and her contract was terminated on June 15, 1865. Due to a war-time eye injury attributed to partial muscular atrophy while imprisoned, she was awarded a disability pension of $8.50 per month starting June 13, 1865. Her injury was painful, did not respond to treatment and resulted in her wearing glasses. After Walker's considerable political campaigning, the pension was raised to $20 per month in 1899.

Presidents Abraham Lincoln and Andrew Johnson were both

aware of Walker's services. President Johnson asked Secretary of War Edwin M. Stanton to look into the merits and legality of presenting an award to someone never commissioned by the Army. In his twelve page report to the Secretary, the Judge-Advocate commented: "The case of this lady, when her sacrifices, her fearless energy under circumstances of peril, her endurance of hardship and imprisonment at the hands of the enemy, and especially her active patriotism and eminent loyalty are considered, may well be regarded as an almost isolated one in the history of the rebellion; and to signalize and perpetuate it as such would seem to be desirable."

Acting on that recommendation, President Johnson bestowed the Congressional Medal of Honor for Meritorious Service on the diminutive lady; she was only about five feet tall. Her citation from the Executive Office commented that she: "rendered valuable service to the Government, and her efforts have been earnest and untiring in a variety of ways ... devoted herself with much patriotic zeal to the sick and wounded soldiers, both in the field and hospitals, to the detriment of her own health ... endured hardships as a prisoner of war four months in a southern prison while acting as a contract surgeon; and ... in the opinion of the President an honorable recognition of her services and sufferings should be made ... and that the usual medal of honor for meritorious services be given her."

Many years later, Walker said that she was awarded the Medal of Honor because she went into enemy territory to care for the suffering inhabitants when "no man surgeon was willing to respond for fear of being taken prisoner."

However, the awarding of the Medal was not the last of it. An Act of Congress mandated that the award should be made for action "involving actual conflict with an enemy, by gallantry or intrepidity, at risk of life, above and beyond the call of duty." A following June 3, 1916 Congressional Act ordered the Army and Navy to review the records of all Medal of Honor recipients since the decoration had first been awarded in 1862 to affirm the revised standards. Originally, the only qualification was that persons "shall most distinguish themselves by their gallantry in action, and other soldierlike qualities."

A five man board of retired officers reviewed the 2,625 Medal recipients for the Army. Based on the new rules, Walker was among the 911 medal recipients who were disqualified. Her intensive political efforts to have the board's decision reversed were unsuccessful. Nevertheless, she refused to return the two medals; the Army had sent her a new medal with a modified design in 1907. Walker proclaimed that she would continue to wear both medals: "One of them I will wear every day, and the other I will wear on occasions." True to her word, Walker wore her Congressional Medal of Honor every day until her death.

Even after her death, the battle continued. There was a further review by the Army Board of Correction of Military Records. This Board stated that "had it not been for her sex, she [Walker] would in all probability have been tendered a commission in 1861 ... When consideration is given to her total contribution, her acts of distinguished gallantry, self-sacrifice, patriotism, dedication and unflinching loyalty to her country, despite the apparent discrimination because of her sex, the award of the Medal of Honor appears to have been appropriate, and the Award was in consonance with the criteria established by the Act of April 27, 1916, and in keeping with the highest tradition of military services."

On June 10, 1977, the Secretary of War ordered Walker's Medal of Honor reinstated and corrected the official records.

Coincidentally, William F. Cody [Buffalo Bill] was stripped of his Medal of Honor at the same time as Walker. In July 1989, the Army restored Buffalo Bill's medal awarded in 1872 for his gallantry as a scout during the Indian wars. Of the 911 persons stripped of their medals in 1917, Walker, Cody and four other Indian Wars scouts were the only ones to regain their awards.

After the Civil War, Walker's medical practice took second place to her diverse endeavors that "concerned every major social institution: law and the polity; the economy; the family and sexuality; religion; education; cultural definitions of femininity [the lady]; and physical restraints on activity."

Usually, Walker was in her District of Columbia medical office on L Street NW, near the corner of Tenth, from September to June. When Congress adjourned, she switched her base of operations to Oswego from July to September. After 1900, at age sixty-eight, she was mainly in Oswego tending to the family farm and limiting her activities somewhat. Whatever role she played, Walker continued to integrate her lifelong social concerns into each one.

Throughout her life, Walker was unyielding in her campaign to reform feminine attire. Intermittently, Walker wrote articles for *The Sibyl*, a dress reform magazine published and edited by Dr. Lydia Hasbrouck of Middletown, New York.

Walker's attire evolved until by the 1870s, she switched to wearing complete male formal attire including black striped trousers, a stiff-bosomed white shirt with a black bow tie, black frock coat and a black high silk hat. However, she did retain her hair in curls so everybody would know she was a woman. Reflecting society's reaction to her costume, humorist Bill [Edgar W.] Nye facetiously referred to Walker as "a self-made man." Despite the almost complete cross-dressing, there is no evidence that Walker entered into homosexual relationships.

From 1866 to as late as 1913, Walker was arrested a dozen or more times for "masquerading in men's clothes." Newspaper articles mentioned her "bifurcated garments." New York City's Police Commissioner, Thomas C. Acton, apologized publicly for an arrest on Canal Street on June 14, 1866. Hostile reactions to her male attire and her outspoken nature often resulted in Walker having to endure the taunts of rowdy boys, the throwing of rotten eggs, and dogs attacking her. Even as Walker aged, this hostility persisted. Around Halloween 1913, when Walker was almost eighty-one, she foiled a "band of young miscreants' when they tried to tar and feather her at her Oswego home.

As a practical contribution to society, Walker designed a "Dress Reform Undersuit" to discourage seduction and rape: "The linen is made with a high neck and loose waist, and whole drawers, and long sleeves with wristbands attached; thus making a complete undersuit in one garment. The drawers are folded over the ankles and the stockings are adjusted over the drawers, thus keeping the ankles warm and also keeping the stockings arranged without elastic or other bands, or any troublesome or injurious arrangement, most of which impede the circulation and produce varicose veins, and weariness in walking."

In an obituary, the *Literary Digest* declared that "her eccentric dress drew attention from her real achievements." That article quoted the *New York Sun* deploring the fact that "the trousers, frock coat, starched shirt and collar, and high silk hat, in which she chose to attire her little body, effectively overshadow the work she did."

As a member of the Central Women's Suffrage Bureau in

Washington, Walker solicited funds to endow a chair in medicine at Howard University to be filled by a woman professor.

Walker and a few suffragists attempted to register to vote in 1871 but were immediately turned away by the election board. Registrars contended that legally none but males could vote. Walker scolded the registrars: "... you but add new proof that this is a tyrannical government sustained by force and not by justice."

Frequently stating publicly that there was no need for a constitutional amendment to enable women to vote, Walker aroused the wrath of the suffragettes. To formally present her views, Walker published her "Crowning Constitutional Argument" in 1907. Essentially, Walker insisted that the Constitution and some States already granted women the right to vote. To the discomfort of the organized suffragette movement, Walker personally testified so at U.S. House of Representatives hearings on woman suffrage in 1912 and 1914.

Walker delivered formal and informal lectures. Her topics reflected her special interests: hygiene, medicine, dress reform, suffrage and women's rights. In 1866, Walker sailed to Great Britain with Dr. Susannah Way Dodds of St. Louis as an invited delegate to the annual meeting of the Society for the Promotion of Social Science. After being invited to address the assembly, Walker spoke on: the prevention of infanticide; decried capital punishment; urged female dress reform; and encouraged equal rights for women. Walker observed at a number of hospitals and facilities. Hoping to facilitate the acceptance of women in medicine, James Edmunds, President and principal promoter of a female medical society, arranged for Walker's appearances and lectures.

At precisely eight o'clock on November 20, 1866, Walker gave her first lecture at St. James' Hall in London. Her subject was "The Experiences of a Female Physician in College, in Private Practice, and in the Federal Army." Most British newspapers were complimentary, although the reviews were mixed. Reporters denounced the hecklers in the gallery as: "a mob of unruly boys, alleged, we hope falsely, to be medical students [who were] noisy and vulgar [and] even indecent [but she] cowed the gallery-full of stupid gentlemen." A reporter, using the pen-name Melampus, labeled the behavior "cowardly ruffanism" and designated the hecklers as "drunken costermongers." Melampus concluded: "Let them [women] study medicine if they desire it." Newspaper reviews led to an additional thirty lecture invitations including a ten city Scottish tour arranged by an agent, Monson Kyle.

Spiteful American medical journals selected harsh criticism from their British counterparts. Under "Varia," the *New York Medical Journal* cited a picturesque example: "The *Medical Press & Circular*, with a bitterness and intensity of satire surpassed only by its coarseness, styles her [Walker] the American Medical Non-descript, and suggests as an attractive subject for her public entertainments, 'Why Not? or, Clitoridectomy and its Uses.'"

After the strenuous lecture circuit, Walker was off to Paris in June 1867 for a visit to the Exposition, sightseeing and a few hospital visits. Back to London in July, she spoke before the Female Medical Society and the London Dialectical Society before returning to the United States.

Beginning in 1868, Walker toured the American lecture circuit speaking about her war experiences and medical activities. She gave her impressions of European women's suffrage to an audience at the Universal Franchise Association in Washington in May 1868. After an introduction by suffragette Belva Lockwood, she lectured on "Pure Love and Sacred Marriage" at Washington's Union League Hall in June 1869.

As her income from lecturing diminished and her eye problems and other ailments limited her ability to practice medicine, Walker became desperate for money. She had only $8.50 per month from her disability pension, so she searched for a job. After considerable legislative politicking, Walker was appointed a mailroom clerk in the Interior Department Pensions Office in April 1882. Considering Walker's background, her work was routine. She was "sought to give prescriptions and loan small sums of money, and do little offices of kindness that I invariably responded to." D. L. Gitt, Walker's supervisor, complained of her excessive absences; she missed 112 days in one year. Walker's complaints included her eyes, her chest, her right arm and finally the left arm. Gitt labeled her as "violent, high tempered and abusive ... aggressive and insolent." In June 1883, Walker returned to Oswego and shortly thereafter received a discharge notice from Secretary of the Interior H. M. Teller. Outraged, she fought her firing through five months of appeals all the way up to President Chester Arthur. However, her discharge was upheld and that ended her government service.

In 1877, Walker eagerly intensified her lecture activities. A professional agency, Kohn and Middletown, suggested a tour of sideshows and dime museums in Buffalo, Chicago, Cincinnati, Detroit and other mid-western cities at a fee of $150 per week. A March 25, 1893 *Toledo Blade* article headline announced her week-long appearance at Wonderland: "DR. MARY WALKER. From the Platform of Princes to the Stage of Freaks:"

Other features in the Curio Hall included: Captain Sydney Hinmann, captain of the life-saving crew at Coney Island, with his complete life-saving outfit; Professor Stendell with his experiments in electricity; the Mexican feather workers; and Stephen Stephens and his London Punch and Judy show.

Using picturesque language and an energetic rapid-fire delivery, Walker lectured on the science of dress, women's franchise, labor unrest, the evils of tobacco, human electricity and the curiosities of the brain. At New York City's Vine Street Dime Museum, she declared that the constant swaying of crinoline spread over hoopskirts on the hips of women caused nervous afflictions.

In the Armory over Old Central Market in Washington, D.C, on February 17, 1897, Walker addressed about two thousand people attending the first Congress of Mothers. That organization became the National Congress of Parents and Teachers.

Although speaking engagements were infrequent in 1912, Walker nonetheless added a lecture on "A Safe and Sane Fourth of July" to protest the deaths and injuries from fireworks.

When not on the lecture circuit, Walker forcefully lobbied Congress regarding dress reform, equal rights for women and a myriad of other liberal causes.

She also lobbied for personal reasons. Between 1874 and 1898, at least thirteen bills were presented to Congress: for the relief of Dr. Walker; to increase her pension; for war claims; and to reimburse her for a botched appointment as a clerk in the Treasury Department. Finally, she got her pension increased and did receive $900.00 from the Treasury Department.

Active in New York State politics, she declared herself a candidate for the U.S. Senate in 1881 in a letter published in the *Oswego Times*. Among her qualifications Walker listed "her ownership of a brain that is never made abnormal by the use of anodynes or stimulants; her ignoring attire that destroys health, ruins morals and deranges finance; her moral courage and moral worth - these combined excellences guarantee both faithfulness and fitness ..."

A family descendent described a memorable moment resulting when Walker made a political medical referral: "Through a friend, Mary Walker, Anna [Dr. Anna Easton Lake] received the presidential appointment to come to the White House as physician to President Grover Cleveland's daughter who was a victim of cerebral palsy. The appointment came at the beginning of Cleveland's second term."

Around October 1, 1913, the annual meeting of the New York State Historical Association convened in Oswego. Congressman Luther Mott introduced the elderly Walker to one of the speakers, Assistant Secretary of the Navy Franklin Delano Roosevelt. Walker spoke to FDR about her misgivings about the other Roosevelt [Teddy], but assured FDR that he appeared to be a different kind of person.

As the U.S. entered World War I, Walker fired off a telegram to Germany's Kaiser Wilhelm offering the use of her Bunker Hill farm as the site for a peace conference. Her cablegram was reprinted in full in the *Oswego Palladium* of April 11, 1917. There appears to have been no reply to the offer.

While evidence is not certain, Walker may also have been an inventor of sorts. A number of sources credit Walker with originating the postal card return receipt for registered letters, with improving third class mailing procedures, with advocating the use of the sender's return address to prevent mail from going astray and with inventing the inside neckband on men's shirts to protect the skin from being rubbed by the collar-button.

Since Walker's practice over the years was minimal, Walker was out of touch with medicine. Yet, she still spoke her mind on professional topics and hygiene. Sometimes her theories demonstrated future remedies. At other times, she completely missed the mark.

In 1910, she belittled the "humbug" theory that germs caused tuberculosis: "No microbes or germs can live in the live tissues of the lungs. They are not the cause of tubercules, but the result of worn-out tissue. Tubercules are formed by smoke, and tobacco smoke is worse than any other kind because the cinders are more poisonous, containing nicotine."

In response to a newspaper advertisement one year later, Walker offered to sell her "living right index finger" for enough money "to erect a consumptive ward on my estate." Walker wrote that because she believed tuberculosis was not contagious, money was not forthcoming from other sources. She was seventy-nine when she offered up her index finger.

In the *Oswego Palladium* of May 9, 1910, Walker revealed how to prevent heart failure caused by overwork, mental strain or spasmodic coughing. Her CPR-like remedy: "When unusual palpitations occur, place the left hand just below the heart with the fingers pointing to the center of the chest. Place the right hand over the left with the fingers touching the left wrist. Apply pressure until the heart beats normally again."

Walker opposed compulsory vaccination for smallpox. In 1911, she testified in Albany before the Health Committee of the New York Senate and Assembly. She contended that the claims for prevention of the disease were grossly exaggerated and that vaccinations were being done for the fees involved. Walker advised onions as a preventive and supported the proposed McManus-Boylan bill allowing unvaccinated children to attend school when their parents conscientiously opposed vaccination.

As late as 1916, Walker expressed her views on infantile paralysis in the *Knickerbocker Press*. Denying that poliomyelitis was contagious, she condemned quarantine and attributed causation in children to their consuming more milk than adults and their inability to shed the poison of tobacco.

Late in the nineteenth century, Walker reiterated all her medical theories and social concerns in autobiographical books.

Between her lecturing and lobbying, Walker wrote two books. In 1871, the puzzlingly entitled *Hit. A Woman's Thoughts About Love and Marriage, Divorce, etc.* was published with a dedication to: "My Parents, and also to the Practical Dress Reformers ... and also to My Professional Sisters ... and lastly to that Great Sisterhood which embraces women with their thousand unwritten trials and sorrows that God has not given to men the power to comprehend."

Walker held men in low regard. She believed that the idea of women needing male protection was a man-made myth and a scheme for man's tyranny. To male readers, she said: "You are not our protectors ... If you were, who would there be to protect us from?" To the point, in 1895, Walker founded a colony for young women, a Utopia she called "Adamless Eden." Women would pledge themselves to single blessedness and go forth as models of the new womanhood. This idea did not succeed and "Adamless Eden" remained a colony of one.

In one hundred eighty pages, *Hit* included chapters on love and marriage, temperance, women's franchise, divorce, labor and religion. Each chapter described the inhumanity of men to women and urged "God given rights" for women.

Addressing a woman's franchise, Walker announced: "As a Physician, the author believes that her duties are not <u>all</u> in the sick room ... she finds herself loudly called to diagnose the great body politic ..." Championing gender equity, Walker urged that women be taught useful occupations and receive equal pay. Even new gender terminology was suggested: "Let men and women stand as equals ... A woman must be called *Mrs.* to let all the world know she is married, and if there is a necessity for this, why not call a man *Misterer* for the purpose of enlightening the world as to his condition?"

Walker proclaimed that "Tobacco poisons the happiness of domestic life ... children suffer from weak digestion and morbid tastes because father's mouth is a nicotine distillery." Alarmingly, she announced that tobacco poisoned every tissue in the body resulting in paralysis and insanity.

On dress reform, she said: "From the crown of the head to the soles of the feet ... The greatest sorrows that women suffer today are those physical, moral and mental ones, that are caused by their unhygienic manner of dressing! The want of the *ballot* is but a *toy* by comparison." However, Walker didn't mean to denigrate the importance of the "Natural Right" to vote to achieve "unqualified individuality."

Seven years later, Walker published *Unmasked or the Science of Immorality, To Gentlemen by a Woman Physician and Surgeon*. She felt that it was "natural to suppose men might benefit by a treatise by a woman M.D." Walker deplored the fact that boys learned about sex and inherited debased ideas from older playmates. Thus, youngsters believed it cunning to seduce and to take advantage of women. Men were classified into six types:

**CLASSIFICATIONS OF MAN**

| | |
|---|---|
| CODE 1 | MAN WHO TRULY RESPECTED HIS WIFE, AND TREATED HER WITH THE SAME DEFERENCE AS HIS HONORED MOTHER OR SISTER. [THIS TYPE WAS QUITE UNCOMMON] |
| CODE 2 | MAN WHO FIRST "SOWED HIS WILD OATS," THEN MARRIED TO HAVE A PURE GIRL, AND ASSUMED THERE WAS NONE BETTER THAN HE. |

| | |
|---|---|
| CODE 3 | SIMILAR TO *CODE 2*, BUT MAN CONTINUED TO HAVE SEXUAL RELATIONS WITH SO-CALLED RESPECTABLE WOMEN. |
| CODE 4 | MAN WHO HAD WOMEN IN VARIOUS PLACES SIMULTANEOUSLY, AND DESERTED THEM AS HE TIRED OF THEM. |
| CODE 5 | MAN WHO VISITED HOUSES OF PROSTITUTION FOR EXTRA-MARITAL RELATIONS. |
| CODE 6 | MAN WHO WAS CONSTANTLY ON THE PROWL FOR VICTIMS TO SATIATE HIS SEXUAL DRIVES. |

This amazingly frank book for 1878 shocked even the uninhibited. Walker ventured into topics suitable for today's scandalous tabloids: types of deformities in hermaphrodites; emotional male morning sickness simulating a wife's pregnancy; kissing spreading diseases such as Syphilis and being especially injurious to children kissed on the mouth; overemphasis on hymens as proof of virginity when medical evidence demonstrated intact and broken hymens without sexual intercourse; seminal discharges were natural and not depraved; barrenness may be from sexual excesses but there are physical factors involved; and the effects of tobacco and alcohol on social disease.

In a 1961 psychohistorical analysis, a psychiatrist concluded that Mary Walker "simply failed each time she attempted her hand at medicine." Sounding very much like an 1860s traditional physician, he delivered a devastating professional psychohistorical analysis:"Psychiatrically, a review of Mary Walker's history clearly indicates a well-established diagnosis of paranoia, representing a compromise with reality unwelcomingly thrust upon a militant and determined ego that revolted against its sex, rebelling - not in a mere turn to homosexuality - but in an open, and as complete as possible, switch to the opposite sex. At best, Mary Walker was a poorly adjusted and chronically unhappy wretch of a woman."

Certainly, the disparaging criticism and the humiliating psychiatric analysis did not deter the U.S. Postal Service and others from still honoring Dr. Mary Edwards Walker. All the egotistical and dubious claims about Walker, many self-initiated, may or may not be true. Even though a New York Times reporter labeled her "That curious anthropoid," Walker was, and still is, the only woman ever awarded the Congressional Medal of Honor.

During one of her political forays in Washington, Walker fell while climbing the Capitol steps. She never completely recovered from that severe injury and died about two years later on February 21, 1919 in

Oswego at age eighty-six.

Two trail blazing feminists set the stage for Walker's diverse accomplishments. In an 1854 speech on women as reformers, Lucretia Mott verbalized Walker's ideals: "Let woman then go on, not asking favors, but claiming as right, the removal of all hindrances to her elevation in the scale of things ... let her strive to occupy such walks in society as will benefit her true dignity in all the relations of life." Throughout her tempestuous life, Walker followed the pioneering advice of Sarah Grimké: "To me it is perfectly clear that whatsoever it is morally right for a man to do, it is morally right for a woman to do."

## SECTION THREE            MANAGED MEDICINE

There is an old aphorism that "there is nothing new under the sun." This section clearly illustrates the truth of that saying. People may ask if it is imperative to seek out the old before installing the new. This is somewhat akin to the cynical Diogenes going forth with a lantern to seek an honest man who had not lost his honor and integrity. This vision of the Greek philosopher in his flowing white robes wandering the countryside can accompany readers of the material in this section.

More than 4,000 years ago, a number of Semite kingdoms in the far east already had written edicts incorporating the modern concepts and tenets of a managed care organization, a health maintenance organization or a preferred provider group. Professional fees were specifically listed along with a sliding scale of reimbursement. There were harsh "an eye for an eye and a tooth for a tooth" mandates to control the quality of care. Prescriptions were included in the fee and records were kept to document therapies. Even the marketing and public education was included as the edicts were copied and distributed throughout the kingdom. Patients who could not read for themselves were advised to have the edicts read to them in front of the statue of the king. Codex Hammurabi was only one example of this managed medical care effort at the dawning of civilization. Are there any lessons to be learned by studying the 282 mandates of the Codex Hammurabi?

Medical malpractice is currently in a cycle of ups and downs. Professionals are refusing to undertake specific procedures because they can not afford the malpractice insurance premiums. Physicians are forming political organizations to lobby legislators to reform the tort laws, to place a cap on total awards and to reduce the ability to sue for monetary awards for pain and suffering. Again, this is not new and the first malpractice crisis in the United States occurred almost two hundred years ago. Attitudes, actions and actual verbiage could easily be interchanged with modern day counterparts involved in a malpractice law suit. By merely updating the language, the participants in malpractice suits would have their testimony and statements already scripted. Early on, improperly healed fractures and dislocations were the major cause of discontent with medical care and those problems remain with us today. Relevantly, the malpractice crisis was not resolved in the nineteenth century either.

Education of health care professionals is a constant concern in the industry. Some critics deplore the influence of corporate America upon the medical care system that turns the "calling" into an "industry." Faculty committees continually study the curriculum to discover the necessary subject matter to teach their students. In addition, the faculty members investigate the best educational methods and techniques for imparting their wisdom to their eager students. In the nineteenth century, many of our medicals schools were little more than diploma mills. As late as the 1870s, even the Harvard Medical School qualified for that derisive appellation. Therefore, it should not surprise anyone that the New York Medical College was unique in its approach to educating physicians. Interestingly, because they did things differently, this school was bedeviled by competing medical schools, by practicing physicians and by professional organizations. Travails cited in the material about the New York Medical College are not uncommon in the existing educational system for health professionals.

# MANAGED MEDICAL CARE IN BABYLONIA IN 1700 B.C.E.

At the dawn of civilization, about four thousand years ago, the concepts and practices of providing medical care to the population were mandated and transcribed into written form. Using cuneiform, a wedge-shaped hieroglyphic writing invented by the Sumerians about five thousand years ago, the mandates were inscribed on a massive column of stone and numerous copies were written on clay tablets. Codex Hammurabi established a sliding fee schedule for services, included outcome measurements with harsh penalties, created medical records that documented diseases and therapies, included prescription benefits, explained patient's rights, and marketed and advertised the edicts of the King. Even though the medical care was authoritarian, there were legal actions to insure justice and equity particular to each social class in the kingdom. Tempered by time, the medical care rulings of Codex Hammurabi can still be considered the beginning of the concepts of managed medical care.

There is no doubt that the volume of complaints about the health care delivery system in the United States remains constant or rises regularly. In the film *As Good As It Gets*, a mother complains bitterly about her bad experiences seeking health care for her child from a health maintenance organization [HMO]. When she finishes complaining, theater audiences, showing their complete agreement, broke out into spontaneous applause. It is amazing to ponder an ancient system that may have served people needing medical care better than nations do today.

Currently, reform of the health care delivery system remains uppermost in the minds of legislators, courts, elected executives, health care professionals and the medically burdened and economically overwhelmed public. Managed medical care emerged as the consensus choice for resolving the top priority of controlling the rapidly escalating costs. In its approach, managed medical care integrated the health care system attributes of reasonable fee schedules for professional services, standards to monitor the quality of care rendered, assurance of patient's rights and satisfaction and competitively marketed health care services.

Amazingly, health care reformers need not have labored so hard to reinvent the wheel! In ancient civilizations, a number of nomadic

Semite tribes had already documented managed medical care techniques to apply to their own basic health care delivery systems. Managed medical care concepts were enduringly inscribed in the written clay tablet compilations by Urukagina of Lagash about 2400 B.C.E, Eshnunna around 2100 B.C.E., and Lipit Ishtar of Isin about 1800 B.C.E. When the scribes wrote letters on clay tablets some four thousand years ago, wellness wishes frequently appeared as divine prayers to the gods: "May Shamash and Marduk give thee health."

During the golden age of King Hammurabi of Babylon, he adapted managed medical care choices from these earlier codes and endorsed seven principles in writing in stone in the Codex Hammurabi:

♦ Rate setting established specific fees for general surgery, eye surgery, setting fractures, curing diseased muscles, and other specific health care services.
♦ Fees were set according to a sliding scale based on ability to pay.
♦ Owners were required to pay for health care for their slaves.
♦ Objective outcome measurement standards assured the quality of care
♦ Outcomes information included data collection and evaluation.
♦ Consumer and patient's rights were publicized, explained and known to all.
♦ Marketing and advertising promoted the adoption of the plan.

There is no consensus as to the dates when Hammurabi ruled even though most experts agree that he was the sixth king of the first or Amorite dynasty of Babylon. Calculations placed his forty-three year reign within periods ranging from 2123 to 2080 B.C.E. or 1948 to 1905 B.C.E. or 1728 to 1685 B.C.E. A comparison of eight different authorities placed Hammurabi's reign at different dates between 2067 to 1669 B.C.E. Regardless of the exact date, managed medical care principles were literally set in stone and inscribed on clay tablets between the seventeenth and twenty-first centuries B.C.E., eternities before health care evolved from priestly incantations, magical applications, omens and evil demons. Despite the dominating presence of supernatural gods, Babylonian society was cultured and sophisticated. Babylonian society, medicine and managed medical care are all interrelated.

King Hammurabi's kingdom took its name from its major city. Babylonia encompassed the fertile crescent between the southern Tigris and Euphrates rivers. This kingdom was about six hundred miles long and two hundred miles wide. Today, that land is Iraq.

Due to its strategic geographic location, Babylon was a flourishing commercial city under King Hammurabi. During his reign, Babylon was already one of the richest cities in history. Its citizens were wealthy, cultured, and sociable. Caravan trade routes criss-crossed through the city's streets that were laid out in regular straight lines with intersections at right angles. Merchandise in bales had clay tags called bullas inscribed with the merchant's name for identification and delivery purposes. Traders and tourists from all parts of the existing world gathered in the bustling marketplaces. Their foreign languages and differing cultures created an incomprehensible mixture of the verbal noise of bargaining and physical body movements. Tower of babel was the name given to the ziggurat, a multistory building, where the traders met to conduct their business. Vegetation flourished utilizing an interconnected irrigation system of canals. Agriculture was the major industry producing wheat, grains and dates. Babylonians wove wool and turned leather from animal hides into attractive clothing. In addition to dressing fashionably, Babylonians took frequent baths with soaps, used perfume and rouge freely, applied depilatories, and colored their gray hair with sage extract and vegetable dyes. Mud and clay bricks were used to build substantial dwellings. Houses were amply furnished and manicured gardens bloomed. Palaces and houses contained ceramics, colored tile works, enamels, engravings, mosaics, paintings, and sculptures. Using cuneiform, scribes recorded a multitude of commercial transactions and intellectual information on sturdy clay tablets.

A considerable percentage of the population was literate. There were libraries containing material on astronomy, botany, chemistry, geology, mathematics and medicine. Schools for boys, girls, and adults were usually administered by the temples. Education included special training for astronomers, engineers, judges, medical healers, priests, and surveyors. Musicians played bells, cymbals, drums, flutes, harps, lyres, oboes, tambourines and trumpets. Babylonians also engaged in choral music.

Babylonian society was distinguished by three social classes: awelum, mushkenum, and wardum. Awelum were the upper class: aristocrats, businessmen, feudal lords, free men, gentlemen, large landowners, military leaders, palace officials, professionals, and temple priests. Mushkenum equated with the middle class: free men who could be poor or could have money, commoners who could own small properties, tenant farmers, craftsmen, merchants, hired laborers, and even former slaves. Wardum were male and female slaves. Awelum may have been racially qualified as the "true citizens" of Babylonia because they were of West-Semitic or Amorite stock. In any event, the awelum and wardum are clearly classified while the intermediate group, the mushkenum, are less so. Regardless of social class, assess to medical care was unrestricted. Since Codex Hammurabi used a sliding fee scale by social class for reimbursement of medical care services, those social class distinctions are vital.

Illness was believed to be caused by the intervention of foreign supernatural forces such as demons, evil spirits, ghosts of the dead, or the wrath of the gods. People became ill for committing a sin or by being victimized by outside agents such as cold, dust or a bad smell. Ashakku was the demon of consumption, Irra the spirit of pestilence, Alu caused blindness, Nergal gave a fever, Tiu caused headaches, and Namtar was the evil spirit responsible for the plague. With these beliefs, it is not surprising that medicine belonged to the priestly class and was largely magico-religious with three types of healers; diviners, exorcists, and physicians. In addition, veterinarians and barbers are mentioned in the Code. Barbers, called gallabu, performed plastic surgery as they branded slaves or removed slave markings, and performed surgical procedures such as dental operations.

Diviners or Baru, were essentially internal medicine specialists who interpreted omens and foretold the course of the illness. Semitic peoples believed that the liver was the seat of the soul and the center of vitality. For this reason, Barus practiced hepatoscopy. A sick person breathed into the nostrils of a sheep and the animal was slaughtered. After the sheep's liver was removed, the Barus compared a concisely coded clay model to the liver to make a diagnosis. This clay model was divided into a number of sections with each section specifying a different ailment. After witnessing the destruction of Jerusalem, Ezekiel the prophet went into lifetime exile in Babylon. In his writings, he refers to Babylonian medical foretelling as he comments about the Baru that "he looketh at the liver."

Exorcists or Ashipu inquired about the nature of the offense to the gods. After discovering the sin, the Ashipu drove out the evil spirits.

They attacked the disease with incantations, prayers, recitations, sacrifices, and ceremonial rituals beseeching the gods for a cure. A typical exorcist prayer used strong language and emotional commands: "Whoever or whatever you are, evil ghost or evil devil, evil god or evil fiend, or sickness or death, or a phantom or wrath of the night, a fever or deadly pestilence, whatever or whoever you are -- get out! Take yourself off before me! Get out of this house! For I am the priest of EA, I who recite the incantation for the relief of the man who is sick. Be exorcized by heaven! Be exorcized by earth! <u>Get out</u>!" [EA was the god of waters, spells and incantations]

Both, Ashipu and Baru used physical examinations to discover signs and omens.

Physicians or Azu were educated in schools associated with the temples and administered by priests. Students learned from the records in the clay tablets and from practical experience observing and giving care to sick people. In keeping with the religious site of their schooling, an Azu worshiped Gula, the goddess of medicine and healing and her husband, Ninurta. Ninazu was the lord doctor, the patron of physicians. His son, Ningishzida, a healing god, carried a round staff with a double-sexed two headed serpent named Sachan. That symbol was adapted by professional medical societies years later. An Azu discovered the illness by listening to the patient's telling their medical history, not by physical examination. Hundreds of clay tablets recorded descriptions of ailments such as abscesses, apoplexy, appetite control, colic, constipation, cough, ear, eye, fevers, gallbladder trouble, heart disease, intoxication, nose and throat disease, phthisis, plague, rectal prolapse, rheumatism, skin disease, tumors, and venereal disease. Long before psychiatry was invented, forty tablets dealt with interpreting dreams and avoiding nightmares After the diagnosis, the Azu prescribed drugs and medications, preformed surgery, set fractures, treated visible sores, and attended to snake bites. Medical instruments included bronze lancets, metal tubes to blow remedies into bodily orifices, tubes for catheters and spatulas. More than two hundred fifty medicinal plants, one hundred twenty mineral substances and one hundred eighty other drugs were used in combination with alcoholic beverages, bouillon, fats, honey, milk in various forms, oils, wax, and parts and products of animals. Medications were prepared by grinding, straining, and filtering substances for ointments or plasters to spread on a piece of thin leather to apply.

External medication applications used solvents from bark, flowers, fruit skins and juices, plants, resins, sea-kelp, seeds or turpentine dissolved in beer or milk and mixed with wine, fats and honey. Narcotics came from hemp, mandragora, opium and solium temulentum. Prescriptions could specify administration via enemas, laxatives, lotions, ointments, pessaries, pills, poultices, powders, salves, and suppositories. A patient's prescription could be "enveloped in the aroma of burning feathers and liberally dosed with dog dung and pig's gall." When they set up practice, Azus created their own seals with inscriptions such as: "O Edinmagi, Servant of the god Girra, who helps mothers in childhood, Ur-Lugaledina the physician is your servant."

Within this Babylonian society and culture of medicine, the stele, the stone pillar, with the inscribed Codex Hammurabi emerged as a unifying force throughout the nation.

In 1902, at Susa in Persia, French archaeologists unearthed a large black diorite stele almost eight feet tall with a six foot circumference at the base narrowing to five feet at the top. After deciphering more than three thousand five hundred lines of cuneiform writing, the archeology specialists called Assyriologists identified the hard stone pillar as a proclamation of the code of laws of King Hammurabi.

Strictly speaking, the Code is not composed of laws and the prologue on the stele describes the exact content of the Code: "These are the just verdicts that Hammurabi, the experienced King, has imposed in order to establish firm discipline and good governance in his country." Hammurabi collected and classified "the most just decisions, the wisest, the most sagacious, the most worthy of an experienced ruler." However, the Code is not the totality of the law of the land. There is no organization of the justice system. There is no trace of criminal law and there are numerous omissions. In effect, the code is a collection of judicial decisions and verdicts, not laws. Judgements followed the harsh rule of "Lex Talionis," the traditional "eye for an eye, tooth for a tooth" punishments of the Semite tribes. Hammurabi replaced the priestly administration of justice with civil judges, local magistrates and palace officials. Furthermore, these edicts are rigorously structured in a grammatical style with a protasis, a proposition beginning with "if", followed by the apodosis, the conditional clause. "If a man's body is yellow, his face is yellow, and his eyes are yellow, and the flesh is flabby, it is jaundice." There were two hundred eighty two mandates covering all aspects of everyday life in Babylonia. Mandates applied to offenses against the administration of justice; offenses against property; land and houses; conducting trade and commerce; marriage, family, and property; assaults and retaliations; professional men; agriculture; wages and rates of hire; and slaves. Professional men included surgeons, veterinary surgeons, and the barber-brander.

Augmenting the decreed Codex, the stele served as a symbol of the greatness and justice of Hammurabi's reign. A finely sculpted engraving, about two foot square in bas relief on the stele, portrays the god Shamash seated on his throne receiving the homage of Hammurabi. Portrayed as an ordinary worshiper adoring his deity, the king stands before him in an attitude of prayer. Two contrary interpretations of the engraving exist. One states that Shamash was handing the code to Hammurabi. Another version contends that Shamash may be offering Hammurabi the circle and scepter as insignia of the King's sovereignty in mandating the Codex. Shamash was "the god of truth and justice, the conqueror of the powers of darkness and the maintainer of morality and justice."

Furthermore, the choice of diorite for the stele carried its own significance. Since the material was not found naturally in the kingdom, "it became an object of great value worthy of respect in its own right." Diorite is a very hard and durable substance ensuring that the code would withstand the test of time. Today, the stele is on display in the Louvre Museum in Paris, France. This enduring stele forms the basis for a comparison of the four thousand year old concepts of managed medical care with those existing currently, beginning with the status of physicians. Clearly, the Code of Hammurabi reveals that the medical profession advanced far enough in the public esteem to be rewarded with adequate fees, carefully prescribed and regulated by law.

Currently, key managed medical care precepts are concerned with a number of commonalities: control of care by management, defining the population covered; establishment of a fee schedule for provider health care services; an administrative division of labor; a credentialing process for providers; deselection of providers; specialty referrals, consultations, and denial of care; pharmaceutical benefits; medical records documentation; patient rights and satisfaction; disenrollment; and quality assessment including practice criteria, outcome measurement, and penalties; and marketing the product. Does the Code of Hammurabi also address these issues?

By modern standards, would Hammurabi's government be considered as regulators of medical care? In 1981, the legal ruling in the *Stewart v. Midani* case defined management control. This federal court identified factors that determined whether an institution affected a physician's judgment or behavior. Specific elements in the relationship between the physician and the institution focused upon the answers to eight questions regarding the services of physicians:

Who directly supervises their work?
Did a contract specify their tasks or services?
Who controlled their work time?
Who was authorized to inspect their work?
Who provided their supplies and/or facilities?
Who could terminate the contract?
Who could evaluate their degree of skill?
Who determined the payment method?

If a preponderance of these variables proved a relationship, the court claimed that the physician was under the influence of the employer. In effect, the employer was, at least, partially responsible.

Based on the medical care related sections of the Code of Hammurabi, the Babylonian government did have the right to inspect the physician's work, if the care was questioned by the patient. In addition, the government set forth the amount of payment for services and penalties for malpractice. However, evidence from clay tablets indicates that the physicians of Babylon were frequently independent of the government. In practice, the physicians handled their own patient contracts as well as the specific services and supplies utilized.

Applying the eight questions in the court ruling, Hammurabi and his government could not be held accountable for the actions of a physician. Furthermore, the Babylonian government did not hold itself out as a care giver, did not receive money from the patients for the physicians' services, and did not limit the patient's choice of a physician. In effect, the Code of Hammurabi presents a mixed bag as compared to controlling actions from a managed care organization. Nevertheless, as a four thousand year old document, the Codex Hammurabi still stands as an innovative arrangement influencing the origin of managed medical care concepts.

Everybody in Babylonia, including the people in the conquered nations, were covered by the health care system specifically identified in the Code. All of the two hundred eighty-two edicts were applicable within the unequal distinctions based upon the three social classes. Fifteen sections mentioned physicians, veterinarians, barbers, or wet-nurses. About twenty sections dealt with injuries in a brawl such as damaging an eye, breaking a bone, knocking out a tooth, striking a cheek, causing a miscarriage, or blows resulting in a death. However, those sections do not mention health care services but only access monetary fines or "eye for an eye" penalties. A welfare-type coverage was in force for slaves as their owners were required to pay for their health care services.

Today, managed medical care organizations control the costs by employing or contracting with health care providers who agree to accept salaries or set fees for their services. Similarly, Codex fees were based upon the patient's social class and the ability to pay in addition to the seriousness of the procedure. Awelum paid the most, mushkenum less, and the wardum's owner paid the least as illustrated in the precise language of the Codex's scheduled fees:

§215 If a surgeon has made a deep incision in the body of a gentleman with a lancet of bronze and saves the man's life or has opened a caruncle in the eye of a man with a lancet of bronze and saves the eye, he shall take ten shekels of silver.

§216 If the patient is a freeman, he shall take 5 shekels of silver.

§217 If the patient is a slave, the master of the slave shall give 2 shekels of silver to the surgeon.

A comparative examination of Hammurabi's Code quickly reiterates the successful and unsuccessful fee setting and penalties methodology. Fees are possibly omitted for unsuccessful bone setting and sinew mending because the outcome is usually not fatal. Operations can be repeated until the result is satisfactory. A reasonable explanation for the omission of fees for the general operation and eye operation on Mushkenum is that the scribe somehow or the other skipped a section. Based upon comparable sections of the Codex, it is likely that a monetary penalty would be applied.

| SUCCESSFUL OPERATIONS | AWELUM | MUSHKENUM | WARDUM |
|---|---|---|---|
| SETTING BONE OR MENDING SINEW | 5 SHEKELS | 3 SHEKELS | 2 SHEKELS |
| GENERAL OPERATION | 10 SHEKELS | 5 SHEKELS | 2 SHEKELS |
| OPERATION ON EYE | 10 SHEKELS | 5 SHEKELS | 2 SHEKELS |
| **UNSUCCESSFUL OPERATIONS** | | | |
| SETTING BONE OR MENDING SINEW | -------------------- | -------------------- | -------------------- |
| GENERAL OPERATION | LOSS OF HAND | -------------------- | SLAVE FOR SLAVE |
| OPERATION ON EYE | LOSS OF HAND | -------------------- | ½ SLAVE'S PRICE |

For a comparable economic understanding of the fee, a free craftsman earned five to eight grains of silver per day and had to work about one year to earn ten to fourteen shekels. A wooden door cost one to two shekels, earthenware jars sold for from ¼ to ⅔ of a shekel, and a wooden tray for carrying on the head, ½ shekel. A middle class dwelling rented for five shekels a year. Based on these comparisons, it is obvious that physicians were well paid for their services. There were additional specified medical care fees:

§206  If a man strikes a freeman in an affray and inflicts a wound on him, that man may swear "Surely I did not strike him willingly" and he shall pay the surgeon.

§221  If a physician set a broken bone for a man or cure his diseased bowels, the patient shall pay five shekels of silver to the physician.

§222  If he be a freeman, he shall give three shekels of silver.

§223  If it be a man's slave, the owner of the slave shall give two shekels of silver to the physician.

**§224** If a veterinary physician operate on an ox or an ass for a severe wound and save its life, the owner shall give to the physician 30 rains of silver (180 grains of silver = 1 shekel).

Business contracts written on clay tablets survived and indicate the specifics involved in transactions. Both the employer and the employee considered the prevailing economy and deviated from the established fee schedules in the Codex. It is also possible that the fees in Hammurabi's code applied to people working for the King or the temple priests. Furthermore, the fees in the code may have included food and lodging or similar benefits.

In today's terms, the Code of Hammurabi established a uniform fee-for-service schedule with a sliding scale based upon ability to pay. Considering the relative lack of specific diagnoses mentioned, the Code may have initiated the first Diagnosis Related Groups (DRGs) used to calculate reimbursements as currently applied in the U.S. Medicare program. There was no annual reimbursement rate such as capitation. Because of the sliding fee-for-service, there was no level of uncompensated care. This eliminated the need for physicians to apply the Robin Hood payment technique of overcharging the upper classes to cover the cost of care for the needy and indigent. Similar to current payment schedules, the established fees caused the physician to absorb any additional expenses of treatment beyond the set fee. Obviously, it is not a modern problem for the physician to be forced to be cost-conscious while treating patients.

Though there was no utilization review by any voluntary or governmental regulatory body, the Code forced Babylonian physicians to constantly be reminded of the need for efficient operations. Efficiency and effectiveness still haunts physicians today as many managed medical care organizations withhold a portion of the physician's compensation until their practice patterns can be analyzed. "Pricing cannot compensate for inefficient delivery of services ... Providers will eventually be penalized for inefficient operations." Cost based reimbursements can not be expected; neither in Hammurabi's Babylon, nor in the modern day American health care marketplace.

In its mandates, the Code of Hammurabi identified a division of labor. In a similar fashion, managed medical care organizations utilize a variety of additional providers to render care to their enrolled population. Priestly health care providers, Baru and Ashipu, rendered internal medicine care through their divining and exorcisms. Azu took care of ailments that were unrelated to divine or mystical causation using non-magical means such as the "bronze lancet" or manipulation. Barbers engaged in plastic surgery by removing branding marks from slaves. A veterinary surgeon, literally "the doctor of an ox or an ass," tended to the animals. A wet-nurse could be classified as a nutritionist or dietitian. Particular duties were identified for each provider in the various sections of the Code, except for the priestly physicians, the Baru and the Ashipu.

Physicians were educated in schools run by the temple priests. There were numerous textbooks consisting of clay tablets with recorded descriptions of diseases, prescriptions, and remedies. In addition, the physicians made rounds visiting patients and learned from practical experience. Critics of the contemporary managed medical care system argue that "any willing provider" should be allowed to participate in a plan's program. With the risk of death or dismemberment in Hammurabi's Code, how willing would any medical care provider be to participate? In contrast, Herodotus, the ancient Greek "Father of History," described a different Babylonian medical care system. He found that sick people were brought to the marketplace where passers-by who had experienced a similar affliction could give advice to those lying in the streets. In fact, it was an obligation for passers-by to inquire about the sick person's condition. Anybody advising the sick could be considered a "willing provider" without worrying about the threat of punishment that accompanied the responsibility of providing medical treatment. However, the truth of this description by Herodotus has been disputed by historians.

Deselection means that a medical care provider can be removed from the approved listing of the managed medical care organization. Hammurabi's Code created the harshest form of deselection possible. If the physician erred through omission or commission, his fingers or hands were cut off. Immediately, that physician was stopped from seeing any more patients. This severe punishment for negligence easily weeded out those physicians incapable of delivering adequate care. In addition, the punishment insured that the physicians would not practice again in a different locality. That certain risk that accompanied every procedure probably helped to reduce any chance of any physician surplus. An unquestioned belief in illness caused by demons and magic allowed physicians to invoke that rationale to make a plea for the court to evaluate in unsuccessful treatments. How could a court be satisfied that a death was not the result of divine intervention and was not the surgeon's fault?

There did not appear to be any limitation on making professional referrals or seeking consultations. Kings and aristocrats assured themselves of the services of the most renowned physicians. Royal doctors were loaned to their allies and sent "to visit the courtesans whom they loved." Certainly, there were no financial incentives for physicians to limit specialty consultations. Baru, Ashipu and Azu freely interacted and readily exchanged treatment regimens. Since the health care services were on a fee-for-service schedule, there was no denial of care because the procedure was considered experimental. There is no mention of refusing to care for a patient although one clay tablet text warned medical students "not to touch a patient who is likely to die." That advice seemed reasonable when a negative outcome could result in bodily mutilation for the care giver. By today's medical malpractice standards, such refusal constitutes unprofessional conduct but today's lawsuits involve insurance policies and dollar amounts, not bodily danger.

Payments for health care did not add extra charges for materials used in the huge pharmacopeia of minerals, vegetables, animal parts, liquids, or unguents. All patients needing medications of any type received them from the health care provider. Similar to today's therapies, traditional family remedies were supplied as well by grandparents, parents, distant relatives and strangers passing by.

Thousands of clay tablets recovered by archaeologists document that medical care data were collected and recorded about ailments, causes, treatments, and therapy outcomes. Information management was systematic and routinely entered including the physician's name and constitutes a report card of sorts.

Patients' rights and patient satisfaction were not ignored in the Code of Hammurabi. In the United States, the American Hospital

Association's "Bill of Rights" for patients are posted in hospitals and distributed to new inpatients. Complaints about managed medical care indicate "there is a pattern of dissatisfaction with choice and quality of doctors, access to specialty and emergency care, and waiting time for appointments." Nationally, the American Medical Association strived to assure patients free choice of providers and to allow managed medical care physicians to tell their patients about all medical care alternatives.

Hammurabi's Code anticipated these communication problems and commanded providers to follow the edicts on the stele. But communication is a two way street and there had to be assurance that patients knew their rights. In addition to the huge stele erected on the grounds of the major temple in Babylon for everybody to read, the Codex was duplicated on clay tablet copies and distributed throughout the nation. Certainly, the population was aware of the code and the ramifications. Furthermore, the king specifically called attention to all those seeking justice that the code would tell them what to expect: "Let the oppressed man who has a cause, come before my statute called 'King of Justice' and then have the inscription on my monument read out and hear my precious words, that my monument may make clear his cause to him, let him see the law which applies to him, and let his heart be set at ease!"

No one was left wondering if they received a fair value in their treatment since it actually was inscribed in stone. Reading the Code sections, or listening to others read the mandates, patients learned what to expect from health care providers beforehand and could seek justice from a legal system if not satisfied. However, there is no evidence of either prosecution or defense lawyers in Babylonia.

In an effort to create an ideal conception of the physician-patient relationship, modern researchers devised a normative standard based around the six C's: choice, competence, communication, compassion, continuity, and conflict of interest. While communication and compassion might be difficult to research, Codex Hammurabi strictly enforced competence through severe penalties. As far as continuity and choice, since the Codex fees were the same no matter what physician the patient saw, there is no reason to believe that these aspects would be impeded. With the fees established, both patient and physician knew what to expect and both could refuse the treatment, which should have eliminated any conflict of interest. Babylonians appear to have been adequately prepared regarding the concept of the ideal physician-patient relationship.

While there was no managed medical care organization from which to disenroll, Babylonians could move up or down the social class ladder and thereby change their level of health care.

Codex Hammurabi specified quality assessment, practice criteria, outcomes measurement, and penalties. Nonsurgical intervention was not subject to quality of care controls or to malpractice verdicts. A priestly Baru or Ashipu could not be held responsible for illness or outcomes that were caused by the gods, demons or evil spirits. However, when an Azu used a "bronze lancet" or other means to heal a patient, that nonpriestly provider was accountable for direct human error or aggression. If a patient died or was seriously damaged, the objective measurement was easily observable and the "eye for an eye" penalty imposed. Significantly, the judges regularly omitted any references to the Code in their recorded decisions and appear to have been guided by tradition, public opinion, and common sense. Quality of care edicts in Hammurabi's code left no margin for error on the part of the provider of care. Physicians and other health care providers had to be either flawless or lucky. Conditional clauses in the code certainly made physicians uncomfortable, to say the least.

§194  If a man gives his child to a nurse and the child die in her hands, but the nurse unbeknown to the father and mother nurse another child, then they shall convict her of having nursed another child without the knowledge of the father and mother and her breasts shall be cut off. [ A wet nurses was paid about 3 shekels]

§218  If a physician operate on a man for a severe wound with a bronze lancet and cause the man's death; or open an abscess in the eye of a man with a bronze lancet and destroy the man's eye, they shall cut off his fingers.

§219  If a physician operate on the slave of a freeman for a severe wound with a bronze lancet and cause his death, he shall restore a slave of equal value.

§220  If he open an abscess in his eye with a bronze lancet, and destroy his eye, he shall pay silver to the extent of one-half his price. (Average prices for male slaves ranged from 16-30 shekels)

§226 If a barber has excised a slave's mark without the knowledge of his owner so that he cannot be traced, they shall cut off the fore-hand of that barber.

§227 If a man has constrained the barber and he excises the slave's mark so that he cannot be traced, they shall put that man to death and shall hang him at his own door; the barber may swear "Surely I excised it unwittingly" and he then goes free.

Throughout the code, there were thirty-two decrees with the death penalty administered by burning, drowning, hanging, or impalement on a stake. Other penalties included bodily mutilation and monetary fines. As with the set fees, the quality of care penalties were adjusted by social class with the higher class able to escape death or mutilation by paying a monetary fine.

Managed medical care organizations and their administrators must balance their cost containment efforts with patient expectations as they provide quality leadership to maintain the delivery of a high quality of care. Quality assessment includes multiple factors such as standardized practice criteria, measurement of therapy outcomes, and corrective actions to resolve deviations. Babylonian medicine also was concerned with these variables. King Hammurabi left no doubt as to his leadership and repeatedly told his subjects that he was the wisest, the most just, and the most caring. Practice standards were written on the clay tablets and taught by the temple schools. Outcome measurements were specifically identified in sections of the Code as were the severe corrective actions for improving the practice of medicine. How much more total can Total Quality Management be than to "cut off the hands" of the offending health care provider?

Edicts also cover the marketing and advertising of the Codex. In the introduction to the Code, Hammurabi lavishly applied the ancient advertising rule that if you say something loud enough, often enough and in grandiose language, your audience will believe it. Hammurabi evoked the gods and repeatedly glorified his magnanimous actions undertaken for the benefit of his subjects: "Anum and Illil ... called me by name Hammurabi ... to make justice to appear in the land, to destroy the evil and wicked that the strong might not oppress the weak ...When Marduk commanded me to give justice to the people of the land and to let them have good governance, I set forth truth and justice throughout the land and prospered the people ... My words are choice, my deeds have no rival; only for the unwise are they vain, and for the profoundly wise they are worthy of all praise."

Continuing his self-glorification, Hammurabi proclaimed his being: "a god amongst kings endued with knowledge and wisdom," the "bountiful provider of holy feasts," a gatherer of "abundance and plenty" bringing "overflowing wealth," the provider of "abundant waters for his people," a philanthropist giving out "abundant riches," a military hero and 'a warrior whom none can resist" who "stormed the four quarters of the world" and brought them "to obedience," a ruler who "magnifies "the fame of Babylon." Despite the high powered hyperbole, Hammurabi was actually "a formidable warrior, an astute diplomat, and a diligent, meticulous manager with a sincere interest in the well being of his subjects." In addition, he was an above average communicator. His image gave weight to his self-praise and by syllogism to the mandates in the code. In addition, in a society of multiple deities, the impact of his blessings and curses surely influenced the population. Hammurabi's code has sixteen lines of blessings and two hundred eighty two lines of calamitous curses for those who do not abide by his doctrines.

What is the relation between modern medicine and Codex Hammurabi? Immensely aggrieved modern health care consumers may wish for a return to the harsh "eye for an eye, tooth for a tooth" penalties in the name of justice and/or simply for revenge. However, with the rush toward endorsing managed medical care as the modal type of health care provider, our society may be re-entering the realm of a four thousand year old medical care system. Anybody reading the popular literature and newspapers and listening to radio or watching TV realizes that natural remedies and holistic therapies are the "in-thing." It is possible that the clay tablet prescriptions could re-emerge in the *Materia Medica* of family practitioners. In the late 1980s, Babylonian clay tablet cookbooks from 1700 B.C.E. resurfaced to reveal "a cuisine of striking richness, refinement, sophistication and artistry." Hammurabi's advice might call attention to the fact that he collected the best medical decisions, the wisest, the most sagacious, the most worthy, and that it would be advantageous to follow such dictums. In the prologue and epilogue, Codex Hammurabi even presents lofty moral and ethical goals for managed medical care organizations to emulate with appropriate changes in health care delivery terminology:"... to cause justice to prevail in the land, to destroy the wicked and the evil, to prevent the strong from oppressing the weak, to go forth like the Sun over the Black Head Race [Babylonians], to enlighten the land and to further the welfare of the people ... I brought health to the land; I made the populace to rest in security; I permitted no one to molest them ... I restrained them that the strong might not oppress the weak, and that they should give justice to the orphan and the widow."

## AMERICA's FIRST MEDICAL MALPRACTICE CRISIS, 1835 TO 1865

Between 1800 and 1835, medical malpractice in the United States was virtually unknown. Cases unrelated to amputation or death were particularly infrequent and patients and/or their families seldom won in court. Between 1812 and 1835 the *New England Journal of Medicine and Surgery* and its successor, the *Boston Medical and Surgical Journal [BMSJ]* reported on only three malpractice cases. In 1829 and 1830, there were suits related to midwifery care in France and England and in 1832 there was an American lawsuit. Within the thirty year period from 1835-1865, medical malpractice lawsuits began to inundate the courts and the *BMSJ* reported 48 cases and published numerous editorials and comments on the subject. Initially, the malpractice suits emanated from western New York State, spread throughout New England and then into the upper Mid-West. Dr. Frank H. Hamilton, "a respected Buffalo [NY] surgeon and a perpetual witness," estimated that nine out of every ten physicians in western New York had been charged with malpractice by the mid-nineteenth century. By 1853, the *Western Journal of Medical and Physical Sciences* lamented that malpractice suits "occur almost every month in the year and everywhere in our country." In 1860, a text on medical jurisprudence asserted: "There can hardly be found a place in the country, where the oldest physicians in it have not, at some periods in their lives, been actually sued or annoyingly threatened."

Even though America's first medical malpractice crisis began to evolve more than 150 years ago, many of the factors that gave rise to it have remained constant over the years. Originally, the concepts of medical negligence were founded upon the legal principles in English jurisprudence which the colonists adopted. American case law created original malpractice principles as the law suits traveled through the judicial system. Trial experiences molded the opinions and attitudes of the participants: the judges, attorneys and the jury members. An overwhelming majority of malpractice law suits were related to the outcomes of orthopedic therapy for fractures and dislocations. Further complicating the malpractice crisis, conflicts arose regarding the opposing expert testimony of physicians for the defendants and the plaintiffs. At one point, the better educated and trained physicians stood a much greater chance of being sued for malpractice. Professional disagreements between lawyers and physicians yielded bitter medical opinions about malpractice suits. Not surprisingly, the passage of time has not tempered these strongly held emotional positions.

Despite the surge in malpractice suits, there was a lack of systematically recorded statistical data about cases resolved in local courts without an appeal. Twenty-seven malpractice suits occurring between 1794 and 1861 that were adjudicated in appeals to the respective state supreme courts in sixteen randomly distributed states were analyzed. Most of the states adopted the then existing English common law as a basis for decisions or as an analogous reference.

In contrast to the U.S., England recorded malpractice cases about 500 years earlier. In 1374, Chief Justice John Cavendish on the Court of the Kings Bench in England ruled on a civil liberty action against a London surgeon named John Swanlond for treatment of the crushed and mangled hand of Agnes of Stratton. According to the legal record, Swanlond "guaranteed well and competently to cure ... [the wound] ... for reasonable payment," a statement he later denied making. Ultimately, her hand was severely deformed and she and her husband sued Swanlond for "misfeasance" [poor performance] under a breach of contract theory. This suit charged that Swanlond had "so negligently conducted his cure that her hand was so impaired that it was maimed to her injury and damage." Because of a legal technicality in the writ of complaint, the physician was held not liable. However, the court specifically established a precedent by declaring that if the patient is harmed as a result of the physician's negligence, the doctor should be held liable and the law will provide a remedy. In balancing that edict, Justice Cavendish laid the framework for the contemporary standard of the "ordinary reasonable/ prudent physician": "if he [the surgeon] does all he can and applies himself with all due diligence to the cure, it is not right that he should be [held] guilty therefor, [even] though there is no cure ..."

Additional initial and relevant rulings in England were handed down in 1433, 1435 and 1472. Pertinently, the Constitutio Criminalis of Charles V in 1533 was probably the oldest European document about medical jurisprudence. This edict allowed judges to call expert witnesses to testify in medico-legal cases. While there were legal deviations, frequently the colonists followed the British and European precedents.

Since the American colonists borrowed heavily from English law, the *Commentaries on the Laws of England* by William Blackstone, first published in 1767, were familiar to the legal profession and an 1841 edition was available in the U.S. However, Blackstone categorized malpractice under private wrongs, not under contract or mercantile law. In his definition of *mala praxis*, Blackstone's last sentence is almost verbatim from a 1697 ruling in the Dr. Grovenvelt case: "Injuries affecting a man's health are where, by any unwholesome practices of another. a man sustains any apparent damage in his vigor or constitution ... As by ... or by the neglect or unskillful management of his physician, surgeon, or apothecary. For it hath been solemnly resolved, that *mala praxis* is a great misdemeanour and offence at common law, whether it be for curiosity and experiment, or by neglect; because it breaks the trust which the party has placed in his physician and tends to the patient's destruction."

Using a common law remedy, a lawyer could file a *writ of trespass* for damages caused by a breach of duty, negligence, or carelessness.

Prior to 1860, none of the legal scholars dealt with the issue of medical malpractice in the medical jurisprudence books commonly used as references. Widely circulated works on medical jurisprudence included the first text in English, Samuel Farr's *Elements of Medical Jurisprudence* [1788]. In the U.S., the first notable work was Theodoric Romeyn Beck's *Elements of Medical Jurisprudence* [1823]. Additional popular references included Joseph Chitty's *A Practical Treatise on Medical Jurisprudence* [1834], Alfred Swaine Taylor's *Elements of Medical Jurisprudence* [1836], Isaac Ray's *A Treatise on the Medical Jurisprudence of Insanity* [1838], Amos Dean's *Principles of Medical Jurisprudence: Designed for the Professions of Law and Medicine* [1850], and lawyer Francis Wharton and physician Moreton Stillé's *A Treatise on Medical Jurisprudence* [1855].

In a summary of medical jurisprudence, James Webster's 1824 doctoral [MD] thesis at the College of Physicians of Philadelphia, University of Pennsylvania did not even mention malpractice. Twenty-six years later, in 1850, Webster discussed the "frequency of suits for malpractice" in an introduction to an anatomy course at the Geneva [NY] Medical College. In his lecture, Webster advised physicians to refuse fracture cases among the poor, and he suggested that "judicious witnesses" should be present when surgeons treated patients to record what happened and to keep independent case records.

John J. Elwell, a lawyer and a physician, was the first expert to intensively examine the mid-nineteenth century medical malpractice crisis. Citing the surge of malpractice suits since 1845 and using excerpts from recent cases, Elwell's A Medico-Legal Treatise on Malpractice, Medical Evidence and Insanity, Comprising the Elements of Medical Jurisprudence [1860] aimed "to furnish the medical man that necessary information respecting his legal responsibility as a practitioner." Almost uniformly, medico-legal experts hailed Elwell's book as filling a huge void in medical and legal literature. A review of Elwell's book in the *New York Medical Press* commented that "law and medicine had evolved into mutually incompatible professions." Continuing, the *Press* made remarks that anticipated currently held attitudes toward medical malpractice: "None of the previous works on medical jurisprudence has been at all sufficiently practical ... It is necessary that [a doctor] knows what he should say and do in a contingency which may happen unexpectedly, any time, especially in civil suits for malpractice ... [while valuable for lawyers, Elwell's material was absolutely] paramount to our medical brethren."

This early mid-nineteenth century medical malpractice crisis never really vanished. Malpractice suits continued to rise in absolute numbers as well as in rates. Physicians initiated a variety of protective mechanisms including medical society legal defense funds, mutual defense pledges, and eventually malpractice insurance coverage. Lawyers became better informed about medicine and specialized in malpractice claims. Today, the battle lines and the principles that emerged during the nineteenth century malpractice crisis are deeply entrenched in American society.

In 1794, the earliest recorded U.S. appellate court decision in a medical malpractice suit occurred in *Cross v. Guthrie*. One of Mrs. Guthrie's breasts was surgically removed by Cross, a Connecticut physician, and she died three hours later. In his malpractice suit alleging negligence in the performance of an operation, her husband sued Cross for £1,000 for "his costs and expense, and deprivation of the service and company of his wife." Plaintiffs argued that the physician ignored his duty to perform a mastectomy safely and skillfully and that his professional performance as a surgeon was unskillful, ignorant and cruel, "contrary to all the well-known rules and principles of practice in such cases, and that the patient survived by but three hours, and that the defendant had wholly broken and violated his undertaking and promise to the plaintiff to perform said operation skillfully and with safety to his wife." Even though the jury's verdict favored the surviving husband, he was only awarded $40 in damages for the loss of companionship.

Fundamental legal principles about medical malpractice evolved as state justices rendered judicial opinions. Analyzing *stare decisis* [case law], twenty-one pre-Civil War appellate court decisions between 1845 and 1861 were classified into five groupings of rationales for medical malpractice:

1. *Dealing with education and knowledge*: A medical practitioner was held legally responsible for what he said he was able to do. In 1856, the Tennessee Supreme Court held that a physician "contracts with those who employ him that he has such skill, science, and information as will enable him properly and judiciously to perform the duties of his calling."

2. *Opinions about the nature of the skill*: Ordinary, not extraordinary, skill was all that was required by law. In 1860, the Illinois Supreme Court held that "the principle is plain and of uniform application, that when a person assumes the profession of physician and surgeon, he must, in its exercise, be held to employ a reasonable amount of care and skill. For anything short of that degree of skill in his practice, the law will hold him responsible for any injury which may result from its absence. While he is not required to possess the highest order of qualification, to which some men attain, still he must possess and exercise that degree of skill which is ordinarily possessed by members of the profession."

3. *Nature of care*: Physicians contract to use reasonable and ordinary care in their application of their knowledge and skill. An 1860 Georgia Supreme Court observed that "he [the physician] undertakes that he will bring to the work a fair, reasonable and competent degree of care and skill in reference to the operation to be performed." He does not undertake that he will, in all events, safely and without injury care for the patient.

4. *Dealing with mistakes or errors of judgment*: Where there were reasonable grounds for diagnostic doubts and differences of opinion about treatment, the physician who exercised his best judgment was not responsible for errors of judgment or mistakes. However, errors of

judgment were not to be excused where what was well known and clearly indicated was not used in treatment. An 1853 New Hampshire decision asserted that "freedom from errors of judgment is never a part of a contract with a professional man."

5. *Opinions about cure*: Legally, physicians were not required to guarantee or insure a cure. While the law did not prevent the writing of contracts for cure warranties, the law would not uphold compensation claims if there was no absolute cure. In addition, the law would not support a malpractice defense by a physician if an absolute cure had been promised.

As the malpractice crisis continued unabated, physicians attempted to ensure that they would not be sued by requesting that patients sign a waiver. Dr. G. W. Butler told the patient that the compound fracture and crushed bone injury were severe and dangerous and added: "I will not treat your case unless you clear me of all responsibility for the results." Witnesses testified that the injured man replied: "I will clear you of all responsibility. Go ahead and treat my case. I would rather have you than anyone else." Nevertheless, after Dr. Butler's treatment, the leg had to be amputated eight days later and the patient voided the agreement and sued for malpractice. Despite the ambiguous legal nature of contracting away the right to sue, a trial judge ruled that the patient had the right to make the pretreatment agreement and accepted its validity. Jurors were told that if they believed that such an agreement existed, Dr. Butler was not liable for the loss of the leg. After brief deliberation, the jury returned with a verdict in favor of the physician.

These five medical malpractice principles were illustrated in a discussion of an actual suit by Dr. William M. Wood, a U.S. Navy doctor, in the *American Journal of Medical Sciences* in 1849. Dr. Wood was summoned as a witness in several trials for malpractice. In this case, a farmer suffered a compound fracture of the left thigh bone when a heavy piece of timber fell on him. His physician tried to save the leg but gangrene developed and the leg was amputated downward from the lower third of the thigh. Two days later the farmer died and a malpractice suit was filed. "Malpractice was attempted to be shown from all the following points: [1] The operation not being primary; [2] The time occupied; [3] Not bandaging and enclosing the limb in firm splints from the beginning; [4] The application of cold water; [5] Fastening the foot to the foot-board; and [6] Making incisions."

A 'botanic' and a "homeopathic" physician testified that the incisions and the failure to bandage the crushed and contused limb were serious medical practice errors. In defense, a "regular" physician testified that the physician's treatment was in accord with appropriate and proper medical practice. A justice heard this case without a jury and rendered a verdict in favor of the physician. Dr. Wood commented: "What would have been the result before a jury, is by no means certain."

In fervent statements to the jury, prosecution lawyers often exploited the anti-professional and anti-social class prejudices of the public. Ruminating about malpractice, a physician found "the interests and prejudices of the whole class [lower socioeconomic] are against the acts and doings of the regular practitioner.' A writer in the *Boston Medical and Surgical Journal* said that "juries have seemed to act with a determination to cripple the profession." During an 1848 case in New York, the patient's attorney criticized the medical profession as an "oppressive and aristocratic monopoly." After objections from the defense, the judge instructed the jurors to disregard the remarks. Despite the emotional appeal to their biases, the jurors rendered a verdict for the physician. A farmer serving as a juror in a malpractice trial characterized the subjective feelings of the jurors and their reactions to the testimony of the expert medical witness: "A jury of laboring men ... go into the jury box with feelings excited against the surgeon, because they think his business should produce no better pecuniary returns than their own; the surgeon's bill is always deemed exorbitant by them; and he is generally looked upon as almost a swindler, and living luxuriously upon their hard earnings; therefore they are always inclined to render a verdict against your profession, and in favor of one of their own class ... [Re expert witnesses] After a few questions are answered, they sneer and laugh at you [physicians], and make up their minds long before they leave the box."

Editorially, the medical journal agreed that the jury's decision was formed while they were still in the box. The writer confirmed that "a great number of these trials in various parts of the Union, but especially amongst farmers, are terminated in this way." He concluded: "The trial of a professional man for an alleged malpractice by a jury of laborers is farce and a disgrace to our country." Disgraceful aspects appeared in other malpractice trials. In the 1857 New Hampshire case of *Leighton vs. Sargent*, a sick juror was allowed to drink brandy while the verdict was being decided. Upon appeal, the defendant was acquitted by the state's Supreme Court "for the cause that brandy was furnished to the jury, and drank [sic] by several of them while deliberating upon the cause, after retiring to form their verdict. We think the verdict must be set aside."

Judges displayed a variety of attitudes towards medicine and physicians as they and the jury pondered if the medical treatment was rendered with "due and proper care, skill, and diligence." In an extreme opinion, a judge contended that the number of unqualified practitioners would be reduced if patients were encouraged to bring malpractice accusations more frequently. Pennsylvania Supreme Court justices revealed a sensitivity to the distinctions between medical and legal judgments. They discussed appropriate techniques for treating fractures and two of the three justices cited a number of professional texts. In contrast, the third justice emphasized that surgical questions had not been adjudicated: "But when we decide the legal point we are done with it. We are not authority on the questions of surgery."

After citing the avarice of the community, the influence and opinions of charlatans, the acute management of the bar, and the ignorance of juries, a physician argued that the only remedy lay with the bench: "Let judges make themselves acquainted with what should be the qualifications required of medical men, according to the *standard justified by their location*, and charge juries definitely and clearly upon that point. There may be other modes of setting things right for the advantage of all parties, and I shall be most happy to see them suggested."

Medical knowledge, or lack of it, by juries, lawyers and even judges, may have led to emotionally based rather than rational decisions. Scientific information about the treatment of fractures and results were not widely known among professional and/or lay circles.

After 1835, orthopedic outcomes became the most common reason for malpractice suits. Elwell claimed that "nine-tenths of all the cases of malpractice that come before the courts for adjudication arise either from the treatment of amputations, fractures, or dislocations." Litigation involved less than perfect results following dislocations and fractures with deformities such as a frozen position following a compound fracture, deformed or crooked limbs, or noticeably shorter limbs. Disgruntled patients could easily demonstrate for the courts their unequivocal and measurable damage as a result of the physician's alleged unskillful treatment. Similar to the situation today, technological advances, particularly in the treatment of fractures, generated unrealistic public and professional expectations and stimulated medical malpractice suits.

A history of fracture therapy traces treatment as far back as the Neolithic age and noted that fractures occurred ever since mankind has been in existence. Throughout history Egyptian, Greek, Roman, Arabian, American Indian and European physicians and healers treated fractures using a variety of splints and mechanical devices. Interestingly, and with relevance to defense arguments in later malpractice suits, a sixteenth century English physician, Peter Lowe [or Love], warned against refracturing a vicious union: "Better suffer a little deformity of the part than loss of the whole body."

In translations of the Byzantine manuscripts of Hippocrates [460-377 BCE], Galen [131-201 AD], and Oribasius [325-403], much of the work dealt with fractures and dislocations and included woodcut illustrations of instruments and mechanical devices. Furthermore, Hippocrates discussed the danger of sepsis in his 48 part, 12,000 word document, *On Fractures*. Similar reviews focused on the history of the treatment of compound fractures and discussed the therapies of Hippocrates, Galen, Theodoric, Bishop of Cervia [1205-1296], Paracelsus [1493-1541], Hieronymus Brunnschweig [1450-circa 1512], Leonardo Botallo [1530-1600], Pierre Joseph Desault [1744-1795], and others. In the eighteenth century, most physicians agreed that compound fractures should be treated by immediate amputation. "It was generally believed that sacrificing the limb before wound complications ensued would enhance the chance of survival." With the introduction of ether in 1846 and chloroform in 1847 as anesthetics, the complications involved in setting bones and doing surgery eased somewhat. To prevent sepsis and avoid subsequent amputation, improved bandaging, splinting and packing techniques were used. Concepts of antisepsis were not introduced until Joseph Lister's series of articles appeared in *The Lancet* in 1867.

About 1755, Dr. Percivall Pott, surgeon to St. Bartholomew's Hospital in England, complained of the "notorious" practice of his peers when treating fractures. He asked: Why were broken thighs and legs "often, *very* often, left deformed, crooked and shortened?" Subsequently, Dr. Pott sustained an open fracture of one of his legs in 1756. Acting against medical advice to amputate, Dr. Pott chose to be treated conservatively and his leg was saved. Pott observed: "In every instance of compound fracture, the surgeon should carefully weigh the risk of conservative treatment against the hazards of operation." Likewise, in 1780, Scottish physician, Dr. Thomas Kirkland, exclaimed that it takes more skill to save a limb than to sever it: "A man must be very ignorant, who cannot take off a leg, an operation to be performed by any blockhead." Nevertheless, despite occasional digressions, primary amputation remained the treatment of choice well into the nineteenth century. "Compound fractures of the limbs with attendant sepsis remained mostly unmanageable and staggering morbidity and mortality could be anticipated."

Dominique Jean Larrey, Napoleon's chief military surgeon, was a pupil of Desault and adhered to "debridement" in the treatment of compound wounds. French military surgeons advocated amputation as the standard treatment for compound fractures. In September 1812, during and after the battle of Borodino in the ill fated Russian campaign, Larrey performed some 200 amputations in about 24 hours.

In 1830, famed Philadelphia physician, Dr. Samuel D. Gross, authored a 389 page book, *The Anatomy, Physiology and Diseases of the Bones and Joints*, the first American book on orthopedics. This title may not indicate that the book deals with fractures. However, in his 1887 autobiography, Dr. Gross commented: "The title was unfortunate; it should have been *A Practical Treatise on Fractures and Dislocations With an Account of the Diseases of the Bones and Joints*."

Dr. Astley Paston Cooper's 1822 book, *A Treatise on Dislocations and On Fractures of the Joints*, was the principal reference in the United States and Great Britain for 30 years. In 1835, Dr. Cooper discussed perfunctory amputations in cases of compound fracture: "Formerly, and with my recollection, it was thought expedient for the preservation of life, by many of our best surgeons to amputate the limb in these cases, but from our experience of late years, such advice would in a great majority of instances be now deemed highly injudicious."

In his 1860 book on medical jurisprudence, Elwell observed changes in the treatment of fractures: "An amputation that would have been justified by the rules of surgery and the operator protected in the court, twenty years ago or even less time than that, would now be repudiated by the best authority and the operator justly charged with malpractice."

In the late 1840s, while he was a surgeon on the faculty at the University of Buffalo [NY] medical school, Dr. Frank H. Hamilton began collecting and analyzing statistical data on the treatment and the outcomes of hundreds of fracture and dislocation cases. Taking precise measurements, adding relevant comments and matching the results with the treatments, Hamilton recorded and compiled "fracture tables" noting imperfect alignments, shortened limbs and other malformations. In contrast to the claims of many practitioners about their excellent results, Hamilton dispelled the myth that properly treated bones unite perfectly; perfect restorations were uncommon. In 1855, he authored a 99 page book on *Deformities After Fractures* that debunked the alleged perfection of the surgeons: "Neither in Great Britain nor in the United States, nor in any other part of the world, has the art of treating fractures attained that degree of perfection which surgeons have almost universally claimed for it ... Students will continue to go out from our hospitals with a belief that perfect union of broken bones is the rule, and that exceptions imply generally unskillful management ... Physicians testify that they have seen and treated ten fractures of the femur, in adult persons, and not one of them [the limbs] is in any way shortened or deformed."

Hamilton said that this last comment could be attributed to self-preservation and the silence of practitioners about the true outcomes. Implying that the surgeons may not tell the truth in the courtroom, he remarked: "They may hesitate to regard the sanctity of an oath!" In response to the query about why medical failures should be exposed, Hamilton responded that the first step towards improvement "must be factual exposure of wants and deficiencies."

As a defense witness, Hamilton commiserated: "Surgeons themselves have believed, and taught, and testified that in a large majority of cases, broken limbs may be made perfect, while the fact is not so!" In one study, forty of the fifty fractures [80%], of the lower extremities healed with deformities or shortening of the limbs. By 1853, a Hamilton publication contained data about 461 fracture cases. Hamilton's statistical data were published in pamphlets, medical journals and books and reached a wide audience. A series of three articles in

*Transactions of the American Medical Association* totaled almost 500 pages and included drawings and a listing of treatments. Often, expert witnesses and defense attorneys relied on Hamilton's publications or even used him as an expert witness. An 1860 review of Hamilton's works evoked a hope that his work would: "erect something like a standard which may be generally agreed upon for the protection and satisfaction of all parties who may hereafter be involved ... in the miseries of a prosecution for 'malpractice.'"

However, this wish was not achieved and uncertainty remained in approaches to treatments for fractures. Hamilton's data were not irrefutable and his selected treatments were not unanimously embraced. Despite the lack of a consensus, Hamilton's prominence led him to become president of a number of professional organizations: the New York State Medical Society [1855]; New York Medico-Legal Society [1875-76]; and the New York Society of Medical Jurisprudence [1880-84].

Related to the scientific principles involved in treating compound fractures, there were deep-seated existing professional conflicts governing the medical practices of regular versus irregular physicians. These conflicts surfaced in malpractice litigation as expert medical witnesses testified in opposition to each other.

In the early nineteenth century, most of the state medical licensure laws were either weak or nonexistent. Competition for patients and fees among regular physicians and between regular and irregular doctors spurred the early increase in medical malpractice litigation. To improve their own status, individual physicians willingly denigrated the therapeutic practices of their competitors. Such public criticism may have encouraged patients to file lawsuits.

Regular or orthodox physicians received their training at medical schools, perhaps loosely linked to a university. Supposedly a three year program, medical schools followed varying curriculums that required two separate four to five months series of academic lectures with surgical demonstrations and a one year apprenticeship in a practitioner's office. By 1851, Dr. Nathan S. Davis, an outspoken critic of medical education, declared that regular medical school graduates were "tolerably well-versed in the ordinary details of medical and surgical practice." Yet, a regular medical education was of notoriously low quality, unevenly regulated and disorganized enough to allow students to earn a medical degree in fewer than three years.

Irregular physicians included "[American] Indian doctors, urine doctors, root doctors, water doctors, steam doctors, and homeopaths, preying upon the community." While irregular physicians secured their medical education in a variety of ways, all the teaching was quick and easy. Mary Edwards Walker earned a medical degree as a hydropath after only a three months education at the Hygeio Therapeutic College in New York City in 1862. John Ordronaux, a lawyer and a physician and author of a 1869 book on medical jurisprudence, declared that "the quack, the pill-vender, the life-elixir compounder, the panacea concocter ... may permanently injure health, or even steal the breath from a man's nostrils without being charged with misdemeanor or felony." In discussing jury trials for medical malpractice, the *Western Medical and Surgical Journal* expanded the professional opinion "that the chances are altogether better for the acquittal of an ignorant, uneducated pretender to medical knowledge, who is really guilty, than that of an intelligent, well-educated surgeon to whom no fault can justly be charged."

Most regular and irregular schools were proprietary and considered a good business venture. Regular schools required a minimal facility and five or six academic lecturers. Irregular schools could be conducted with physician aspirants purchasing self-study books and/or medical kits, through short-term lectures, or through a curriculum approaching the regular school but based on unorthodox healing theories. Efforts to regulate the profession of medicine were initiated during the late 1840s as the newly organized American Medical Association recommended reforms in medical education. "Ignorant and impudent pretenders, under a great variety of humbugging titles, come before the public with equal rights, and a better chance for popular favour, than the regular practitioner ... Hence, ignorance and charlatanism become the rule, and intelligence the error."

Ironically, the most knowledgeable and technologically advanced physicians became frequent targets of medical malpractice suits involving the care of fractures. Several factors resulted in the better physicians being sued more often rather than the host of amateurs and alternative doctors.

1. *Improved techniques and more careful training produced advances in therapeutic measures.* With these professional advances, physicians opted to try to save limbs in difficult cases. About twenty years earlier,

the majority of patients with compound fractures would have had their affected limbs amputated. Physicians would have been following safe and standard procedures and there would not be a malpractice suit.

2. *To avoid internal infection, the physician required sophisticated knowledge of wound dressing and bone setting.* Often, better regularly trained physicians would try to save the limb in difficult compound fracture cases, even if the result was less than perfect. A physician might rationalize that even a slightly deformed limb was better than no limb. In contrast, amateur or inexperienced healers would never pretend to possess the skill to properly dress the wound and to set the fracture.

3. *Irregular healers could not be sued for malpractice since no standard procedures existed for them.* Regular physicians utilized educational textbooks and manuals that could be considered norms or standards in court suits. On the other hand, irregular physicians could not be sued for undesirable results because no standards existed. Each patient came for the individual herbal drugs, hot baths, or water therapies. A regular physician expressed his frustration: "It is better to be without a diploma; for then, besides having the sympathies of the community, the practitioner can say, "I make no pretensions, I offer no certificate of ability, and only gave my neighbour in his sufferings such aid as I could."

4. *A deep pocket theory already existed.* Patients were not inclined to sue irregular doctors who had few assets when the regular practitioners were more prosperous and the award might actually be collected. Part of this attitude arose from the anti-professional and social class ethos of the period. In addition, there was "the avarice of those disposed to escape their doctor's bill, and willing to take the chance of making money out of their injuries."

To avoid this swindle, physicians found it easier to forgive the bill or settle a claim rather than legally fight the accusation and risk dire consequences. In reflecting on the frequency of medical malpractice suits in the Northern states, Dr. Hamilton claimed "that many men abandoned the practice of surgery, leaving it to those who, with less skill and experience, had less reputation and property to lose." Trepidation about a possible malpractice suit gave rise to intense emotional feelings among regular physicians.

A chronology of items appearing in the *Boston Medical and Surgical Journal* between 1844 and 1855 clearly illustrate the intense reactions of medical practitioners toward the surging malpractice crisis.

On September 11, 1844, the *BMSJ* discussed the malpractice case against Dr. Azariah B. Shipman who was forced into a "legal hopper" and could possibly be "ground up": "Western New York is becoming dangerous for a surgeon ... A man may be ever so qualified for practice, and yet be constantly liable to vexatious suits, instituted by ignorant, unprincipled persons, sometimes urged on, it is presumed, by those who have a private grudge ... unless a better state of things could be brought about, the medical practitioners in that part of the country would unitedly refuse to render any assistance to case of fractures and dislocations."

A prominent New York physician, Dr. Alden March, discussed a case of alleged malpractice in surgery in the August 4, 1847 *BMSJ*: "Legal prosecutions for mal-practice occur so often that even a respectable surgeon may well fear the results of his surgical practice."

In August 1851, Dr. Shipman's letter to the editor of the *BMSJ* commented on a malpractice suit against Dr. G. W. Edwards by Morgan Stewart. Stewart was "somewhat addicted to the use of ardent spirits" and was kicked by a horse resulting in a compound fracture of his tibia. However there was a minuscule displacement and a slight shortening of the limb. None of the medical witnesses attributed the claimed shortening to the treatment of Dr. Edwards. Stewart walked with crutches and impressed the jury. He was awarded $500 in damages. Dr. Shipman concluded: "Since the trial he [Stewart] has thrown away his crutches and walks much better than before ... I have known many a poor cripple, who could not walk without the aid of crutches, on the termination of a trial, get the use of his limb in a most surprising and miraculous manner .. The frequency of suits for mal-practice is having a most decidedly pernicious influence on our profession ....I know several good surgeons who will not touch a case of fracture, and others who will only do so under a guaranty that ... they shall be protected ... If it was only the ignorant and unskillful men who were the sufferers, it would be a relief to the profession; but it is not so. In nine cases out of ten it is some well-educated and eminent man."

On June 2, 1851, a letter to the *BMSJ* referred to a suit against Drs. Poole and Carpenter. This writer noted the tedious eight day trial before court approved referees and the expert testimony that cited the average results in cases of fractures of all kinds as compiled by Dr. Hamilton. In this case the decision was favorable to the defendants.

Furthermore, this letter noted an "unjust attack" in a malpractice suit against a Professor of Surgery at Darmouth [VT] Medical College, Dr. Dixi Crosby, "a gentleman of affluence and high standing." He continued: "Such suits are exceedingly oppressive and cruel to humble physicians, of limited means. The public must be combated into a proper understanding of what constitutes a physician's legal responsibility ... No physician who has the means will infamously submit to be plundered by 'buying his peace.' And a gentleman of Dr. Crosby's wealth and well-earned celebrity, will not shrink from doing his part to combat and check this unnatural crusade against one of the most useful of professions."

In the "Medical Intelligence" section of an 1852 issue, the *BMSJ* commented that Massachusetts was "taking the lead in the persecution of surgeons." It was claimed that the "best operators in New England expose themselves to a vexatious lawsuit" when the result is not satisfactory to the patient in all respects. A case was cited of a physician's "alleged unskillfulness and negligence" in the treatment of a broken arm. "The damages were laid at the moderate sum of $4,000! By the good sense of the jury, the plaintiff recovered but *one dollar* ... Some of the most worthless men in the State ... have made a fractured bone the stepping-stone to personal independence." In summary, the article painted a bleak picture: "It is impossible to predict whose turn may come next ... there is a cherished disposition among certain classed of persons to ruin every surgical practitioner, if possible, by seizing his property. A pre-text of malpractice ... [and] an unrighteous suit at law ... [causes] the ruin of the defendant's professional influence ... even if his last dollar is not taken."

During an 1853 discussion of the liability of physicians and surgeons, the *BMSJ* talked about written agreements to protect against malpractice suits and stated that physicians cannot "legally fortify themselves in this manner." Physicians are obliged to render care and "must stand the racket of a law-suit into the bargain, if a patient wants to raise a sum of money." This catch-22 situation damns the doctors if they do or if they don't treat patients: "Either way, lawyers pretend that they have us at their mercy ... no surgeon or physician, having a particle of self-respect or independence of character, would put himself knowingly at the mercy of an unprincipled knave, whose pleasure would be to ruin him if money could be obtained, thereby."

A ten page 1853 report of the Massachusetts Medical Society on the causes and prevention of suits for malpractice was ridiculed by the *BMSJ* as being worthless. Instead, the article presented an alternative preventive method: "Refusing to give one's services to people who are disposed to prosecute their professional advisor in order to cheat him out of a bill, or obtain money for miscalled damages, is the shortest way of keeping out of the difficulty."

A malpractice suit was brought against Dr. Bartlett of Somerville, near Boston, in 1854 for "alleged want of skill in the treatment of a fractured clavicle" in an eight year old girl, Emma Edgely. Damages of $10,000 were asked for by the lawyers. While not yet aware of the court decision, the "Medical Intelligence" article made a strong point: "It is almost a wonder that any surgeon, now-a-days, can be found, with moral courage or humane feeling enough to undertake to remedy a deformity, or treat a case of injury, without a bond from the patient or his legal guardian that he shall not be subjected to a suit for damages, in case he should fail to make the patient as whole and perfect as he was when he came from the hands of his Creator."

In 1855, the 'Medical Intelligence" section of the *BMSJ* followed up on Dr. Bartlett and reported that "the defendant came off victoriously ... without a shilling drawn from Dr. Bartlett's pocket." In addition, the report noted that surgeons were seeking written agreements from patients not to sue before rendering care. There was an opinion that changes for the better would occur "when the courts have the patience to sift out the motive that ordinarily prompts to these unrighteous prosecutions, by unfortunate patients or their friends."

In February 1854, the *BMSJ* reported about the case of a man who suffered compound fractures of the leg in a railroad accident. He was treated by Dr. David Allen who opted to try to save the leg. After saving the leg, the young man walked as if his leg might be a quarter or one-half inch shorter. Dr. Abner Phelps examined the patient and concluded: "In my humble opinion, the skill. ingenuity and strong judgment employed by Dr. Allen in the cure of such a limb, have justly entitled him to far greater and more lasting honor and reputation than he could have acquired by fifty successful amputations."

Dr. Phelps rhetorically asked: "But are not many limbs amputated that might be saved?" Addressing physicians, he encouraged efforts to save a "badly broken limb."

Almost exactly one year later, on February 8, 1855, there was a report from the Massachusetts General Hospital about a female book peddlar who fell under a railroad car at Lynn station. She suffered compound fractures of both feet, a toe on her right foot was completely mashed, and the skin was stripped off her left foot upward behind the ankle. Dr. H. J. Bigelow, Professor of Surgery at Harvard Medical College, was summoned and he decided to amputate her left leg immediately.

In the November 13, 1855 issue of the *BMSJ*, a letter applauded the journal's remarks about the need for "a standard work on surgical jurisprudence." He followed by taking lawyers to task: "This will, in a measure, shield us from those upstart members of the bar, who by their impertinent, irrelevant questions worry and ill-treat members of a profession in every respect equal to their own. Medical men do not fear legal *gentlemen*; yet the protest against the scurrilous attacks of some who claim to be such - who pretend a knowledge in law superior to Blackstone, and in medicine to Galen ... I believe ... this *Vandal* warfare should be carried to *Carthage* ... The change must come."

Changing times do not appear to have substantially differentiated the first malpractice crisis from those that ensued subsequently. There can be no doubt that the frequently heated interactions, accusations and acrimonious verbal assaults between physicians and lawyers have not ceased up to the present time. This hostility may be due to the intrinsic differences between law and medicine: "Much of the hostility existing between the professions of law and medicine is caused by the fact that medicine is a prospective profession, whereas law is retrospective. When a physician does anything to any patient, he is experimenting or medically speculating. But if the patient suffers adverse results and sues, then the court applies what is by definition a retrospective judgment of a particular course of treatment."

Concerns about medical malpractice prompted calls for tort reform from a variety of sources. Technology advances allowed concerned parties to present their views on the super information highway of the computer Internet. Dr. Nancy W. Dickey, Chair of the AMA Board of Trustees, posted the AMA's official comments on malpractice reform in her testimony before a February 27, 1996 U.S. House of Representatives, Committee on Judiciary meeting. She supported a $250,000 malpractice cap for noneconomic damages, a reform of joint and several liability, reductions in statutes of limitations, and allowing juries to be informed when plaintiffs have already collected from insurance companies. Broadening the chasm between lawyers and physicians, Dr. Dickey reminded the legislators that fifty cents of every dollar collected goes to attorneys and not to the plaintiffs. In addition, Dr. Dickey noted that median verdicts in 1995 were up 40 percent, to $500,000.

Using the Internet, lawyers can advertise their medical malpractice services to computer "surfers" seeking an attorney to represent them in a claim against a physician. These lawyers list their biographical data, their special interests, and their legal accomplishments. One law firm highlighted winning awards of $4.2 million for a quadriplegic injury and $2 million for a carpal tunnel injury. In a parallel marketing technique, attorneys purchase frequent advertisements in newspapers alerting the public to their legal right to sue physicians for damages if they are harmed.

While some patients may continue to be regarded with suspicion as opportunists, a majority of physicians tends to blame the lawyers for prompting patients to sue. Attorneys counter that people are entitled to sue if they are harmed. The discourse on this issue between the "mutually incompatible professions" of the mid 1800s, physicians and medical malpractice lawyers, still appears to be as hostile in the 1990s as it was during America's first medical malpractice crisis.

## A VERITABLE OASIS IN THE DESERT: NEW YORK MEDICAL COLLEGE

In the *History of Medicine in New York*, the New York Medical College is labeled "a veritable oasis in the desert of low grade medical education in America at this time ... One very well planned attempt to get away from the unfortunate degradation of medical education which had come over the country was made in New York. This was the New York Medical College, and its founders proved to be a full generation ahead of their time."

A brief review of medical education in the United States in the 1850s lends understanding to the comments about the degradation of physician training.

Kings College [NY] and the College of Philadelphia, the first two American medical schools, had admission and graduation requirements similar to well established European medical colleges. During the Revolutionary War, there was a regression to a medical apprenticeship system. It took more than 100 years to regain the prior high educational standards.

In mid-nineteenth century America, medical education combined lecture courses and apprenticeship. Students tended "to rush into practice with the least possible expenditure of money, time, brains and knowledge." A medical student literally "read" medicine from books in a physician's office for eight months and seldom cared for any patients. During the next four months, the student sat through four to seven lectures daily at a medical college. If required, he attended clinics and/or practiced dissection. To graduate, students had to be 21 years of age with three years of study that included 28 months apprenticeship with a preceptor plus two full four months courses of lectures. Lectures were essentially repeated each year; subject matter was not graded upward in difficulty. Topics included the basic sciences, the theory and diagnosis of disease and the treatment of disease.

Obviously, critics of medical education existed long before and after the New York Medical College was founded. By the 1870s, medical education reforms were well under way in the United States. In the early 1900s, the Flexner report on medical education in the U.S. and Canada popularized the revolutionary changes already underway to reform medical education.

About 1845, Dr. Nathan S. Davis complained in the *New York*

*Medical Journal* that the complex medical college subjects "are all crowded into his [the student's] mind in the short space of sixteen weeks." Medical students were ill prepared for such intensive learning. Compared with 80 percent of theology students and 65 percent of law students, only 26 percent of medical students were then college graduates. An 1846 book on practical education in medicine derided the `half-educated graduates in medicine " who practiced the "rifest and rankest quackery." Lamenting the public's deprecation of the education of physicians, the American Medical Association [AMA] Committee on Medical Education said: "... more pains are often taken by men of reputed good sense in choosing a cook or a coachman than in choosing a physician." By 1860, a *New York Times* editorial deplored the fact that "... a young man can now obtain from our greatest schools his diploma to commence the practice of medicine in eight or nine months from the time that he first enters the walls of a college or the wards of an hospital - nay, the hospital practice is not required at all as a condition of graduation." Quoting a Dr. Reese, the editorial continued: "Any ignorant clown may enter a medical college by paying five dollars and without ever having read a medical book, or, indeed any other, at once be transformed into a student of the most recondite and abstruse sciences of the entire curriculum, by simply paying his fees - this qualification being the only *sine qua non* of regular attendance upon the lectures."

In the 1910 Flexner report, Henry S. Pritchett, President of the Carnegie Foundation, summed up the status of medical education in 1885: "There has been enormous over-production of uneducated and ill trained practitioners ... in absolute disregard of the public welfare and without any serious thought of the interests of the public ... over-production of ill trained men is due to the existence of a very large number of commercial schools sustained by advertising methods drawing unprepared youth out of industrial occupations into medicine ... until recently medical school was profitable business because instruction was mainly didactic."

Considering the opposition's argument that "a poor medical school is justified in the interest of the poor boy," Flexner diplomatically inferred that the rationale may be insincere.

Medical columns of the newspapers advertised that Dr. W.H. Humbert, No. 542 Broadway, devoted his attention to the treatment of all those cases of diseases "termed incurable," and which have baffled both quack and regular practice; Dr. Larmont, 42 Reade Street, applied a Paris and London treatment for private disease with no mercury used. Testimonials from satisfied patients appeared in the ad; Dr. Corbitt, 19 Duane Street, put forth a no cure - no pay offer; Dr. Joseph A Weder plugged his Orange [NJ] Mountain Water Cure where private baths were attached to the patient's room; Hydropathic physician, T.L. Nichols advertised lectures on Suicide, Medical Quackery and Allopathy, and Homeopathy and Hydropathy on Monday, Thursday and Friday evenings at 12½ cents each with ladies free; Dr. J. S. Fancher touted his Grecian Fancheronian Drops to positively cure dyspepsia, chills and fever, jaundice, diarrhea and cholera; Horeshound Cough Syrup sold for 12½ cents; Bryan's Pulmonic Wafers proclaimed freedom from cough in 10 minutes; readers could buy a Vegetable Pain Killer; and Mrs. Burns offered her Antique Ointment.

A medical college was a profitable business because instruction was almost exclusively pedantic; lecture halls were all that an entrepreneur needed. Yet, schools were small and about 50 percent of the schools had incomes below $10,000 per year. In March 1850, there were 42 regular medical schools in the U.S.; two existed in New York City with about 525 students while the comparatively smaller city of Philadelphia had five schools with 1,500 students. In comparing the two New York medical schools, Dr. Alfred Stillé commented that students in New York "prefer that rotten and disgraceful concern [University of New York Medical Department] to the dignified and meritorious College of Physicians and Surgeons."

Established in 1807, the College of Physicians and Surgeons at 67 Crosby Street, was the oldest in New York City. In 1841, the University of New York Medical Department opened free of restrictions of the Regents. Their graduates could practice "without receiving a license from State or county medical societies." At first, courses were held at Stuyvesant Institute on Broadway opposite Bond Street. In 1851, the school moved to a newly erected building on 14th Street.

Typically, a medical school had one main building with two lecture halls. A lower floor was used for chemistry, materia medica, and the theory and practice of medicine. Having skylights, the upper floor was used for anatomy, physiology and surgery. Possibly, there was a museum with paper-mâché body parts displayed, anatomical and physiological specimens and obstetrical models of chamois and leather.

Relative to equipment, Flexner reported that Harvard Medical School announcements first mentioned a stethoscope in 1868-69 and a microscope in 1870-71. Libraries consisted of the personal holdings of the faculty.

Regular lecture sessions in New York City medical schools usually began in October and ended in March. Assertive students could seek out medical schools where lectures began and ended during other months. Finding these schools, students could attend lectures at one school and a second set elsewhere and complete their required lectures in one year. Frequently, the medical schools announced free introductory lectures prior to the regular course. These were open to the public and to professionals and were intended to entice students to enroll in the school. In 1850, only two schools had sessions of five months or more. In about 80 percent of the schools, the lectures went on for 16 to 18 weeks. Five days a week, students sat in lecture halls for up to six hours each day. Individual faculty lectures regularly lasted for one hour.

Usually, each faculty member conducted brief, oral and secret examinations to test students for graduation. Harvard Medical School student James Clark White was asked only one question when he appeared in 1850 to be tested on surgery: "Well, White, what would you do for a wart?" This situation so distressed Charles Eliot, Harvard University's President, that he urged the medical school to institute written examinations in 1871. Dr. Henry Bigelow, Professor of Surgery, responded: "I had to tell him [Eliot] he knew nothing about the quality of the Harvard Medical School students; more than half of them can barely write. Of course, they can't pass written examinations."

Matriculation fees for medical school ranged from $3-5. Each professor issued lecture tickets at about $15 each for all his sessions and earned his salary in that manner; for seven faculty the student's total fee would be $105. Dissecting fees were $5-10. A graduation fee varied from $10-40, but usually around $15-20. Room and board in the neighborhood cost $2.50-3.50 per week. Students paid private practitioners from $50-100 per year for their apprenticeship. In total, students spent from $350-650 for three years of study.

To streamline the process and collect payment in advance, medical colleges initiated a fee for the full course of lectures. In 1849-50, the University of New York Medical Department advertised in the *American Journal of the Medical Sciences*: "The Lectures of the regular winter course will begin on Monday, October 29th, and be continued to the last of February [four months] ... The fees for the full Course of Lectures $105." In the same publication, the College of Physicians and Surgeons announced a $96 charge for the lectures beginning Monday, October 15th and ending the second Thursday in March.

An 1849 AMA Committee on Medical Education survey of 30 medical schools revealed: 17 schools did not require dissection; only four required certification of apprenticeship for the full three year period; 10 did not require any certification from a preceptor; and only seven required hospital attendance. Moreover, there were questionable practices relative to medical school records. Frequently, students were allowed to register after the term began and to leave before it ended. A student could purchase tickets to the lectures and never actually attend. Merely having the tickets was acceptable as evidence of attendance. Less than 50 percent of the students who enrolled actually graduated. From 1844 to 1849, there were 18,899 students at the 30 medical colleges surveyed. Only 6,414 [34 %] were awarded medical degrees. During that time period, two medical schools enrolled and graduated the greatest number of students in the nation; University of Pennsylvania, Medical Department 2,331 and 849 [36 %] and Jefferson Medical College [Philadelphia] 2,327 and 833 [36%].

Spearheaded by Dr. Nathan S. Davis, the Medical Society of the State of New York [MSSNY] advocated medical education reforms in the early 1840s. Shortly after being founded in 1847 and setting $3 dues for the year, the AMA recommended that lecture terms be lengthened, that schools increase the number of their faculty and that the granting of degrees be separated from the school's faculty.

A Harvard Medical School committee consisting of Drs. John Ware, Jacob Bigelow and Oliver Wendell Holmes declared in April 1849 that "it is not expedient to extend the course of medical lectures, given at this institution, beyond its present duration." This committee maintained: "too prolonged an attendance upon lectures ... is likely to beget injurious habits of mind in the student ... four months in the year is quite as large a proportion of the student's time as can be profitably occupied in attendance upon lectures ... the remaining eight [months] may be devoted far more advantageously to private personal study."

"Deficiency of sufficient preliminary education" was cited as a major obstacle in improving medical education. While the report supported "three years at least of full and entire devotion to medical studies," the members believed the three years requirement was "imperfectly enforced." A faculty meeting accepted the committee report unanimously.

After scrutinizing the Harvard Medical School report, the AMA Committee on Medical Education labeled the document as "an elaborate defence of the limitation of the courses of medical instruction in the schools to four months." In response, the AMA Committee stated: "It is absurd to suppose that any effectual improvement can be made ... bringing their instruction up to the present elevation of medical science, while the four-month courses are retained." Significantly, medical schools were overwhelmingly proprietary and cut-throat competition killed any movement toward reforms. In the 1849-50 term, the University of Pennsylvania Medical Department increased its lecture course to six months. Even the lecture fees were reduced to compensate for the student's increased room and board. However, the experiment failed because rival medical colleges did not do likewise. In fact, Philadelphia's Jefferson Medical College continued its four month long lecture series and the class "increased more rapidly than ever before."

There were two unrelated New York Medical Colleges: one, the "veritable oasis," existed from 1850 to 1864; the other originated in 1860 under a different name and after several name changes evolved into the New York Medical College that still exists today.

On April 8, 1850, the New York Medical College was chartered. A regular course of lectures began on October 16, 1850, the first class graduated in March 1851 and the college closed in 1864. While there is no documentation of a cause and effect relationship, the New York Medical College was the first to comply with all of the educational recommendations of the MSSNY and the AMA, the latter newly formed in 1847. Lecture courses were lengthened to a month-long "Preliminary Course embracing subjects not included in the regular Course" plus five months of regular course lectures. Professorships were increased well beyond the usual six or seven, and the granting of medical degrees was disassociated from the faculty and became the province of an independent medical Board of Censors.

Today's New York Medical College was chartered on April 12, 1860 as the Homeopathic Medical College of the State of New York in New York City. Their credo declared: "No medical institution in our country shall be better prepared to impart a thorough medical education." Poet, journalist and civic leader, William Cullen Bryant was elected President of the Board of Trustees and served for ten years, from 1862 to 1872. After several name changes, the school adopted its current name in 1936 and exists today in Valhalla, New York.

Medical education reformers faced bitter, vigorous and continuous opposition from the entrenched proprietary medical schools. Nevertheless, significant medical education reforms persisted and a developing national movement increased in strength. Public acceptance of the Flexner report attracted adherents and abetted medical reformers who had struggled for many years.

Few of the existing medical schools adopted any of the medical education reform recommendations. To counter the obvious deficiencies in medical education, a group of concerned New Yorkers decided to establish a school in which the standards would be higher than those in vogue in other schools. They were determined that the New York Medical College: "be the model medical institution of our country." These citizens - city officials, clergymen, lawyers, merchants, and physicians - applied for and received a state charter for the New York Medical College on April 8, 1850. Prominent lawyer, George Wood, was President of the 32 member Board of Trustees that included three physician faculty members: Drs. Abraham L.Cox, R. Ogden Doremus and Horace Green.

At a cost of $50,000, a commodious building 50 feet wide and 90 feet deep, was erected. A cornerstone was laid on July 31 on 13th Street between Third and Fourth Avenue. Classes began on October 15 of the same year. There were three large halls where all the seats were arranged in a parabolic curve rising one above another for sight and convenience: the anatomical room had 20 skylights with the theater being 40 feet from the floor to top of the dome; the general lecture hall was 18 feet high arranged so every seat had a clear view of the speaker and/or demonstrator; a chemical lecture room had a similar arrangement; next to the first floor lecture room, the whole front of the building was devoted to the chemical laboratory. At his own expense, Dr. Doremus established and equipped the first laboratory in the U.S. for the instruction of medical students in analytical chemistry, toxicology and research. A first floor museum displayed comprehensive anatomical and physiological wax models imported from France as well as a variety of specimens. Water from the Croton reservoir and gas were available throughout the building. Speaking tubes descended from every room to the janitor's apartment.

A summer course was established and the lecture term was lengthened. Realizing the need for clinical instruction, a charter was secured to allow the school to erect a hospital alongside the school. While fund raising progressed, the college opened a 27 bed charity clinic. When hospital beds were established within its own building for teaching purposes, the school was sometimes called the New York Medical College and Charity Hospital. By 1855, more than 2,000 sick poor people were cared for annually. This was the "first attempt at establishing a regular daily bedside clinic for all branches of instruction in the indispensable parts of medical teaching." Bedside teaching supplemented clinical teaching that took place at Emigrant's Hospital on Ward's Island and at Charity Hospital on Blackwell's Island. Referring to the free care, an 1860 *New York Times* editorial praised the school: "Every day, the New York Medical College opens its doors to the lame, halt and blind where they are examined and treated by the faculty ... the foremost practitioners, facilities and teachers rank with the best."

Faculty increased well above the usual six or seven professors to 10 or more. In compliance with the school's state charter, an independent medical Board of Censors examined the students before recommending that the Trustees grant a medical degree. Furthermore, "no fee for graduation shall be exacted from the candidates." Even more, the charter authorized gratuitous admission to the medical college of up to five distinguished "young men of good moral character ... in necessitous circumstances" from the Free Academy [later the College of the City of New York].

Did these students receive a quality medical education? Perhaps reflecting popular opinion, a *New York Daily Times* editorial on medical schools in the city lauded the New York Medical College: "The Faculty are all young men. There are no *old fogies* among them. They are men of wide reputation, full of zeal and determined not to be outdone in nothing that can facilitate the acquirement of a thorough medical education." In the New York Medical College's twelfth annual circular [1861-62], the following self-evaluation appeared: "They [Trustees and Faculty] are happy to state that their efforts to raise higher the standard of medical education, and to furnish increased facilities for thorough professional acquirements are more and more appreciated. Other Colleges have profited by the example originally set by this, and have increased the number of Professorships, and of the branches taught. Our Trustees point with pride to the character of their alumni, as especially shown by their success when competing for stations of profit and honor, both in military and civil service."

In late 1850, people paid two cents for a copy of the *New York Herald* and read the announcement in the "Special Notices'" column:

> The New York Medical College in East Thirteenth Street, near Broadway, will be opened on Wednesday evening October 16 at 7½ o'clock when an address will be delivered by Dr. A. L. Cox. The profession and the public generally are invited to be present.
> R. Ogden Doremus, Secy, Bd. of Trustees

Dr. Abraham L. Cox was Professor, Principles and Operations of Surgery with Surgical Pathology and also a Trustee of the school. Newspapers reported that a "highly select and respectable assemblage of ladies and gentlemen attended for the purpose of giving their countenance to the institution." Entering the school building, people found it difficult to find a seat in the crowded lecture hall on the second floor.

Essentially, Dr. Cox discussed the qualifications of physicians; the education of medical students to "think and act well," the character and standing of the faculty of the new college; the weekly "cliniques," and the plans for a free teaching hospital connected with the medical school to allow "students to become practically acquainted with disease in all its multitudinous forms." Commenting on the deficiency of practical medical teaching, Cox remarked that "it is a great evil that he [the physician] should have to learn on his patients." People attending were stirred to loudly applaud Cox's conclusion: "No efforts ... of the Faculty ... will be spared to render this seat of learning illustrious and serviceable to the public weal ... these guarantees will make the diploma of the New York Medical College one of the most honorable testimonials of professional qualification."

At twelve noon on the next day, the first class of medical students observed "several capital operations in the clinique ... a case of lithotomy, one of cataract, a striking case of double compound hare-lip, and several interesting and important cases of tumors ..."

Students paid a matriculation fee of $5, $105 for the full course of lectures and a demonstrator's fee of $5. Room and board in the area cost $3 to $4 a week. There was a $30 final examination fee.

During the existence of the New York Medical College, from 1850 to 1864, about 305 students graduated and received their medical degrees. While 800-900 students matriculated, only about one-third received medical degrees. Graduating class size ranged from 13 in 1850 to 34 in 1858 with an average of 22 per year. While 41 percent [124] of the graduates came from New York, 25 percent [77] came from 17 other states from Maine to California and 14 percent [42] from nine Southern states. Interestingly, 18 percent [56] of the graduates came from foreign countries including 13 from Germany, six from Cuba, five from England and others from as far as Brazil, the Sandwich Islands and Turkey. In addition, 10 percent [30] of the graduates already had an M.D. degree.

At the New York Medical College's first graduation, Trustee President, George Wood, bestowed the degree of Doctor of Medicine on the graduates. Professor Green delivered the valedictory address on *The Prospective Progress of Medicine in America*. In comparing American to European medicine, Green remarked that "the healing art will make progress among us, because we are characterized by a fondness for novelty and experiments." Green added: "But let us never forget, that the most glorious, though least gainful triumphs of our art, should be to prevent, not to cure disease." Welcoming the graduates to a noble profession, Green declared with impassioned sentiment: "You are the firstlings of our hands and hearts." After listening to Green's speech, a *New York Daily Tribune* reporter commented: "It was well received and exhibited a perfect knowledge of the subject."

In comparison to the 13 graduates from the New York Medical College in 1851, the University of New York Medical Department awarded 116 medical degrees and the College of Physicians and Surgeons accorded 56 degrees.

In celebration, the new physicians and their friends could pay 25 cents to see Christy's Minstrels at Mechanic's Hall; or 12½ cents to sit in the Gallery at the Broadway Theater to enjoy the comedy *Old Love and the New* with Julia Bennett as Camille and Mr. Conway as Sydney; or pay $5 for a private box at Niblo's Gardens where a new vaudeville *La Maitresse Des Langues* and the grand ballet of *Catarina Ou La Reine Des Bandits* were featured.

A distinguished faculty taught at the New York Medical College.

Brief biographical notes about some of the eminent faculty members illustrate the calibre of physicians involved in this reform minded medical college. Advertisements for the New York Medical College always listed the faculty as a means of attracting students. As usual at the time, Nathaniel Wilson, Janitor, was included in the faculty listing. Proprietary medical schools often added the janitor's name to make their faculty list longer.

While only on the faculty for a short time, Dr. Cox lectured on the pathology and treatment of Asiatic cholera and a new apparatus for the removal of enlarged tonsils.

In early 1851, Dr. Cox resigned and was replaced by Dr. John Murray Carnochan, 759 Broadway, who remained on the faculty until 1862. Students were conveyed "each Saturday during the session to the Emigrants' Hospital, where operations will be performed and clinical lectures delivered by Professor Carnochan, the Surgeon-in-Chief of the Institution." Emigrants' Hospital on Ward's Island was then the largest hospital in the U.S. and Carnochan remained as surgical chief for 25 years. Students eagerly read Dr. Carnochan's 1850 book: *A Treatise on the Etiology, Pathology, and Treatment of Congenital Dislocations of the Head of the Femur*. Being a bold, dexterous and innovative surgeon, in 1851 Carnochan was the first to remove the entire lower jaw at one operation when bone necrosis followed a severe attack of typhus fever; the patient fully recovered and was well four years later. That same year, he also was the first to ligate the femoral artery just below the origin of the arteria profunda to cure elephantiasis. Carnochan was the first to exsect [sic] the superior maxillary nerve to cure facial neuralgia in 1856. In 1870, Carnochan was Health Officer for the Port of New York.

With an office at 22 East 14 Street, Dr. Edwin Hamilton Davis, Professor of Materia Medica, Therapeutics and Pharmacy, taught at the New York Medical College for ten years, until 1860. He was probably more renowned as an archeologist than as a physician. Those students who were literate and interested in anthropology, frequently had private conversations with Davis about his original surveys and explorations of the ancient monuments of the Mississippi valley.

Considered the best known obstetrician in the U.S. in his time, Dr. B. Fordyce Barker was Professor, Midwifery and Diseases of Women and Children from 1850 to 1859. Women flocked to his office at 16 Eleventh Street, especially if a difficult labor was anticipated.

Often, Dr. Barker lectured about the pathology of puerperal diseases. After Barker joined the faculty of the Bellevue Hospital Medical College in 1860, he published his clinical lectures on puerperal diseases in 1874. That became his principal work and was translated into French, German, Italian, Russian and Spanish. His book on disease variations of the cervix uteri was a popular professional reference. In 1858, Barker was President of the MSSNY. When the American Gynecological Society was founded in 1876, Barker was elected as the first President. Barker was also the President of the New York Academy of Medicine [1879] and the President of the New York Obstetrical Society [1888].

Dr. Horace Green was a founder of New York Medical College, a Trustee, the President of the Faculty and the Professor of Theory and Practice of Medicine from 1850 to 1855 and then Professor, Respiratory Organs until he resigned from the faculty and as President in July 1860. Prior to relocating to New York, Green was President of Castleton [VT] Medical College from 1840 to 1843. From his office at 12 Clinton Place, he was the first physician to specialize in throat diseases. Students, physicians and the public read Green's book on disease of the air passages because of a continuing public acrimonious controversy that began about 1840. In 1846, Green introduced a probang into the larynx to apply a 40 to 80 grain to the ounce solution of nitrate of silver for local medication. A probang is a curved whalebone instrument about 10 inches long tipped with a tiny sponge. In 1849, Green's second edition of his text on disease of the air passages appeared. In an 1854 speech before the New York Medical and Surgical Society, Green's ideas about applications of medication directly on the laryngeal mucous membrane were met with overt skepticism and bitter opposition. As late as 1857, Green responded to his persistent critics with a three column long letter to the editor in the *New York Times*. A year later, students and physicians often consulted his newly published 206 page collection of the favorite prescriptions of living American practitioners. After 1860, Green was an editor for the *American Medical Monthly* until his death in 1866. Despite his busy life, Green still had time to father 11 children.

One of the most erudite men in the medical profession, Dr. Edmund Randolph Peaslee, replaced Dr. John H. Wittaker as Professor, Physiology, Pathology and Microscopy in 1851 and remained until 1860. All the students watched as Peaslee performed the first successful ovariotomy in the New England area in 1851. Later that year, Peaslee delivered the introductory address at the Medical School of Maine on the *Comparative Intellectual Standing of the Medical Profession*. Continuing with the reform medical education message, in October 1852, Peaslee delivered the introductory public lecture on the moral character of the medical profession. Peaslee did pioneering work in abdominal and pelvic surgery and was among the very few to be called "microscopists." Renowned as a teacher, writer, scholar and operator, Peaslee seldom, if ever, missed giving a lecture. Peaslee read French, German, Italian and Spanish and held concurrent faculty appointments at four medical colleges. His 54 page book summarized his lectures on general and human physiology and made its way onto many student's bookshelves due to the concise reference notes. In 1872, Peaslee published his best known work on *Ovarian Tumors, Their Pathology, Diagnosis and Treatment, Especially by Ovariotomy*. During his career, Peaslee was also President of the New York Pathological Society [1858], the New York County Medical Society [1867], the New York Academy of Medicine [1871], the New York Medical Journal Association and the American Gynecological Society [1877]. In addition, Peaslee was a fine mathematician and talented as a vocal and instrumental musician.

Students frequently visited with Dr. A. M. F. Eisenlord, curator of the school's anatomy museum and a Prosector in Surgery, to examine the models/specimens and asked probing questions. This valuable museum was donated to Bellevue Hospital Medical College when the New York Medical College closed in 1864.

A founder, Secretary of the Trustees, and Dean of the Faculty, at age twenty-six, Dr. Robert Ogden Doremus was Professor of Chemistry, Toxicology and Medical Jurisprudence and remained from 1850 to 1861. At his own expense, Doremus equipped the chemical laboratory used by students at the New York Medical College. This laboratory occupied most of the front first floor of the school. Students studied analytical chemistry and toxicology in the laboratory learning to conduct research. In lectures, Doremus strongly advocated thoroughly disinfecting hospitals and dwellings. Doremus also helped to found and to teach at two other medical schools: the Long Island College Hospital Medical School and the Bellevue Hospital Medical College. He was also a member of the Committee that established the New York City Health Department. As an inventor, Doremus originated a technique to compress granulated gunpowder into cartridges. Doremus was a friend of Louis Pasteur, a skilled cornet soloist and was three times president of the Philharmonic Society.

In 1850, the faculty included Barker, Cox, Davis, Doremus, and Green. Carnochan and Peaslee were added in 1851. Two new chairs were created in 1852: Medical Jurisprudence for Judge Joel Parker and Dental Pathology and Surgery for physician and dentist, C.C. Allen, the first dental chair in an American medical school. Coincidentally, at this time the newspapers announced a practical treatise on a painful subject - educating medical students about extracting teeth. Few faculty changes occurred after 1852. Faculty physicians prominent in U.S. medicine included the following: Dr. Henry G. Cox took over Theory and Practice in 1855; Dr. Timothy Childs taught Anatomy in 1856; and Dr. Austin Flint, Jr. lectured on Physiology and Pathology in 1859. In the reorganization of 1860, two new departments were created: Dr. Abraham Jacobi chaired Infantile Pathology and Therapeutics and Dr. Bern L. Budd chaired Toxicology, now independent of chemistry. Additional eminent physicians on faculty from 1861 to 1863 included David S. Conant [Anatomy], William Frederic Holcomb [Ophthalmology & Aural Surgery], Emil Noeggerath [Toxicology] and Samuel R. Percy [Materia Medica & Therapeutics].

Even as early as the first graduating class in 1851, Dr. John P. Batchelder asked the New York Academy of Medicine to withhold approval of the New York Medical College. Dr. Batchelder said that the College "assumed an attitude and policy hostile to the honor, dignity and welfare of the medical profession." He criticized the examination process and questioned whether a medical degree should have been issued to one of the graduates. Dr. Green appeared before the Academy and reminded them that the New York Medical College was the only medical college in the city where an independent physician Board of Censors examined the students and recommended the granting of medical degrees. Indignantly, Dr. Green asked: "Why is the New York Medical College being selected for censure?" Intense discussion followed. Finally, Dr. Batchelder withdrew his motion. Nevertheless, embittered antagonism from organized medicine, rival schools and kindred individuals continued unabated.

Having struggled for ten years, from 1850 to 1860, without receiving sufficient patronage, the faculty decided to suspend classes. After all nine faculty resigned, the New York Medical College was reorganized on April 21, 1860. Drs. Carnochan and Doremus carried on and notable new additions included Drs. Abraham Jacobi and Austin Flint, Jr.

An 1860, newspaper advertisement announced the eleventh session and listed the faculty of the New York Medical College. A preliminary course opened September 17 with daily lectures. Regular lectures began on Wednesday, October 17 and continued till mid-March with four lectures daily. Additionally, there were daily clinics in medicine, surgery and obstetrics by the faculty. Demonstrations and practical teaching in chemical analysis, operative surgery and practical anatomy were listed as distinctive features. This ad also noted that chairs in pathology, materia medica and clinical medicine were now vacant but will be filled in time for the lecture sessions. Fees were the same as in prior years.

On the same day as the announcement, local newspapers said that the New York Medical College "ranks among the hard working, useful and energetic of the seminaries of learning."

Toward the end of 1859, with the war between the states threatening, Southern medical students began leaving Northern medical schools. About 75 percent of the students at Philadelphia's Jefferson Medical College came from the South. After a mass meeting at National Hall in Philadelphia, more than 250 medical students left by train for Richmond [VA] and points south. Rumors abounded that the Baltimore & Ohio Railroad would provide free fares and that Southern medical schools would waive fees. A New York newspaper asked "why were medical students 'constrained' to return to the south?" Southern politicians urged the students not to mix in politics and to stay put. Contrariwise, Southern agents may have fomented the medical school secession for propaganda reasons. In an editorial comment, the *New York Daily Tribune* quipped: "We hope they have a good time. Philadelphia survived the blow as late as one o'clock this morning."

A meeting at the University of New York Medical Department attracted 300 to 400 people. After heated emotional repartee, only 14 students stepped forward to pledge themselves to secede. However, when the secession of the Confederate states moved closer to reality, the loss of southern medical students seriously affected the viability of the New York Medical College which drew many of its students from the South.

New York Medical College soon found itself *persona non grata* with the Southern students, with the rival local medical schools and with organized medicine. Rival schools still granted diplomas after two short lecture courses. Another misfortune occurred in March 1859 when a violent storm blew off a skylight and deluged a closet where 30 odd diplomas were ready except for the names of the graduates. New parchments were ordered but the old diplomas were carelessly left unvoided. When the janitor was fired about six months later, the wrinkled diplomas disappeared with him. Afterwards, individuals practiced medicine with bogus New York Medical College diplomas in the U.S. and abroad.

Adding to the school's troubles, a scathing critic, T.V. Paterson, prepared a book prospectus aiming "to expose shams, hoot at false pretences, prick windbags, and divulge some of the *modus operandi* of popularity hunters." His outline was written about 1863 since the faculty mentioned were new people at that time. In a withering satire, Paterson's prospectus listed titillating items for discussion: "the Mutual Admiration Society ... the skysail pole of popular applause and the scupper hole of professional contempt ... the Medical Factory ... a nightly resort of bullies, bawds, and rogues and pimps ... sects warring ... how to use a tool and bait hooks for verdant students ... Chang and Eng, the siamese twins of the Factory ... artful dodges ... the recent fire in the Factory a god-send ... is the Factory a mere Lazeretto of diseased and distempered Medicos?"

An historian concluded that "New York Medical College had its troubles, probably its faults, and above all its enemies." A hodgepodge combination of crisis events included bitter opposition from organized medicine, the withdrawal of Southern students, a damaging fire, the stolen diplomas and the lack of reform progress. These occurrences discouraged a majority of the idealistic faculty in their efforts to improve medica education. It took Harvard 28 years to introduce similar changes or to follow the New York Medical College bedside clinical teaching example. It required 40 years at Columbia for these changes to be implemented.

In 1864, the New York Medical College closed. Up to this time, the medical education reforms of the AMA were "a signal and utter failure." Ideals of the [New York Medical College] faculty were too high for the time, though strictly in accord with the demands of the

AMA for raising the standards of medical education in this country. Reform in medical education had to wait for another generation.

# BIBLIOGRAPHY

Barton WE. *The Life of Clara Barton* Two volumes. NY: AMS Press, 1922.

Böht FMT. *King Hammurabi of Babylon in the Setting of His Time.* Amsterdam: Noord-Hollandsche Uitgevers Maatschappijm, 1945.

Boylston HD. *Clara Barton, Founder of the American Red Cross.* NY: Random House, 1955.

Brandt N. *The Congressman Who Got Away with Murder.* Syracuse University Press, 1991.

Brown FJ. *A Sketch of the Life of Dr. James McHenry.* Baltimore: John Murphy, Printer, Maryland Historical Society, 1877.

Burns CR. Malpractice Suits in American Medicine Before the Civil War. *Bulletin of the History of Medicine* 43:41-56, 1969.

Clephane JO. *Official Report of the Trial of Mary Harris Indicted for the Murder of Adoniram J. Burroughs.* Washington, DC: WH and OH Morrison, 1865.

Caffrey K. *The Twilights Last Gleaming. Britain vs. America 1812-1815.* NY: Stein and Day, 1977.

Conrad E. *Mr. Seward for the Defense.* New York: Rinehart & Co., Inc., 1956.

DeVille KA. *Medical Malpractice in Nineteenth-Century America. Origins and Legacy.* NY: New York University Press, 1990.

Driver GR, Miles JC. *The Babylonian Laws* Vol. 2. London: Oxford University Press, 1955.

Dunn JT. Jones LC. Crazy Bill had a down look. *American Heritage* 6[5]:60-63, 108, 1955.

Elwell JJ. *A Medico-Legal Treatise On Malpractice, Medical Evidence, and Insanity, Comprising the Elements of Medical Jurisprudence.* New York: John S. Voorhis, 1860.

Flexner A. *Medical Education in the U.S. and Canada. A Report to the Carnegie Foundation for the Advancement of Teaching.* New York: Carnegie Foundation, 1910.

Fontaine FG. *Trial of the Hon. Daniel E. Sickles for Shooting Philip Barton Key, Esq., U.S. Attorney of Washington, D.C. February 27th, 1859.* New York: R.M. DeWitt, Pub., 1859.

Gray JP. The Case of Dr. David M. Wright for the Murder of Lieutenant Sanborn - Plea Insanity. *American Journal of Insanity* 20:284-300, 1864.

Gray JP. The Trial of Mary Harris.
*American Journal of Insanity* 22:330-360, 1865.
Hall BF. *The Trial of William Freeman for the Murder of John G. Van Nest.*
Auburn: Derby, Miller & Co., 1848.
Hamilton FH, Boardman J. *Fracture Tables Showing the Results of Treatment in 461 Cases.* Buffalo, NY: Jewett Thomas & Co., 1853.
Harper RF. *The Code of Hammurabi, King of Babylon.*
Chicago: University of Chicago Press, 1904.
Hooker W. [Chairman]. Report of the AMA Committee on Medical Education. *Transactions of the American Medical Association* 4:409-441, 1851.
Ireland RM. Insanity and the unwritten law. *American Journal of Legal History* 32:157-172, 1988.
Irwin BJD. *History of the Great "Tuczon Meteorite" Donated to the Smithsonian Institution.* Memphis: Blelock & Co, 1865.
Irwin BJD. Notes on the Introduction of Tent Field Hospitals in War.
*Proceedings. Assocation. of Military Surgeons* 4:108-136, 1894.
Irwin BJD. The Chiricahua Apache Indians. A Thrilling Incident in the Early History of Arizona Territory.
*The Infantry Journal* 32:368-375; April 1928.
Jacobi A. The New York Medical College 1782-1906.
*Annals of Medical History* 1:368-373, 1917.
Jensen JE. 166 Years Ago This Month: William Beanes: The Doctor Behind the Star Spangled Banner.
*Maryland State Medical Journal* 29[9]:60-65, 1980.
Jordan EL. *A Painful Case, The Wright-Sanborn Incident in Norfolk, Virginia, July-October 1863.* Master of Arts Thesis, Old Dominion University [VA], April 1979.
Kaufman M. *American Medical Education. The Formative Years 1765-1910.*
Westport, CT: Greenwood Press, 1976.
Kelly T. General Sickles Cuts a Swath in Lafayette Park
in *Murders. Washington's Most Famous Murder Stories*
Washington, DC: Washingtonian Books, 1976.
Key-Smith FS. *Francis Scott Key, Author of The Star Spangled Banner. What Else He Was and Who.* Washington, DC: Key-Smith and Co., 1911.
Kimmel SP. *The Mad Booths of Maryland.*
Indianapolis: Bobbs-Merrill Co., 1940.

Lawson JD. *American State Trials, Vol. 12*.
  St. Louis: F.H. Thomas Law Book Co., 1919.
Leix A. The Medical Knowledge of Babylonia.
  *Ciba Symposium* 2:675-680, 1940.
Lord W. *The Dawn's Early Light*. NY: W.W. Norton & Co., 1972.
Mattsson-Bozé MH. *James McHenry, Secretary of War 1796-1800*. PhD
  Dissertation, University of Minnesota. Ann Arbor, MI:
  University Microfilms, 1965.
May JF. Mark of the Scalpel. *Records of the Columbia Historical Society*
  13:51-68, 1910.
McFarland A. Insanity As a Defense, *Chicago Tribune*, June 20, 1889.
Magruder, Jr. CC. Dr. William Beanes, the Incidental Cause of the
  Authorship of The Star Spangled Banner in Larner JB: *Records of the
  Columbia Historical Society*, 22:207-225. Washington, DC: Published
  by the Society, 1919.
Miller JM. James McHenry, MD of Fort McHenry in Baltimore Towne.
  *Maryland Medical Journal* 1992; 41:413-415.
Mohr JC. *Doctors and the Law. Medical Jurisprudence in Nineteenth
  Century America*. New York: Oxford University Press, 1993.
*New York Herald*. Execution of Dr. Wright, October 25, 1863.
*New York Times*. The Case of Dr. Walker, Only Woman To Win [and Lose]
  the Medal of Honor, June 4, 1977.
Norwood WF. *Medical Education in the U.S. Before the Civil War*.
  New York: Arno Press, 1971.
Oates SB. *A Woman of Valor. Clara Barton and the Civil War*.
  New York: Free Press, 1994.
Parsons RL. Review of the Trial of Mary Harris for the Murder of Adoniram
  J. Burroughs. *Quarterly Journal of Psychological Medicine and
  Medical Jurisprudence* 1:186-212, 1867.
Pasewark RA. A Review of Research on the Insanity Defense. *Annals of the
  American Academy of Political Social Science* 484:100-114, 1986.
Pryor EB. *Clara Barton, Professional Angel*.
  Phila: University of Pennsylvania Press, 1987.
Ray I. *A Treatise on the Medical Jurisprudence of Insanity*.
  Boston: Charles C. Little & James Brown, 1838.
Rhodeham JH, Taper L. *"Right or Wrong, God Judge Me." The Writings of
  John Wilkes Booth*. Urbana: University of Illinois Press, 1997.

Sellers L. Commissioner Charles Mason and Clara Barton.
*Journal of the Patent Office Society* 22:803-827, 1940.

Snow J. *On Chloroform and Other Anaesthetics: Their Actions and Administration.* London: John Churchill, 1858.

Spiegel AD. *A. Lincoln, Esquire: A Shrewd and Sophisticated Lawyer in His Time.* Macon, GA: Mercer University Press, 2002.

Steiner BC. *The Life and Correspondence of James McHenry, Secretary of War Under Washington and Adams.*
Cleveland: The Burrows Brothers Company, 1907.

Swanberg WA. *Sickles the Incredible.*
New York: Charles Scribner's Sons, 1956.

Synder CM. *Dr. Mary Walker, the Little Lady in Pants.*
New York: Vantage Press, 1962.

Thompson JH. First Medal of Honor Won by Chicagoan,
*Chicago Tribune* March 8, 1959.

Townsend GA. *The Life, Crime, and Capture of John Wilkes Booth With a Full Sketch of the Conspiracy of Which He Was the Leader and the Pursuit, Trial, and Execution of His Accomplices.* New York: Dick & Fitzgerald, Publishers, 1865.

U.S. Army, Office of Judge Advocate General. *Investigation and Trial Papers Relating To the Assassination of President Lincoln.* Washington, DC: National Archives and Records Service, General Services Administration, Microcopy No. 599, Roll 4, frames 0348-0369, 0442-0485. Washington, DC, April 27, 1865.

*Weekly Pantagraph.* The Trial of Isaac Wyant, April 15, 1857.

Walker ME. *Hit. A Woman's Thoughts About Love, Marriage, Divorce, Etc.*
New York: American News Co., 1871.

Walker ME. *Unmasked or The Science of Immorality in Gentlemen By a Woman Physician and Surgeon.* Phila: William H. Boyd, 1878.

*Washington Post.* A Romance of the Court. Marriage of an Aged Attorney to His Fair Client, November 3, 1883.

Wharton F, Stillé M. *A Treatise on Medical Jurisprudence.*
Phila: Kay, 1855.

Woodward JA. *The Code of Hammurabi: Law of Mesopotamia.*
Los Angeles: National Center for History in the Schools, 1991.

# INDEX

Abolition malice 57
Adams, John 115
   and McHenry 150
Alaska
   gold rush 19
   purchase 19
   Seward's folly 19
   statehood 19
*American Journal of Insanity*
   9, 38, 95
American Red Cross
   approved 177
   disasters 177
   founder 161, 176-178
   mismanagement 177-178
Anesthesia 35-39
   chloroform 36
   ether 35
   nitrous oxide 35
   textbooks 37
   words coined 37
Appia, Louis
   Red Cross 172
Arnold, Benedict
   treason 127
Arthur, Chester
   appeal by Walker 192
   approved Red Cross 177
Assassination
   John Wilkes Booth 103
   James Garfield 3, 113
   Charles J. Guiteau 3, 113
   Andrew Jackson 3, 113
   Richard Lawrence 3, 113
   Abraham Lincoln 103
   Alanson L. Sanborn 64
   John H. Sorhoron 74
   Eben White 74
   David M Wright 64
Association of Medical
Superintendents of American
Institutions for the Insane [AMSAII]
   3, 9, 26, 65, 95, 96

Babylon
   flourishing city 203
   healers 204-206
   illness 204-206
   physician seal 206
   remedies 205-206
   social classes 203-204
   society 203
Bagioli, Teresa
   confession 48
   death 55
   marriage 41
   reconciled 55
Barker, B. Fordyce
   obstetrics 250
Barnes, Joseph K.
   Booth's body 104-106
   spinal spools to museum 107
   surgeon general 104
Barton Clara v, 116, 161-178
   abusive workplace 167
   American Red Cross 176-178
   angel of the battlefield 170
   character 164, 167, 178
   civil war 169-170
   death 178
   equal pay for equal work 167
   female clerks fired 166
   Franco-Russian war 172
   lecturer 177
   Lincoln approved finding
   mismanagement 177-178
   nervous prostration 171-176
   not nurse 161, 169
   patent office 165-168
   phrenologized 162
   prisoners 170
   school teacher 163-164
   set-up Bordentown school
      163-164
   spa cure 174-176
   supported Fremont 168
   symptoms 173

Bates, Finis L.
  Booth alive 108
  mummy exhibited 108
Battle casualties
  battle toll 121
  disease toll 121-125
Beanes, William 117
  career 135-136
  death 142
  Federalist 138
  hospitality to British 135
  jailed soldiers 137
  prisoner 137
  saved 141
  watched bombardment 140
Beard, George M
  neurasthenia 173
Bennett, James Gordon
  newspaper editor 19
Bell, Luther V.
  insanity expert 26
Blackstone, William
  *mala praxis* 221
Blackwell, Elizabeth
  first woman physician 162, 181
Bolles, John A.
  insanity 61
  Judge Advocate 61
Booth, Edwin 101
  hatred 112
  insanity in family 109
  poor crazy boy 109
  re brother 102
Booth, John Wilkes
  vi, 99-113
  and Cushman
  appearance 110
  assassination 103
  Booth not killed 108
  character 99, 102, 112
  crazed by liquor 111
  death 103-104
  earnings 101
  Edwin 102, 109
  fellow actor 110
  heredity 109

  identified 85
  Lincoln applauded 99
  mummy exhibited 108
  not mad 113
  plays 102
  post mortem exam 104-107
  self-glorification 110
  sister 109
Booth, Junius Brutus
  domineering father 112
  envy/hatred 112
Bowen, Lemuel
  bias 69
  clemency 68
  defense lawyer 59
  U.S. Senator 59
Bradley, Sr. Joseph H. 45, 75
  career 79
  cases cited 79
  chief defense lawyer 76
  cross-exam of May 85
  death 98
  kissed Harris 94
  marriage 98
  paroxysmal insanity 79
  Sickles case 79
  testifies 81
Brady, James T.
  confession 48
  defense lawyer 44
  jury instructions 52
Brigham, Amariah
  asylum 8
  career 8
  *American Journal of Insanity* 9
  drop case 9
  insanity defined 9
  post-mortem 18
  testimony 14-15
  therapy 8
Buchanan, James
  ambassador 41
  declined aid 45
  female clerks 168
  President 80
Burroughs, Adoniram J.

career 76
killed 75-76
marriage 76
Burroughs, John C.
  brother of murdered men 89
  defense conflict 89
  witness 89
  writes articles 95
Butterworth, Samuel T.
  advice 43
  watched shooting 43
Carlise, James M.
  closing 52
  insanity 49
  new evidence 50
  prosecutor 45
Carnochan, John Murray
  surgeon 249
Carrington, Edward C.
  career 78
  common sense doctors 85, 88
  false assumptions 38
  Lincoln appointed 75
  prosecutor 78, 82
  summation 90
  Union man 82
  used Greek mythology 82
Carter, David Kellogg
  campaign manager 60
  chief justice 60
Case law
  five groupings 223-224
Chandler, Lucius H.
  bias 69
  clemency 62
  defense lawyer 59
  U.S. Attorney 59
Chase, Salmon P.
  chief justice 19
Clarke, Booth Aisa
  not insane 109
  sister 109
Clephane, James O.
  court reporter 77
Cochise 115
  12 year war 148-149

atrocities 147
character 147-148
raiding 146
Cochrane, Alexander F. I.
  detains Key 139
  Vice Admiral 138
Cockburn, George
  see Red Devil
Codex Hammurabi 201-218
  282 edicts 209
  cuneiform 201
  division of labor 212
  fees 209-211
  Lex Talionis 206
  mandates 201-202
  marketing 216-217
  patients' rights 213-214
  physician education 212
  quality assessment 215-216
  referrals 213
  shekel value 210
  stele 206-207
Cody, William F.
  Buffalo Bill 188
  Medal of Honor restored 188
Colored troops
  recruited 73-74
  Medal of Honor 74
Cooper, Astley Paston
  main references on fractures 228
Cox, Abraham L. 247
Crawford, Thomas Hartley
  adultery 49
  evidence 48,50
  jury instructions 52-53
  similar cases 46, 79
*Cross V. Guthrie*
  first appellate case 222-223
Cuneiform 201
Cushman, Charlotte
  and Booth 101
Davis, David
  insanity plea 25
  jury instructions 31
  military trials 60-61

Davis, Edwin H.
   *materia medica* 249-250
Davis, Jefferson
   clemency appeal 63
Davis, Nathan S.
   critic of medical schools
   230-231, 240, 243
District of Columbia Court
   opposition 60
   rebel sympathy 60
   reorganization 60
Dix, Dorothea Lynde
   mental health crusader 6
Doremus, Robert O.
   chemistry 251-252
Dress Reform Undersuit 189
Dunglison, Robley
   mania defined 2
   medical educator 2
Elwell, John J.
   text 222
Esquirol, Jean E.D. 2
   book 9, 40
*Ex Parte Milligan*
   military trials 61
Fendall, William Y.
   defense lawyer 81
Fisher, George P.
   Associate Justice 60
Fitch, Calvin
   diagnosis of Harris 83
   disappointed affection 83
   uterine irritability 83
Flexner Report
   critical of medical education
   239-240
Fort McHenry
   bombardment 139-140
   history 132-133
Fowler, Lorenzo Niles
   phrenologist 162-163
Fowler, Lydia Folger
   second woman physician
   162, 181
Freeman, William
   beatings 6

   history 18
   insanity 5
   murder 6-7
Gardner, Alexander
   photographed Booth's body 101
Garfield, James
   assassination 3
   supported Red Cross 177
Goodbrake, Christopher 21
   coroner 22
   testimony 24
Graham, john
   defense lawyer 44
   insanity 47
   opening statement 47
Green, Horace
   censure 253
   practice 250-251
   throat diseases 250-251
Grimke, Sarah
   moral rights of women 197
Gross, Samuel D.
   first American book on
   orthopedics 228
Guiteau, Charles J.
   Garfield assassination 3
Hamilton, Alexander
   critical of McHenry 129
   stomach trouble 126
   West Point proposal 130
Hamilton, Frank H.
   expert witness 229
   fracture expert 229-230
   improperly healed 229-230
Hammond, William A.
   permission for Barton 169
Hammurabi 61
   and Samash 207
   moral goals 217-218
   regulation of care 208
   ruled 202
   words on stele 216-217
Harris, Mary v, 75-98
   after trial 96-97
   biography 76
   breach of marriage 77

crossed-in-love 78
feigning 78
indictment 77
institutionalized 97-98
love letters 76
marriage 76
painful dysmenorrhea 78
paroxysmal insanity 78-79, 84
marriage 98
reactions 91-96
verdict 90-91
Herold, David E.
   sold drugs to Booth 99
Hogg, Harvey
   prosecutor 23, 31
Holmes, Oliver Wendell
   anaesthesia 37
   anaesthetic 37
Holt, Joseph
   Booth identification 70
   court martial 70
   Judge Advocate General 63
   legislation 63
Howard, Flodoardo
   career 87
   testimony 88
Hughes, James
   attacked Rev. Burroughs 89
   character 80
   cited Ray 80
   defense lawyer 80
   lay witnesses 81
   Lincoln appointed 75
   summation 90
Hydropathy 174, 181, 183
Insanity 2
   beatings 5
   Booth insane 109-113
   brainstorm 4
   causes 1
   chloroform overdose 3, 21-40
   crossed-in- love 4
   dysmenorrhea 4
   emotional 1, 41-55, 57-74
   exciting 1
   feigning 29, 30, 40

homicidal monomania 2
humbug 82
jurisprudence 1
lunatic 1
mania 2
medical experts 11-16
monomania 2
moral mania 2,3
paroxysmal 78
plea 4,5
predisposing 1
public attitude 33
Shakespeare 3
temporary 4, 45
Irresistible impulse 31,79
Irwin, Bernard J.D. 2, 115, 143-159
   Army medical corps 144-145
   belongings torched 150-151
   biography 143-144
   family 143, 158-159
   field tent hospital 152-153
   hanged Indians 148
   married 158
   Medal of Honor 149, 159
   medical advertisements 144
   medical articles 156-157
   medical education 143-144
   purveyor 157-158
   retired 158
   Smithsonian 151
   weather diary 152
   West Point 154-155, 157
Jackson, Andrew
   assassination attempt 3
Jefferson, Thomas
   West Point 6, 11, 130
Johnson, Andrew
   and Walker 187
   awarded Medal of Honor 187
Johnston, Williams P.
   career 87
   cross- exam 87
   hysteria 87
Key, Francis Scott 41, 115, 132-142
   family 142
   Federalist 138

letters to parents 138
Madison approved 138
national anthem 142
*Star Spangled Banner* 140-141
urged to intervene 138
used words earlier 141
watched from own sloop 140
wrote poem 140-141
Key, Phillip Barton vi, 41-55
adulterous affair 4
career 41
killed 43, 46, 75, 79
Kirkbride, Thomas S.
re Harris case 96
Lafayette, Marquis de 115
Lamon, Ward Hill
Lincoln's partner 23
Larrey, Dominque Jean
200 amputations in day 228
Napoleon's medical chief 228
Lawrence, Richard
assassination attempt 3
Lee, Robert E.
and Sickles 75
and Walker 185,187
at West Point with Mason 82
civil courts 59
clemency 57, 62-63, 70-71
graduated No. 2 82
Lincoln, Abraham
assassination 4, 77, 103, 111
beard 21
chloroform overdose 3, 21-40
head picking 30
insanity plea 25
jury 23
law partner 23
medical experts 26-30, 65
military trials 60
missing prisoners 170
politics 57, 69, 73
*prima facie* case 23
sacked symbol 110
saw Booth act 99
summation 31
too harsh 34

verdict 32, 67
witnesses 23-25
Lincoln, Mary T vi, 55
flowers to jail 75, 90
Malpractice 219-237
231-232
AMA comments 237
amputation 228
anesthetics 227
better physicians sued more
cases 233-236
deep pockets 232
early texts 221-222, 228
expert witnesses 225
first appellate case 222-223
history of fracture case 227-230
in England 220-221
judges 226
jurors 225-226
lawyer tactics 225
legal advertising 237
mutually incompatible
professions 237
patient waiver 224
reasonable skills 223
*stare decisis* 223-224
targets 231
unknown 219
Mania 2
Madison, James
approved negotiations 138
Managed medical care
complaints 201
precepts 207-208
Mason, Charles
chief judge of Iowa 81
defense lawyer 165-168
patent commissioner 75, 81
West Point graduate 82
May, John Frederick
Booth monomaniac 111
Booth 85, 99-113
career 85, 102-103
cross-exam 86
death 102
heredity of Booth 109

hysteria 85
identified Booth 104-107
inconsistencies 106-107, 113
insanity of Booth 109-113
Lincoln re relative 75, 103
pain insensitivity 109-110
physical appearance 110
self-glorification 110
son helped 100
surgical scar 105
testimony 85
treated Lincoln 103
May, Samuel J.
  abolitionist 19
McCulloch, Hugh
  eye witness 81
  Treasury Department 81
McFarland, Andrew
  as witness 29
  career 29
  feigned insanity 29
  remarks re Wyatt 33-34
McHenry, James 115, 117-134
  and Adams 130
  apprentice to Rush 118-120
  captured 125
  career 117-118
  constitutional convention 128
  critics 131
  Federalist 127-128
  flying hospital 126
  Fort McHenry 132-133
  Hamilton critical 129
  Hamilton 126-127
  marriage 133
  medical education 118-120
  mishandling money 131
  naval affairs 129
  papers 133
  poetry 133
  politics 127-128
  resigned Army 127
  Secretary of War 129-131
  treated troops 121-125
  Valley Forge 126
  West Point proposal 130

Mead, Edward
  feigned insanity 40
  verdict 40
Medal of Honor
  colored troops 74
  history 150
  Irwin 149
  Sickles 56
  Walker 91, 187
Medical advertisements
  144, 241
Medical education
  AMA survey 243
  criticism 103, 230-231
  curriculum 239
  earliest schools 118, 239
  exams 242
  fees 242
  Flexner report 239-240
  graduates 243
  sectarian schools 181, 225
  typical school 241-242
Medico-Legal Society
  established 1
Military commission
  vs court martial 59
Miller Thomas
  career 87
  testimony 87
Mitchell, S. Weir
  treated neurasthenia 173
M'Naghten Rule
  know right from wrong 26, 84
Monomania 2
Moore, Clifton H.
  prosecutor 23
Moral insanity 3
Morton, William T.G. 35
  ether 38, 37
Mott, Lucretia
  women's rights 197
Murdered
  Adoniram J. Burroughs 75-76
  James Gordon 5
  Phillip Barton Key 43, 46
  Abraham Lincoln 103

Anson Rusk 22
Alanson L. Sanborn 58
Van Nest family 6-7
Murderers
   John Wilkes Booth 103
   William Freeman 6-7
   Daniel E. Sickles 43, 46
   David M Wright 58
   Isaac Wyant 22
   Henry G. Wyatt 5
Neurasthenia 174-175
New York Medical College
   vi, 239- 255
   bogus diplomas 254
   civil war 253- 254
   credo 245
   critic 254
   fees 248
   history of 244- 245
   oasis 143, 239
   questioned exams 252
   students 248
   two different schools 245
New York State Lunatic Asylum
   at Utica 8
Nicholas, Charles H
   and Lincoln 75
   credibility 84
   disloyal 64
   expert witness 84
   M'Naghten rule 84
   paroxysmal mania 84
   sanity expert 64
Olin, Abram B
   Associate Justice 60
Orme, William Ward
   defense lawyer 23, 31
Ould, Robert 79
   angry words 49
   prosecutor 45
Parsons, Ralph L.
   eight insanity principles 96
Peaslee, Edmund R.
   physiology 251
Phrenology
   know thy self 162

   theory 162
Pinel, Philippe 2
Prichard, James C, 2
   book 9
Ray, Isaac 2
   homicidal monomaniac 2
   insanity indications 80
   mental illness defined 26
   monomania 110
   moral mania 2, 110
   Nichols' testimony 95
   treatise 2, 9, 26
Red Devil
   attacked Americans 140
   council of war 135
   denounced Beanes 139
   destroyed newspaper 136
   ethereal mix 142
   pillaging 136
   Rear Admiral George Cockburn 135
Ross, Robert
   attacked Americans 140
   British general 135
   burned Washington 136
   killed 140
Roosevelt, Franklin Delano
   and Walker 193
Roosevelt, Theodore
   upset Red Cross 178
   Walker's misgivings 193
Rush, Benjamin 2, 115
   apprentices 118- 120
   blood letting 119
   health of soldiers 123
   insanity 2
   miasma 120
   pathology 119
   patriotism 119
Rusk, Anson
   feud 21
   killed 22
Sanborn, Alanson L.
   career 57
   murdered 58
Segar, Joseph Eggleston

defense lawyer 59
U.S. Representative 59
Seneca Falls Convention
   women's rights 179
Serendip v
Seward, Frances 7
   inhumanity of prison 17
   read books 9
Seward, William H. 3, 5-19,
   appeal 17
   governor 6
   insanity expert 8, 54
   insanity plea 5
   medical experts 11-16
   prejudice 10
   read books 9
   Seward's folly 19
   summation 16, 18
   witnesses 10
Shaw, Lemuel
   irresistible impulse 31, 67
Sherman, William T.
   Walker's clothing
Sherwood, Luman
   prosecutor 10
Sickles, Daniel E. vi, 41-56, 75, 79
   amputated leg 56, 75
   and Lincoln 75
   career 41
   civil war 55
   death 56
   jailed 44
   jury 46
   kills Key 43, 46
   lawyers 44
   Medal of Honor 56
   murder indictment 45
   reactions 54-55
   temporary insane 45,47
   unwritten law 45
   verdict 53
   wife's confession 42
   witnesses 42, 50-51
   Yankee King of Spain 56
Simpson, James Young
   used chloroform 35-37

Skinner, John S.
   letters from British soldiers 139
   prisoner-of-war agent 138
Snow, John
   royal births 39
   used chloroform 39
Spencer, Thomas
   faculties of the mind 13
Stanton, Edwin M.
   Booth's autopsy 107
   defense lawyer 44
   legal bully 49
   moral closing 51
   moral mania 79
   Sickles case 79
*Star Spangled Banner* 115, 117
   Ft. McHenry flag 142
   history 135-142
Strong George Templeton
   diary entry 41, 48
Surratt, Mary
   hanged 77
Swanlond, John
   1374 malpractice case 220
Swett, Leonard
   chloroform insanity 21-40
   insanity expert 29
   measured chloroform 29
   news item re Wyatt 33
   witnesses 26
Taney, Roger B.
   Key's brother-in-law 139
   re Beanes 139
Tuke, Samuel
   book 9
Uncontrollable impulse 31, 79
Unwritten law 45,88
Van Buren, John
   prosecutor 10
Van Nest, John 6
Van Nest, George W. 6
Van Nest, Sarah 6
Voorhees, Daniel W.
   attacked Rev. Burroughs 89
   Greek hero 82
   lawyer 75

oratory 81
summation 89-90
Walker Mary E. v, 116, 179-197
   attire 189-190
   arrested 189
   biography 180
   career 179-180
   civil war 183-187
   death 197
   dress reform 179,189,195
   dress reform undersuit 189
   eye injury 186
   FDR and Teddy 193
   at Harris trial 91
   heart failure 194
   hydropath 183, 231
   ideals 197
   inventor 193
   and Lincoln 185
   lecturer 190-191
   lobbyist 192
   mail room clerk 191-192
   man classified 196
   marriage 182
   Medal of Honor 91, 180,187-188, 197
   medical school 181-182, 184
   peace conference 193
   polio 194
   politics 193
   practice 182-184, 188
   prisoner 186
   psychohistorical analysis 196
   smallpox 194
   spy 185-186
   suffrage 190, 195
   tobacco 195
   tuberculosis 193-194
Walker, Robert J.
   career 47
   emotional instability 48
Walpole, Horace
   serendipity v
Washington, George 115
   blood letting caused death 119
King of U.S. 128
   troops cleanliness 122
Weed, Thurlow 9
*Weekly Pantagraph*
   trial coverage 23
Wells, Horace
   dentist 35
   nitrous oxide 35
West Point 115
   medical officer 154
   proposed 130
West, Richard
   urged Key 138
West Virginia
   statehood 59
White House
   burned 136
   critics of burning 136
   saved Washington painting 136
Whiting, Bowen
   judge 6, 7
   jury charge 17
   sanity ruling 11
Wilson, Nathaniel
   assistant prosecutor 82
   cross-exam of Fitch 83
Woodward, Joseph Janvier
   Booth's autopsy 107
Women physicians
   discrimination 180-181, 184
   first physician 162, 181
   second physician 162, 181
Wright, David M. 57-74
   bribe 70
   chose coffin 68
   clemency petitions 62-63
   daughter's marriage 68
   escape 69-70
   family 68, 72
   funeral 71
   hanged 70
   insanity 61
   jailed 58
   killing 58, 64
   military commission 59
   rabid secessionist 59

    resolution in honor  71-72
    sanity  65-67
    self-defense  61, 64
    slave owner  58
    trial  59-61
    verdict  62
Wright, Silas  6
Wyant, Isaac
    arrest warrant  22
    jailed  22
    murder trial  21-40
    released  34
    sent to asylum  32
    verdict  32
Wyant, Henry G.
    insanity  5
Wylie, Andrew  79
    associate justice  60
    expert witness  84
    letters as evidence  81
    Lincoln appointed  75
    threatened  60
    wait for verdict  90
Wyndham, Charles
    progressive insanity of Booth  109
Young, Noble
    career  36
    testimony  87

## ABOUT THE AUTHOR

Allen D. Spiegel, PhD, MPH, is Professor of Preventive Medicine and Community Health, State University of New York, Downstate Medical Center, College of Medicine, Brooklyn, New York. His experience includes a wide range of activities in medical and health care services, comprehensive health planning, public health education, health and medical communications and the history of medicine.

Formerly, Dr. Spiegel was with the New York City Health Department, The Medical Foundation, Inc. of Boston and a Special Research Fellow at Brandeis University.

Dr. Spiegel received an AB from Brooklyn College, an MPH from Columbia University and a PhD from Brandeis University. He also earned a Special Diploma in Radio and Television from New York University.

As a consultant, Dr. Spiegel's services have been sought on health and welfare projects by an assortment of private, voluntary non-profit and governmental agencies at all levels.

He has authored and co-authored more than twenty-five books and hundreds of articles, reports, and mass media material on health care. His books include the following: *Perspectives in Community Mental Health, Medicaid: Lessons for National Health Insurance, Basic Health Planning Methods, The Medicaid Experience, Curing and Caring, Medical Technology, Health Care and the Consumer, Rehabilitating People With Disabilities Into the Mainstream of Society, Home Health Care: Home Birthing to Hospice, Strategic Health Planning: Methods/Technologies Applied to Marketing/Management, Risk Management in Health Care Institutions,* and *Abraham Lincoln, Esquire: A Shrewd, Sophisticated Lawyer In His Time.*

www.ingramcontent.com/pod-product-compliance
Lightning Source LLC
Chambersburg PA
CBHW050839230426
**43667CB00012B/2063**